Power & Powerless 1980

read that chapter

how powerless act to self

in their own domination

How does this mechanism

play itself out in cities

Harold Washington

and the Neighborhoods

Progressive City Government in

Chicago, 1983–1987

EDITED BY

Pierre Clavel and Wim Wiewel

Rutgers University Press
New Brunswick, New Jersey

Library of Congress Cataloging-in-Publication Data

Harold Washington and the neighborhoods : progressive city government in
    Chicago, 1983–1987 / edited by Pierre Clavel and Wim Wiewel.
        p.   cm.
    Includes bibliographical references and index.
    ISBN 0-8135-1725-7 (cloth)   ISBN 0-8135-1726-5 (pbk.)
    1. Chicago (Ill.)—Politics and government.   2. Chicago (Ill.)—Economic
policy.   3. Community development, Urban—Illinois—
Chicago.   4. Political participation—Illinois—Chicago.   5. Washington,
Harold, 1922–1987.   I. Clavel, Pierre.   II. Wiewel, Wim.
JS714.A1N45 1991
352.0773'11—dc20   91-9430
                                                                            CIP

British Cataloging-in-Publication information available

Contents

Preface

This volume came about beginning in 1988 when several persons in Chicago's community development movement and inside the city administration, all of whom had supported or worked for Mayor Harold Washington, agreed to collaborate with us on a set of memoirs whose purpose would be to help record and define their experience. Some hesitated, and for some it was very hard because, having committed themselves so wholly to what Washington stood for, they were in the midst of dealing with his tragic death in office a year earlier and the partial dissolution of his program. Later, while these chapters were still under revision, some had to deal as well with the defeat of Washington's successor, Eugene Sawyer, and their own shifts out of city employment.

Clavel had followed the events in Chicago at some remove while at Cornell where two of the authors, Mier and Giloth, had been graduate students. He had written an earlier work, *The Progressive City*, on cities that responded to grassroots movements for participation and redistribution, and he had continued gathering material on progressive city administrations. He came to Chicago in 1988 as a visiting professor at the School of Urban Planning and Policy at the University of Illinois at Chicago (UIC) and during that time laid the groundwork for this book.

Wiewel had been at the UIC's Center for Urban Economic Development since 1979 and had become its director in 1983 when founder Robert Mier moved on to become Harold Washington's commissioner of economic development. The center provides technical assistance and research in the area of economic development to Chicago's community organizations and local governments. Wiewel was interested in assessing the lessons to be drawn from the Washington administration because of what they might hold for the Center's work, the future of Chicago, and progressive cities elsewhere.

These circumstances of the inception of this volume provide some explanation of what we attempt to do here. Many of the authors note the strong background of community organizing that preceded Washington's election, but this volume primarily represents one segment of that organizing, the part we have called the "community development movement." We only partly represent other parts of the movements and broader coalitions that came together to elect Washington.

We have used other criteria for inclusion as well: except for the editors, all of the authors represented here either worked in the Washington administration or in the community organizations (or in direct support of them in one case). Thus, it is a book by insiders, offering their interpretation of what they tried to do and why. We aimed for a truthful account but not necessarily one that included all viewpoints, certainly not those of Washington's opponents.

We focused on economic development and the neighborhood components of other program areas such as housing or social services. The emphasis on economic development arises in part from our backgrounds and contacts, but there is also a thematic reason: many cities in the United States have strong neighborhood movements that focus on a variety of concerns, but Chicago developed earlier and more extensive, neighborhood-level economic development activities. We felt this was an important feature and wanted to see how far a city administration sensitive to neighborhood issues could carry an economic development program with this sort of base.

We benefited from the writing that has already appeared complementing what we have attempted here. There is, first, important work on Chicago's grass-roots movements and their struggles, including the increasingly sophisticated literature criticizing the "growth coalition," such as Larry Bennett and associates' *Chicago: Race, Class and the Response to Urban Decline* and Anne Shlay and Bob Giloth's work on the World's Fair.[1]

There is a body of journalistic and other work, some of it superb, on the Washington administration and the neighborhood movement in Chicago. Gary Rivlin's articles in the Chicago *Reader* is one case in point. There is other work on Washington himself and on the politics of black empowerment: Alkalimat and Gills's *Harold Washington and the Crisis of Black Power in Chicago*, and memoirs of Washington by Dempsey Travis and Alton Miller.[2]

We have complemented our work on this book with a document collection project carried out jointly with the authors, the Center for Urban Economic Development, and the Chicago Historical Society. We have collected many papers from the authors and others pertaining to the Washington administration. We have deposited them in an archive called the Harold Washington Neighborhood and Economic Development Papers at the Chicago Historical Society. We invite readers to use and contribute to this collection. Both editors want to thank the Chicago Community Trust, and particularly Judith Stockdale, for providing funding for the Archives Project, which greatly helped the preparation of this book. We also thank Archie Motley at the Chicago Historical Society for supporting the idea and housing the archives, and Thom Clark and Charlie Serrano for help in collecting material.

Clavel wants to acknowledge Kenneth Reardon's work on Chicago, as well as that of his students at Cornell who participated in preparing the "Annotated Bibliography on Progressive Cities."[3] He also expresses his appreciation to Charles Orlebeke, director of UIC's School of Urban Planning and Policy, and to the Center for Urban Economic Development, for affording him the opportunity to spend time in Chicago.

Wiewel gratefully acknowledges the insights provided by many people who worked for the Washington administration and others, particularly Steve Alexander, Lauri Alpern, María-Theresa Ayalla, Michael Bennett, Mary Bonome, Margarette Delgado, Tom Dubois, Ken O'Hare, Roz Paaswell, Julie Putterman, Arturo Vázquez, Wanda White, and Wendy Wintermute. He also thanks the staff of the Center for Urban Economic Development for the supportive environment and helpful comments provided by Deborah Bennett, John Betancur, Virginia Carlson, Bill Howard, David Ranney, and Pat Wright. Sasha D'Austin and Soyla Villicana provided assistance in producing the manuscript. At home, Janice Weiss provided encouragement and support, as well as editorial advice.

Finally, we want to express our deep appreciation to the authors of these chapters. Their enthusiasm, commitment, and insights are at the core of this book; we hope we have done justice to them and to what they stand for.

Pierre Clavel
Wim Wiewel

NOTES

1. Larry Bennett, Kathleen McCourt, Philip Nyden, and Gregory Squires, *Chicago: Race, Class, and the Response to Urban Decline*, (Philadelphia: Temple University Press, 1987); Anne B. Shlay and Robert P. Giloth, "Social Organization of a Land Based Elite: The Case of the Failed Chicago 1992 World's Fair," *Journal of Urban Affairs* 9, no. 4 (1986):305–324.

2. Abdul Alkalimat and Douglas Gills, *Harold Washington and the Crisis of Black Power in Chicago* (Chicago: Twenty-first Century Books, 1989); Alton Miller, *Harold Washington: The Mayor, The Man* (Chicago: Bonus Books, 1989); Dempsey Travis, *"Harold," The People's Mayor: An Authorized Biography of Mayor Harold Washington* (Chicago: Urban Research Press, 1989).

3. Kenneth Reardon, "Local Economic Development in Chicago, 1983–1987: The Reform Efforts of Mayor Harold Washington" (Ph.D. dissertation, Cornell University, 1989); Pierre Clavel, with Victor Chang, Carol Chock, Mark Fitzstevens, Robert Giloth, Catherine Hill, Renee Jakobs, David Lynn, Ann Murray, and Frances Viggiani, "Annotated Bibliography on Progressive Cities" (unpublished manuscript, Cornell University, 1989).

Notes on Contributors

ROBERT BREHM has been executive director of Bickerdike Redevelopment since 1978. Bickerdike is a community organization active in affordable housing and economic development in Chicago's largely Hispanic West Town area.

PIERRE CLAVEL is a professor at Cornell University's Department of City and Regional Planning, where he has been on the faculty since 1967. He is the author of *The Progressive City* (Rutgers, 1986), *Opposition Planning in Wales and Appalachia* (Temple, 1983), and co-editor of *Urban and Regional Planning in an Age of Austerity* (Pergamon, 1980).

DONNA DUCHARME is the founder and executive director of the Local Economic and Employment Development Council of the New City YMCA in Chicago. She is also the president of the Chicago Association of Neighborhood Development Organizations.

DOUG GILLS is assistant director for community development at the Kenwood Oakland Community Organization in Chicago and president of the Chicago Community Workshop on Economic Development. Previously, he was the executive director of the Chicago Rehab Network and a charter member of the Taskforce for Black Political Empowerment. He is co-author of *Harold Washington and the Crisis of Black Power in Chicago* (Twenty-first Century Books, 1989).

ROBERT GILOTH is executive director of the Southeast Community Organization/Southeast Development, Inc., in Baltimore and has taught at the University of Maryland and at Tuft's University. During the Washington administration he was deputy commissioner of the Chicago Department of Economic Development.

ELIZABETH HOLLANDER is director of the Government Assistance Project of the Chicago Community Trust. She was commissioner of the Chicago Department of Planning from 1983 to 1989. Previously, she was executive director of the Metropolitan Planning Council in Chicago.

JOHN KRETZMANN is director of the Neighborhood Innovations Network of Northwestern University's Center for Urban Affairs and Policy Research. Through his work with the center and the Associated Colleges of the Midwest, where he has been a long-time faculty member, he has been involved in a wide variety of neighborhood issues.

ROBERT MIER is a professor at the School of Urban Planning and Policy at the University of Illinois at Chicago and the founder of its Center for Urban Economic Development. He was Washington's commissioner of the Department of Economic Development and assistant to the mayor for development.

KARI J. MOE is legislative director for Senator Paul Wellstone (Minnesota). During the Harold Washington administration, she worked in the Mayor's Office and was commissioner of General Services.

MARÍA DE LOS ANGELES TORRES is an assistant professor in the Department of Political Science at DePaul University. She was the executive director of the Mayor's Commission on Latino Affairs in Harold Washington's administration.

JUDITH WALKER is a consultant and executive director of the Wells Community Initiative, a public housing improvement project in Chicago. She was Washington's commissioner of the Department of Human Services and chair of the Community Services sub-cabinet, after stints at the U.S. Department of Housing and Urban Development and the Provident Community Development Corporation.

WIM WIEWEL is director of the Center for Urban Economic Development and associate professor in the School of Urban Planning and Policy at the University of Illinois at Chicago. He is co-editor of *Challenging Uneven Development: An Urban Agenda for the 1990s* (Rutgers, 1991).

TIMOTHY WRIGHT is an attorney at Sachnoff and Weaver. He held several positions in Washington's Mayor's Office, including special counsel and director of Intergovernmental Affairs. He also served as commissioner of the Department of Economic Development during the administration of Mayor Eugene Sawyer.

Harold Washington and the Neighborhoods

Introduction

PIERRE CLAVEL and WIM WIEWEL

Harold Washington's period as mayor of Chicago in 1983–1987 will be remembered as one of the high points in the history of American cities. It would be enough for this that he was the city's first black mayor, that he put together the first successful major rainbow coalition, and that his reforms marked the end of the notorious "machine" identified with Richard J. Daley. This book documents another, less noted side of Washington's mayoralty: a redistributive economic development agenda, pursued by a network of neighborhood-oriented organizers and professionals, which played a crucial role in legitimizing the administration generally and made it possible to initiate, and occasionally to institutionalize, major reforms. Once in the city government, these activists pursued such policies as the reallocation of city investments from downtown to the outlying neighborhoods, the reorientation of city economic policy to provide good jobs for residents rather than real estate development projects, widespread use of community-based organizations as delegates for carrying out city policy, and a commitment to broad public participation.

These initiatives occurred at a time when national policy had withdrawn from urban affairs in many areas, and they confounded mainstream academic and public opinion—just when the dominant literature was suggesting the difficulties of redistributive policies, asserting the impossibility of public ownership and management and regulation in numerous specific areas, and denying the effect of racial discrimination.[1] Therefore, Harold Washington's economic policies have wide significance, both because of what he set out to do in one city and because of what this showed about the potential for redistributive policies anywhere.

Economic Change and City Policy in the United States, 1970–1983

Part of the significance of Mayor Washington's policies comes from the context: the 1980s was a time of increasing economic, racial, and political instability in the United States and particularly in its major cities. There had been economic and social dislocation for some twenty years. The rift between the relatively poor segments of city populations and the middle and upper class grew wider, exacerbated by race and geography. The result was that, just as the challenge of urban problems was greatest, the capacity of city governments to respond seemed to dissolve in political and social polarization, worsening condition, and the retreatism and avoidance of the nation's business leadership.

Observers noted the end of the coalitions that had governed U.S. cities, and there seemed to be a "new political terrain."[2] One of the possible new options was the formation of coalitions that could mobilize the relatively poor populations which formed the bulk of the urban electorate. But mobilizing the poor alone threatened political order. It was also necessary to maintain sufficient legitimacy with a city's business elites so that economic growth could continue and provide some of the resources to distribute. The Washington administration represented such a coalition, which managed to juggle the demands for redistribution made by its poor constituents with the need for broader support. It did this in part by expanding participation, in part because it adopted a new economic policy agenda that had evolved over a decade of work by the city's neighborhood organizations. In the process of developing and implementing this agenda, the rules of the game and the nature of the political structure of the city were fundamentally altered. The innovations were referred to as "progressive"—an approach to governance that harked back to early-twentieth-century reform movements which also combined the radical redistributive demands of the "have-nots" with a pragmatic acceptance of the necessities of governance imposed by the larger array of social classes.[3]

Economic Growth

A number of key developments at the national level created this set of circumstances, and also played themselves out in Chicago. National economic growth, led by a long cycle of increasing productivity in manufacturing, slowed by the early 1970s.[4] John Mollenkopf has laid out the implications for urban geography and politics.[5] The cycle began in the 1930s with what was still recognizably the nineteenth-century city of highly concentrated industrial employment and residence with a predominantly white, though ethnically diverse, working class. There followed such organizational and spatial rearrangements as (1) the administrative separation of office and factory, which made possible (2) the concentration of offices and services in the city and (3) the dispersal of manufacturing and population to suburb and sunbelt. This created a new prosperity driven by manufacturing, supported by the consumption of consumer durables associated with the growth of suburban housing and by the replacement of city housing and manufacturing by office construction and the growth of services. The result was the transformation of the economic base, the spatial structure and the population composition of most cities during the postwar period.

Racial Change

This new economy was affected by—and partially helped to create—a new demography in the cities as first blacks and later Hispanics and others were forced off rural agricultural settings and migrated to the cities. Unlike earlier ethnic migrations, these occurred in the aftermath of World War II just after manufacturing employment had peaked, severely limiting economic opportunity. At the same time, racial discrimination in jobs and housing was more virulent and easier to impose than had been the case for previous migrations, so that the new populations concentrated in low-income ghettos.[6]

Growth Politics

This economic growth and racial change was supported by a certain kind of political coalition and urban policy. This was created nationally and locally out of a New Deal preoccupation with ending unemployment and building a constituency for employment-oriented programs, and a growing business constituency for creating a mass consumption society; but recent research increasingly portrays both coalition and policy as a spatially organized system. The earlier, concentrated city had featured a succession of politics: the indulgence of political machines by elites who used them to defuse working-class radicalism; then the progressive, good government movement against the urban machines.[7] The New Deal urban programs, central to dealing with the 1930s unemployment, created a kind of "reform" version of the earlier type of political machine. Its basis was federal subsidies for public works, housing, and economic development that the cities administered or shared in administering and that were successful in stimulating private investments and profits. But what proved crucial later was that the new policies also transformed the cities toward a dispersed geography with suburban single-family housing, central office and retail, and inner city slums. Players included real estate developers, lawyers, design professionals, newspapers, service sector businesses that benefited from population growth, and unions, particularly those in construction trades. These new forms of political machines lasted into the 1960s, and in some places (like Chicago) for another decade or so. Because of their emphasis on "growth," they came to be called "growth machines" or "growth coalitions."[8]

These political coalitions have been described repeatedly and with different emphases, but two key features stand out. First, they were *producer* coalitions that depended for success on executive leadership, the use of indirectly accountable boards and commissions, and a quiescent consumer base. The urban renewal and highway programs of the 1950s did a great deal to insulate leadership: federal and state subsidies amounted to 75 and 90 percent of local public costs; eminent domain power could be concentrated in appointed boards; and public entrepreneurs developed the art—first practiced on a large scale by Robert Moses in the 1920s—of generating political support from key beneficiaries while projecting spectacular gains in traffic circulation and public space designs to the public at large.[9]

The second feature was the claim that the coalition and its growth-oriented policies could solve problems of racial conflict. Part of the claim was the simple argument that "a rising tide lifts all boats," compelling to some, but also used to justify an array of compromises to gain segregationist support. But there was also a part of the coalition that was committed to racial integration. From this came a deeper claim on the race issue, which played a part in many of the attempts to adapt the growth program to the new race-induced pressures that arose in the 1960s. In Philadelphia at the beginning of the 1960s, Richardson Dilworth's reform mayoralty agonized over the prospect of losing racial balance, and thus the prospect of achieving goals of race integration in the city, owing to white out-migration. Model Cities, Community Action, and other urban programs were, in most cities and especially in the earlier stages, attempts to adapt growth policies to the cities' newly mobilized minority populations.[10]

Through the 1970s and in the face of protests that had brought specific growth programs—like urban highways and urban renewal—to a halt in many places, growth coalition leaders maintained minority participation without changing the formula in a basic way. In hindsight, it is easy to see why these leaders would take such a tack. It had the political advantage of co-opting both white liberals and blacks committed to the goals of the civil rights movement; and of offering material incentives to selected minority politicians, contractors and others, without fundamentally altering the formula for the coalition. The disadvantage was in the economic weakness of the minority constituencies, which placed increasing redistributive burdens on machine policies—burdens that became a crisis with the fiscal stringencies of the 1970s.

When black or Hispanic mayors gained control over cities, starting in the late 1960s, growth coalition managers generally stayed in the game. White political control, however bitterly relinquished, was a less fundamental issue than was the persistence of the growth formula for governing; blacks and Hispanics generally had to go along. This generally was true until the 1980s, and the list of minority mayors it applies to is long: Carl Stokes in Cleveland, Richard Hatcher in Gary, Maynard Jackson in Atlanta, Kenneth Gibson in Newark, Tom Bradley in Los Angeles, Coleman Young in Detroit, Lionel Wilson in Oakland, Wilson Goode in Philadelphia, and Marion Barry in Washington, D.C. Many of these mayors struggled against it, but for the most part the formula was to trade support for growth constituencies, for the chance to make marginal economic and civil rights gains: increase the numbers of minority contractors, hiring of minority professional administrators and other city workers, and support for social programs within the constraints of the cities' diminishing resource base. No alternative formula or coalition emerged.[11]

Economic Decline and Political Decay

This situation might have gone on indefinitely, with minorities inheriting political control from other ethnic groups as their numbers came to dominate city populations, if the economy had held up. As long as manufacturing and worker incomes continued to increase, most groups benefited and growth coalitions might have survived even the dislocations of urban riots in the 1960s. But by the 1970s this situation changed. Oil price increases may have been the biggest shock; but in the context of a general decline in profits, major business support defected from the long-term commitment to Keynesian policies supporting consumer demand, which had favored the older Northeastern and Midwestern cities, toward a defense spending orientation associated with sunbelt constituencies and with antilabor policies.[12]

But the decline of the growth coalition was not just a matter of slowing economic growth. As academic and journalistic commentary began to show, its arguments were wrong on two other counts as well. One, argued by John Mollenkopf, was that the seeds of decline were there in changed demography and income distribution inherent in the growth strategy itself, which had essentially governed the country since the New Deal. Most fundamentally, the policy of building new owner housing in the suburbs while redlining the inner city ghettos and demolishing low-rent properties for offices and highways created and exacerbated inequalities in the basic constituencies. These inequalities had not been so stark when the policies were first enacted in the early postwar period.

But as time passed, much of the original working-class constituency migrated to suburban and sunbelt locations, where they became the base for a politics of urban neglect. Meanwhile, within the cities there emerged a more bifurcated population of the poor and dependent, on the one hand, and a new professional middle class on the other—both created by the new service economy that the growth policy helped to generate. This laid the basis for conflict, which put inordinate strains on the economy and politics. The conflict erupted in the 1960s: social programs were invented to respond, but they were too little, too late, and too expensive. They resulted in a conservative backlash that was the basis for conservative policies after 1968. Local business coalitions, which earlier had adopted central city reconstruction as main priorities, now lost interest and sometimes moved their offices to suburban locations, their main leadership now relatively more preoccupied with a shift to world-scale financial manipulations. Urban neglect in the 1970s exacerbated trends that were underway. The competition between central city and suburb, rustbelt and sunbelt, intensified while capital investment of all types slowed. Cities' financial crises heightened while their populations became increasingly concentrated with minorities, the elderly, and the poor.[13]

The growth coalition was also wrong, tragically, on race. The suburban development program separated the races. Economic growth was, essentially, bought at the cost of a failure to face the issues of race. These problems came home beginning in the 1960s. If as much energy and money had gone to search for better ways to accommodate racial differences as went into highways and urban renewal and home ownership subsidies, some of the fundamental problems of the 1980s might have been lessened—education would have been better, political regimes more effective, factories less quick to leave urban populations stranded.

New Coalitions?

From these changes there emerged, by the 1970s and 1980s, a new situation. First, at the local level cities had relatively more choices in what policies to attempt than previously and it seemed a situation of experiment. This may seem an odd statement in the light of the withdrawal of federal resources and the new fiscal stringencies that were affecting cities everywhere, but as the federal government withdrew from any strong urban policy initiatives, localities were more free to design their own solutions to local problems and they did so.[14] Second, as Mollenkopf argued, there was a new political terrain, different from that of the earlier period when the original coalitions had formed, which any new effort must adapt to. The earlier urban constituency was much more homogeneous: there had been a geographically concentrated, white, ethnic, blue-collar vote in the cities; and a WASP, Republican vote in the suburbs. Now the city vote was increasingly diverse, partly white-collar, racially divided, still usually Democratic, but with Democrats less committed to the redistributive programs that had proven successful for them earlier. But the suburban vote was also more divided, though tending to be Republican and conservative. Particularly in the cities, but in the suburbs as well, local politics had produced new constituencies: community-based organizations, new middle class groups like environmentalists, and new public sector and service sector labor unions.

What experiments would succeed? Mollenkopf's posing of the issues is useful: By the end of the 1970s, there seemed to be three main contenders for any national policy, each of which had at least some local variant as an exemplary case: traditional liberals who wanted to rebuild the Democratic party; conservatives who wanted to consolidate their gains; and advocates of community-based organizations, who were pressing an alternative policy in many cities and dominated a few.[15] But the key part of his analysis was that any new urban policy, to emerge more generally, had to solve the problems that had sunk the old one. It had to bridge the conflicts that existed within the cities, that is, *address the inequalities* now separating different local constituencies. It had to bridge the conflicts between central city and suburb, and rustbelt and sunbelt, that is, it had to be a *national* policy. It had to devise a system of *accountability* to replace the discredited "iron triangles" of bureaucracy, legislatures, and interest groups that were too removed from the mass of voters. Among the variants Mollenkopf identified, no candidate was completely satisfactory.

The *liberal* alternative was most completely formed, though in retreat. Nationally, the last vestige of the old New Deal/Great Society hangovers, still dominant in most cities, had been the urban policies of the Carter administration, which first tried targeting Urban Development Action Grants (UDAGs) to low income areas, but later reduced aid as part of a budget-cutting economic policy, which then undercut its political support in the cities. Part of the problem was a lack of leadership: this first alternative was simply a revival of the Great Society programs without any attempt to solve the main problems of the coalition: UDAGs went to help downtown interests, and there was neither accountability nor any attempt to mobilize suburban or southern Democrat support.

In the cities, these latter-day growth coalitions varied greatly in success. Some competed vigorously and successfully for the diminishing pool of federal funds and for increasingly footloose private capital. Others limped along, with diminished business support, generally stalemated by the conflict within their boundaries and the diminishing federal resource base.

Black mayors were an increasingly prominent part of the picture, but the problems of the liberal alternative applied to them with particular force. In places like Newark, Detroit, and Oakland, then Philadelphia, Baltimore, and Hartford, they made brave efforts to attract business while placating demands for services from neighborhoods that were going under economically and socially.

The second possibility, given much attention by conservative research institutes and Reagan administration spokespeople and at least partially adopted in many cities, was a *conservative alternative*: defund the left, spend on the military, rely on the states, favor the sunbelt, cut social spending, and work through the private sector. Enterprise zones were the main urban policy initiative: a federal bill furthering such zones was never enacted, but many state bills were passed that aimed to cut the regulatory and labor costs of business in designated places.[16] But this approach had as many *political* drawbacks as the liberal alternative. It was destructive of productive capacity: it defunded the social services, wasted productive assets in the older cities, and shifted assets to defense, the least productive sector. Second, even in the areas it favored, the social costs of growth would ultimately be destabilizing for the conservative coalition. Finally, by confronting the poor, the Northeast, and the very broadly defined "left" the conservatives provided a focus to unite their enemies. These difficulties were apparent in many cities, and there are few examples of the appearance of such a conservative version of the growth coalition at the local level.[17]

The third possibility was the *neighborhood movement alternative*, characterized by citizen participation and neighborhood control, with an economy of self-help and small enterprises, a focus on rehabilitation rather than big projects and helping networks rather than bureaucratized social services, as well as opposition to free market policies. There were many partial and a few more or less complete local examples by the early 1980s, entailing a shift in budget priorities and a shift in the organization of the "delivery system." The first would be a shift of federal grant monies like the community development block grants and UDAGs from downtown to neighborhoods; and of federal resources generally from the military to cities and to social services. The second would be the shift of the service delivery system from city and other public bureaucracies to community-based organizations; and the enlarging of such federally funded employment programs as CETA (Comprehensive Employment Training Act) and VISTA (Volunteers in Service to America), which supported public service employment while delegating control to such agencies. The combined effect of these shifts would be to augment a decentralized, "third sector" delivery system while also increasing the possibilities of alliances between the urban poor and the new professionals.

With the idea of a neighborhood based alternative to the growth coalition, Mollenkopf was summarizing a set of thoughts that, while provocative, had never seemed quite realistic. Early in the 1970s some observers, impressed by the gains of 1960s protest organizations, were quite sanguine about the potential of low income neighborhood organizing. Stephen L. Elkin had noted the emergence of new service agencies supported by their constituencies and federal government largesse; and the most powerful statement had been made in James O'Connor's *The Fiscal Crisis of the State*, suggesting the susceptibility of government employees to alliances with their clients.[18] But a decade later these potentials had still not been reached, although certainly there had been a dramatic increase in neighborhood and other populist based organizations. Few would argue that this was a *viable* political coalition at the national level, but the outlines were there.

In a later piece, Susan Fainstein reviewed the potentials: urban grassroots activity became more sophisticated after the 1960s; while the unifying force of the race issue decreased, activists increasingly took a sophisticated view of the relation of the productive economy to local conditions. Goals now included items like linkage for housing, worker control over runaway plants, and local development corporations doing commercial projects. But while noting a real new potential for joining workplace and community organizing, and new objective conditions for alliance between low- and middle-income workers, she thought the actual formation of coalitions remained an issue.[19]

Thus the idea—frequently suggested in academic and popular writing—became one of cross-class neighborhood alliances. Mollenkopf thought there were inherent limits on such a coalition: a tendency toward localism, "neighborhoodism," and a focus on "service" rather than on the underlying problems (e.g., unemployment, low incomes) that caused the need for the services. But he added a further thought: that the potentials depended on "progressive mayors" who could mobilize their support while also addressing the underlying problems, perhaps by generating a national, supralocal constituency.

One problem that impeded support for such alliances and the possible role of mayors in cultivating them was the negative experiences of many such movements during the 1970s. A number of mayors tried to co-opt the neighborhood constituencies while playing the growth coalition game. This was the "liberal" model growth coalition, extended to situations where there was both the beginnings of a citizen movement and serious economic hardship that made the neighborhood organizations vulnerable— they needed real relief and got symbolic support, or perceived it that way. Rebelling, they turned against city hall.[20] More generally, since the 1960s, there had developed a sense of the fragility of populist social movements, and the ease with which participation in a municipal governing coalition can destroy them. Manuel Castells, in his account of the citizens movement in post-Franco Madrid, lays this possibility out with dramatic finality. There are other such accounts, such as Derek Shearer's description of electoral victory, followed by (temporary) defeat, in Santa Monica.[21] An initial proposition, then, suggests a negative effect, for any social movement, of electoral involvement.

Other evidence suggests the story is not so straightforward. Early U.S. experience with municipal socialism tell of strong social movements at their base that appear *not* to have been destroyed by the governments built upon them.[22] In Rod Bush's collection in *The New Black Vote*,[23] several authors detail breaks from the liberal growth model under black leadership: Chicago, Boston, Oakland, and elsewhere. The popular movement in Boston appears not to have been crippled by the election of the populist Raymond Flynn as mayor, perhaps because a major part of it occupied a position to Flynn's left and so remained distinct and in some conflict with his government.[24] Other examples have been described for such places as Denver, San Antonio, Seattle, Portland, San Francisco, and Minneapolis; and there is important evidence from such long-term "progressive cities" as Santa Monica, Burlington, and Berkeley.[25]

The Experience of Progressive Municipal Government Through 1983

One might well ask what such accounts, often focused on smaller cities with no substantial minority populations, can tell us that is relevant to the larger U.S. cities. Perhaps they tell part of the story. In the larger cities one sees substantial neighborhood and other social movements but very strong resistance to any takeover of city government, so there is little actual experience of governing by a progressive coalition from which one can learn. In some smaller places the takeover has been easier and there has been a governance experience, leading to a whole new set of issues. Their experiences were not uniformly happy ones. But at a minimum, one can view the efforts of progressive local governments as instructive: look for partial gains—for example, the development of new leadership and the emergence of techniques for encouraging organization at the grass roots. In this perspective, Mollenkopf's community organization alternative begins to take on new meaning.

Events of the 1980s, and some in the 1970s, were at least mixed: if anything more sanguine than Fainstein's general statement. Progressives did take over mayoralties in a number of smaller and larger cities, and neighborhood and other social movements did mature and begin to debate the most fundamental problems, through such national organizations as the Conference on Alternative State and Local Policies and, increasingly, the U.S. Conference of Mayors.

When grass-roots interests moved from individual projects and coalition building *outside* of government to support for and occasional participation in majority takeovers of local government itself, their degree of sophistication moved to a new level. An early example was in Hartford, where Nicholas Carbone became majority leader of the city council in the 1970s and initiated such innovations as a city real estate program, a neighborhood police experiment, and various new client-oriented services such as a city energy policy for low-income tenants and support for the nationally known Hartford Food System. The real estate program may have been the most important innovation. It was based on the realization that the city had few resources but some land and tax abatement authority; that it could trade land and tax abatements for control over the operation of downtown projects—hiring during construction and later operation, for example, of the Hartford Civic Center shops; guarantees of city resident, minority, and low-income hiring and tenancy. These policies, later known as "linkage" in such other path-breaking cases as Santa Monica, San Francisco, and Boston, were successfully put into place in eleven major downtown projects.

In Santa Monica, a rent control coalition succeeded in establishing the nation's strongest rent control law in a 1979 initiative, and then used its organization to gain control of the city council two years later. The result was a series of reforms that persisted through a subsequent Republican mayor and council and later a second generation of the original coalition's leadership. Most notable were a set of "linkage"-type development agreements and enhancement of citizen participation across a range of issues. Berkeley's progressives gained access to the city council in 1971 and controlled it except for two years after 1979: their innovations included several rent control initiatives (including some struck down by court decisions) and a "Fair Representation Ordinance" that dramatically increased participation in city boards and commissions. In Burlington, Vt., socialist Bernard Sanders was mayor from 1981 to 1989, when he stepped down in favor of his community development director, Peter Clavelle. In San Antonio, Mayor Henry G. Cisneros implemented economic development and educational reforms supported by a grassroots organization, Communities Organized for Public Service (COPS).

In cases like these, where the experience goes a step beyond the promise of social movements and of potential or actual coalitions among single-interest constituencies and we witness the actual takeover of the instruments of legitimate power, the implications are enormous—as we shall see in the following subsections.

Agenda Setting

First, once a populist coalition gained majority control over a government, it offered the possibility to stake out terrain in a dramatic—often conflictual—way, thus changing the agenda of public debate. Thus, in Burlington, Sanders was an "avowed socialist," and he used this identification to claim a city voice and interest in disputing the claims of businessmen and developers to control city economic policy. Through a series of disputes, and after gaining reelection, city working-class and antidevelopment interests gained a great deal of control over the agenda of debate. In Santa Monica, the rent control coalition established its authority over the development process—and attendant debate—by setting a moratorium on construction at its first council meeting and establishing three citizen task forces to determine what to do with pending projects. Similar initiatives occurred in other places.

These sorts of conflicted beginnings served a tactical function, welding the progressive coalition together as its members realized the intransigence of the opposition, and discrediting die-hard defeated factions for not giving the new regime a fair chance. But it was also a strategic challenge: Was there substance around which to organize, a set of goals truly worth fighting for when once in office? What were these, and where did they come from? Some of this agenda came from long periods of organizing or from minority positions in government prior to gaining control. Some of it was improvised by progressive leadership or in group discussion. The more exact nature of this agenda-setting function is not clear, and we shall later explore its Chicago variant.

Relating to the Base

There opened up the possibility of using the municipal government to mobilize the base as a mass movement. In Berkeley, radical coalitions, lacking majority control of city council, used the initiative process to do this: proposals like rent control, police reorganization, a utilities takeover, and a neighborhood protection ordinance brought out the vote for electoral purposes and dramatized popular support for legislation the progressives supported. In Burlington, Sanders gained support when he confronted the developer-oriented planning board over development projects and an unpopular "southern connector" highway that threatened city neighborhoods.

Progressives could also exploit the mass base. Later in Boston, the existence of a mass base to the left of Flynn, one organized partly around the strong mayoral bid of populist black candidate Mel King, gave Flynn leverage to initiate new linkage and housing policies. Activists in Berkeley and Santa Monica credited a vocal left, not under the control of the governing coalition, with increasing their own freedom of action.

It was a more long-run issue and often neglected, but these governments could also *nourish* the base that elected, supported, and sometimes pushed them to do more than they felt able to do. Perhaps most obvious was the channeling of funds to community-based organizations and providing them with access to government officials. This happened in all of these cases.

But nourishing the base became a problem, a subtle one: community organizations, which gained part of their strength from their ability to fight city hall, now had to find other ways to maintain their legitimacy with their constituents; and what if they disagreed with their "friends" in city hall? There were other problems as well. City hall, by hiring organizers away from neighborhood organizations, could sap their leadership. Even while funding them, they could turn popular advocate agencies into service providers.

There was clearly a need for adjustment on both sides. But what may be most interesting is the extent to which these adjustments were successful, resulting in a continuing and growing base. In Berkeley, eighteen years of participation in government did not destroy the grass-roots energy of the progressive coalition there; in Santa Monica and Burlington there remained a constituency for the programs initiated by progressive governments. Both the local movements and the governments appeared to recognize certain principles: movement and government needed to remain separate and independent; granting of funds to neighborhood organizations did not obligate them to give up a political role.

Transcending the Base

The problem with the mass base was that, however organized and vigorous, it was often narrow in its aims, while the city government needed support from a wider coalition if it was to survive. This problem had the potential to destroy both the base and the government. Progressive governments tried various strategies, not all of them successful. In some cases progressive mayors, having ridden to victory on grass-roots support, quickly reached out to more conservative elements at the cost of diffusing grass-roots support. Another approach was a "pragmatic" populism: dole out some city resources—Community Development Block Grants were the usual ones first tapped—to neighborhood organizations while placating business interests who supported growth projects. This did not work too well either.

Race was both the most divisive and the most powerful motivating force in the grass-roots movements of the larger U.S. cities, and progressive mayors tried to devise strategies to cultivate grass-roots support across race lines. One strategy was what Mayor Dennis Kucinich of Cleveland called "urban populism" in a well-publicized speech. He argued that the city should focus on economic issues, since these united various city consti-tuencies, but that it should avoid "social issues." But the most important social issue was race in his tragically divided city, and race baiting, when he allowed it to creep into his reelection campaign, destroyed his chances of uniting the city's black and white working-class neighborhoods against the banks. Mayor Flynn of Boston took a tack that was at least superficially similar a decade later. His left opposition argued for a more thoroughgoing populism confronting problems of race head-on.[26]

Remarkably, many progressive governments found ways to transcend grass-roots narrowness and even to change and broaden the movement. In Berkeley there were many small victories in the attempt to weld blacks and white progressives in a coalition that had a history dating back to the 1960s.[27] Moving beyond narrow agendas was easier where race was not the main factor. In Santa Monica, for example, rent control interests learned to negotiate with developers and homeowners around common and broader objectives.

But progress toward such broader aims was always a problem. Creation of a general theory of the relationship of a progressive government to its mass base, or simply a set of rules and focused "problems," is an obvious need: more focused versions of such requirements as that of recognition of the difference between a movement and a government, and that of mutual respect for the fragility of movement organizations and the rigidity of gov-ernment bureaucracies. Cities varied in these things.

Progressive Expertise

There was a buildup of management experience and technique in pro-gressive cities, distinct from what went on before, and which could become a resource for the future. This is an obscure but vital point: progressive gov-ernments tended to begin as creatures of a "movement," and independence from the existing city machinery sometimes seemed more important than professionalism. But the problem was not independence but control, and that depended crucially on key appointments even in the beginning, and the development of an independent and innovative kind of professionalism was crucial to their continued success. In Hartford, Carbone depended on such staff people as John Alschuler, David Smith, and Michael Brown; in Santa Monica the roles of City Attorney Robert Myers and City Manager John Alschuler (who moved from Hartford), in Berkeley Assistant City Manager Eve Bach, in Cleveland Planning Director Norman Krumholz, and in Burlington key contributions by Peter Clavelle, Jonathan Coleman, and Michael Monte were crucial. Later, as these governments evolved, staff expertise developed and grew, and a new management style emerged, as well as what amounted to a new doctrine of city economics, legal practice, and city planning.

Management style was important because it helped break down the bureaucratic form of government that progressives were reacting against. Progressives did this partly by hiring better administrators generally; but they were aided because their governments were built upon social movements. Thus they could draw many top administrators from that movement. The result was the frequent introduction into city government of a capacity to relate the bureaucratic routines of agency life to the informal and often highly charged styles of street organizing; this went beyond style, in some cases, to include a capacity to make contact across class lines and even race lines that was quite foreign to the city bureaucracies that existed before the progressive regime, even in the smaller cities. This capacity to reach out from city hall to the neighborhoods came at a price: intense conflict within agencies and among agencies, for example, for the changes were uneven. But there were also changes, sometimes dramatic, that occurred in the outlooks of people who participated in progressive governments, usually from more traditionally professional to more interactive, perhaps more conscious of class, race, and gender.

The other part of the new professionalism was the new uses it made of the techniques of planning, budgeting, and other management work. Planning, which tended to be distorted and constrained by the market fetishism of growth coalition governments and by the assumption that private sector initiatives were presumptively good, took on new life and usefulness under progressive regimes. Budgeting became creatively redistributive and participatory as in the case of Berkeley's Citizen Budget Review Commission, in which thirty-six persons executed a significant upward redistribution of budget cuts in 1979.[28]

But the catalog of management and administrative experience under progressive governments—not to say any theory or codification—remains unexplored territory at this point, with little or no literature despite the growing experience.

Professionalism and Diversity

The new professionalism was more than technical. Many members of these city governments testified to the transforming experience of day-to-day contact with economic classes and races that had been outside their previous experience. The catalyst for this was often political rather than professional work, and the boundaries between the two, jealously guarded in traditional city government bureaucracies, often blurred. Norman Krumholz, Cleveland city planning director during most of the 1970s, described the experience of working for black mayor Carl Stokes as pivotal; sitting on a suburban-dominated regional board as Stokes's representative, he felt their antipathy to Stokes and Cleveland blacks as racism directed at *himself*, and this fed his own commitment to oppose it.[29] Later, he was able to foster close interaction between his own staff professionals and the organizers of the Cleveland neighborhood movement. Harry Fagan, a figure behind much of the organizing, said, "We had kids working for each other, who dated each other. . . . It was an instinctive feeling about the same things. Someone would say 'that son-of-a-bitching RTA is going to go to a buck' and we both know that blacks were likely to get screwed."[30] Nicholas Carbone, who was the dominant political figure in Hartford during the same period, described a transformation in his own consciousness resulting from his willingness to encounter black leaders during a series of riots there in the beginning of the 1970s:

> In June of 1969, I was at the state capitol when the word came about the first of the riots . . . I was shocked and aghast at what I saw, because this was outside the realm of my experience. I never understood anger which was so great as to be totally violent. . . . First I came down on the side of the officials. This had to be looters, thugs, etc. . . . The more I examined and talked to people, the more I learned about the extent of poverty. I had never known real poverty before. . . . It took like a year of going through this.[31]

These encounters resulted in a series of personal changes. White middle-class students and professionals got in contact with low-income blacks and other low-income persons through organizing work, which they later built on in professional schools and in government work. Low-income blacks and others worked their way into city government positions, or other leadership roles, through union work or neighborhood organizing work. A series of alliances across classes and racial lines developed.

The result was the development of abilities to see into the interests of a variety of groups that differed from the normal practice of professions or city bureaucracies, and differed also from the practice of political figures who, though they thrived on the widest net of contacts, often retreated into the isolation of the groups from which they came. The progressive city experience was different from this: politicians led the way, but professional staffs became infused with norms of contact and consultation across class and race lines. This made a difference in everything they did.

Institutionalizing Reform

Once a grass-roots coalition got control of a city government, there was the question of which reforms could be made permanent and institutionalized, given the massive resistance that often came from city bureaucracies, the press, and holdover city council members. Several things worked in favor of this, though the book is still open on which ones worked most effectively. There were new possibilities for legitimizing and protecting specific constituencies and interests. Burlington and Santa Monica set up Women's Commissions, for example. Burlington protected its vision of the city interest in development by setting up a Community Economic Development Office (CEDO) in which it installed much of its key staff. These new offices got strong constituency support, which would make them hard to eliminate once established.

Another front was the fight to build alliances between a new government in control of, say, the city council or the mayor's office, and existing city administrative centers. A good example is the police. Once in power, the coalition has formal control over the police. There is now a battle over how the police shall operate, but the struggle has moved to a new level and new terrain. In Santa Monica, the rent control coalition, once it got control over the city council, moved immediately to cultivate the cooperation of the police. The city attorney began to give police a new level of efficient service on citizen complaint cases, which had long been a problem for them; and the city council began a neighborhood policing initiative that built community support for police.

Getting Outside Connections

Local governments are notoriously limited in what they can do, and progressives, once in office, invariably noticed the constraints put on them by state governments and an increasingly hostile federal government environment. But there was also the knowledge that some changes were possible at the local level and that there was much to be gained by showcasing innovations elsewhere and learning from other places. Progressives exploited the chance for outside contacts vigorously.

Many of them wrote and spoke extensively; some organized small research and technical assistance institutes that facilitated national networking. There was the Conference on Alternative State and Local Policies, which former activist Lee Webb established in Washington, D.C., in 1974 and which produced national conferences through 1980. Associates and members of progressive governments won higher political office or peopled administrative positions. Tom Hayden became an assembly member in California.

There was also the support these governments gave and got from academia. Universities hired personnel and provided student interns; their informal role may have been much more important in some cases, as in Berkeley, where a major part of the radical community would not have existed except for the existence of the University of California campus there. Finally, a network of consultants developed. They varied in how successful they were, but consulting made possible a cadre of highly skilled professionals that could transfer skills learned in one municipality to another, or from one level of government to another.

Economic Background
and the Community-based Agenda in Chicago

The essays that follow describe many of these same phenomena in Chicago. During Harold Washington's mayoralty in 1983–1987 the grassroots organizing in the black community and in the community development organizations emerged from the periphery of local politics and economic decision making to a more central position. In this the community development movement played an important role. Its leadership—the main representation in this book—in part moved into official government positions. Mier, Moe, and Giloth represent this group. These people, along with other sympathetic figures drawn from elsewhere—like Hollander, Torres, Walker, and Wright—had a chance to see how far, and over what obstacles, Mollenkopf's suggestion of a neighborhood-based alternative to the growth coalition could be implemented. Other members of the community development movement stayed outside city hall but, from one vantage point or another, found themselves playing supportive or critical roles in the same experiment. This characterizes others whose work is represented below: Gills, Kretzman, Ducharme, and Brehm. There were a host of others in each category.

For the community development people at least, their later experience in and around the Washington administration was conditioned by a set of economic and political developments during the 1970s that set the agenda for them. These developments paralleled what went on in other cities but also had their unique aspects. One aspect that was particularly well developed in Chicago, more than in other places, was the evolution of consciousness, analysis, and program ideas by the community-based network. This can be seen as a prepolitical but formative phase and is worth special mention here. Gills's chapter, below, provides a good deal of the stimulus for our emphasis, and we believe it informs other chapters as well, though their main focus is on Washington's administrative performance as related to the community development movement. The main features of this prepolitical phase in Chicago include those discussed in the following subsections.

Economic Changes

The nationwide economic changes of the postwar period hit Chicago somewhat later than other parts of the Northeast and Midwest. Its diversified economy withstood the effect of business cycles better than the specialized economies of cities like Detroit, Pittsburgh, Cleveland, or Buffalo did. Also, its main industries, based on major consumer goods, agricultural equipment, food processing, and machinery were more resistant to imports from low-wage countries than, for instance, the shoe and apparel industries of New England.

Nevertheless, until 1983 the City of Chicago had been losing manufacturing jobs steadily since its peak of 668,056 in 1947 and after 1967 the Chicago region as a whole declined in manufacturing employment. The decline was particularly devastating between 1967 and 1982, when a quarter of a million, or 46 percent of the city's manufacturing jobs, were lost.[32]

These manufacturing job losses provided a context of decline and dislocation. This sense was probably strongest during the period of Harold Washington's 1982/83 mayoral campaign, when a long period of decline was capped by the worst recession since the Great Depression. Many of the manufacturing jobs had been located throughout Chicago's neighborhoods, and everywhere outside of the central business district there was visible evidence of economic decline in the form of abandoned factories. The counterpoint to this was provided by the gleaming office buildings going up at record pace in Chicago's Loop and the suburbs, which, however, were not providing jobs for Chicagoans. Indeed, manufacturing decline was not made up by growth in nonmanufacturing jobs in the city, which actually declined by 45,000 between 1972 and 1983, for a total decline of 222,000 jobs. Nonmanufacturing jobs did grow in the suburbs, by a whopping 48 percent, or 316,000 jobs.[33] Also, many more suburbanites

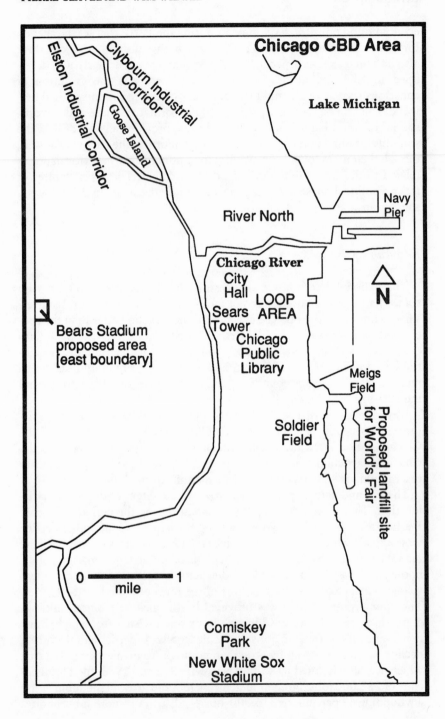

Chicago CBD Area

Elston Industrial Corridor

Clybourn Industrial Corridor

Goose Island

Lake Michigan

River North

Navy Pier

Chicago River

City Hall

LOOP AREA

Sears Tower

Chicago Public Library

Bears Stadium proposed area [east boundary]

Meigs Field

N

Soldier Field

Proposed landfill site for World's Fair

0 ———— 1
mile

Comiskey Park

New White Sox Stadium

O'Hare
Airport

Northwest
Side

North
Side

Chicago River

Lakefront

Lake Michigan

Uptown

Lincoln
Park

West
Town

River
North

CENTRAL
BUSINESS
DISTRICT

West
Side

*Bears
Stadium

Lawndale

South
Loop

City
of
Chicago

Pilsen

Near
South
Side

Little
Village

Kenwood-
Oakland

Lakefront

Southwest
Side

Woodlawn

South
Side

∧
N

*Proposed

0   miles   5

commuted into Chicago than the reverse, with about a third of Chicago's jobs held by suburbanites.[34]

Racial Change

The suburban job growth followed on the heels of the suburban population growth, which largely consisted of whites. Of the metropolitan area's black population, 86 percent lived in the city in 1980. Chicago's white population decreased from 60 percent of the population in 1970 to 47.6 percent in 1980; blacks increased from 33 to 40 percent, and Hispanics to approximately 8 percent. Total population size declined slightly, to just under 3 million, out of a metropolitan area population of about 7 million.

These changes were accompanied by a general deterioration of socioeconomic conditions of Chicago residents. In constant dollars, per capita income in the city declined by 6.6 percent from 1979 to 1985; in the United States it grew by 3.7 percent during the same period.[35] Minorities bore the brunt of the worsening circumstances. Median family income for blacks in Chicago declined between 1970 and 1980 from 77 to 68 percent of that of whites. Similarly, the percentage of families with incomes below the poverty level declined for whites in the city, but increased from 21 to 29 percent for blacks and from 16 to 23 percent for Hispanics.[36] Thus, by 1983, the city's economic structure, population composition, and income levels had changed drastically from the situation even ten or fifteen years earlier.

Chicago's Growth Coalition

As in other cities, Chicago has had a clearly discernable growth coalition, or "growth machine," which aided and abetted some of the major postwar changes but also sought, in vain, to reverse others.[37] As elsewhere, the main participants in this coalition were the economic sectors with large fixed investments in place, with the fewest options to leave: the major downtown banks, especially Continental Bank and First National Bank of Chicago; department stores such as Marshall Field's; utilities; newspapers, particularly the *Chicago Tribune*; real estate developers and architectural firms, especially Skidmore, Owings & Merrill; and occasional other corporations with headquarters downtown. Usually these firms acted jointly, represented over time by different organizations, such as the Central Area Committee, Chicago United, and the Commercial Club. Of these, only Chicago United included significant numbers of minorities, since it was originally established in the early 1970s as a coalition of the main Chicago businesses and minority leadership. Before this, minorities were largely invisible in these circles.

During the 1950s and 1960s, this business sector formed a strong coalition with city government under Mayor Richard J. Daley and with the labor unions. The plans it put together were generally aimed at maintaining a very strong downtown and consequently favored service sector employment over manufacturing, investment in centrally focused transportation networks over infrastructure improvements in the neighborhoods, and housing for the middle class over low-income housing.

Most plans formulated by the growth coalition focused on land use but made explicit assumptions about the economy in doing so. Specific economic planning was focused on targeted areas, such as the Mid-Chicago Economic Development Project.[38] The first real citywide economic plans were published in the mid-1970s by the Mayor's Council of Manpower and Economic Advisors, a private sector–dominated advisory group. A series of reports identified the strengths and weaknesses in different economic sectors and, in an interesting display of candor, analyzed three policy options.[39] The equity-based approach would focus public resources on those areas and residents that were worst off; a triage policy would focus on those rated average, with upward potential; and the economic growth policy would focus resources on the areas and industries with the greatest potential to generate jobs and on the residents who could most easily be retrained. The reports recommended the last approach on the assumption that the highest possible growth would be of most benefit to the city.

This approach was reiterated in the 1984 economic plan of the Civic Committee of the Commercial Club.[40] Entitled *Make No Little Plans: Jobs for Metropolitan Chicago*, the report called attention to the poor performance of the Chicago economy, both in absolute terms and compared to the nation. It strongly supported an emphasis on entrepreneurship and growth industries such as financial services, the information industry, health care, high technology, and tourism. An interesting new twist to the report was its focus on the region, rather than just the city, reflecting the decreasing importance of Chicago itself. The report argued that improving the attractiveness of the business climate and quality of life were the main tasks for the region. The study hardly mentioned manufacturing at all.

Political Change

Although the growth coalition's views of the city as an administrative and financial services center had in many ways been realized by the early 1980s, the goal of maintaining a demographically balanced population had clearly not been achieved. The city's population was poorer than it had been, and for the first time whites constituted a minority of the population.

The traditional power base of Chicago's political machine had been the coalition between business interests and the white working class represented by unions. The city administration under Mayor Daley provided the glue holding it together in the form of business and development opportunities and union-scale wages for all city projects. Blacks received token representation and were generally powerless. The city council consisted of fifty ward-based aldermen, who largely controlled the delivery of city services in their wards. [NB: In Chicago, city council members are traditionally all called alder*men* regardless of their gender.] They also controlled land use decisions, in that no zoning changes were approved without the consent of the affected alderman. All city employees essentially served at the mayor's pleasure, and a recommendation from the local alderman was a prerequisite for most city jobs.

The dramatic demographic and economic changes of the 1960s and 1970s shattered this arrangement. As the white working class moved to the suburbs, support at the polls became ever more precarious. The civil rights movement introduced the first attempts at political independence in the black community. Finally, the middle-class professionals in the financial and business services sectors, residentially concentrated along the Lakefront, were not integrated in the traditional union and political machine system, and supported the election of a host of independent aldermen to city council.

After Daley's death in late 1976, the machine hung on to power with the election of Daley's floorleader, Michael Bilandic. But the erosion of its electoral support became clear when Jane Byrne, running as a proneighborhood and antimachine candidate, defeated Bilandic in the next primary, in 1979.

The machine was not yet dead though. Although Byrne's independent candidacy helped elect even more independent aldermen, she quickly turned to, or was encapsulated by, the old guard. As Douglas Gills writes in his chapter, her four-year tenure was marked by increasingly bitter fights between her administration and the progressive and black communities that had helped elect her and that were subseqently strengthened by four years of opposition. These fights also reflected the increasing resource scarcity imposed by federal policies and the city's own changed socioeconomic conditions.

In addition to the economic, demographic, and political changes affecting the viability of the machine, legal proceedings took away one of its key resources: patronage jobs. The Shakman consent decree, entered into by Mayor Washington in 1983, outlawed the firing of city employees for political reasons and exempted only about 800 out of the 40,000 city jobs. Thus, one of the main tools for rewarding supporters and punishing opponents was not available to Washington. His inaugural statement, that "the machine, as we know it, is dead, dead, dead" was indeed true.

The Black and Neighborhood Movement

While the aforementioned changes were a necessary condition for the demise of the machine, they were not sufficient. Certainly they were not sufficient for the replacement of the machine by a progressive black mayor and his administration. Gills presents the history of black political development in Chicago to explain how the combination of demographic change and black political mobilization prepared the terrain for Washington. An important additional set of conditions derives from the growth of the neighborhood movement in Chicago. While this movement could hardly supply all the votes needed for an election, it delivered some of the energy and enthusiasm needed for the voter registration drive that made election possible. Most importantly, it supplied many of the ideas and people that constituted Washington's neighborhood and economic development policy, which was the cornerstone of his agenda. The history of this community movement in Chicago has not yet been written and is ultimately beyond the scope of this book. However, we need to sketch it briefly to allow for a proper understanding of what transpired during the 1983–1987 period.

The history of Chicago's neighborhood movement starts with the nineteenth-century settlement houses and the often racist neighborhood conservation groups of the early part of this century.[41] The strongest organizational influence can be traced to Saul Alinsky's work in the 1930s in the Back of the Yards area. His coalition of churches, fraternal organizations, block clubs, and other groups emphasized immediate, easily identifiable, and, most importantly, winnable issues as the route to creating power for ordinary citizens.[42] The model was widely replicated, and Chicago still has a large number of Alinsky-style coalition organizations, especially in the white and, increasingly, Hispanic working-class areas.

The antipoverty programs of the 1960s brought a second wave of neighborhood organizations to Chicago. Unlike the Alinsky organizations, these new groups were established to provide services or to channel citizen participation in the planning process. Thus, they had a more direct relationship with city government, especially since local government always maintained more control over the Great Society programs in Chicago than was the case elsewhere. Nevertheless, these programs created an organizational infrastructure of trained organizers and leaders, especially in poor and minority neighborhoods.

As funding for these programs diminished, the organizations that survived became more diverse. Some became involved in housing rehabilitation and formed such coalitions as the Chicago Rehab Network. Others developed into purely protest and advocacy organizations and were engaged in struggles around the plans of the growth coalition. For instance,

opposition to one of the major proposed expressways, the Crosstown, gal-
vanized succesful organizing efforts in many of the neighborhoods in its
path. Similarly, several neighborhoods organized to oppose the Chicago
21 Plan, one of the major downtown redevelopment plans, and two neighborhoods on the Near West Side developed their own counterplan. On a
larger scale, Gale Cincotta's National People's Action developed from individual struggles around redlining issues and was ultimately succesful in
getting the federal Community Reinvestment Act and Home Mortgage
Disclosure Act passed. This pattern of succesful organizing by coalitions of
individual neighborhood organizations continued through such diverse
activities as the establishment of the Neighborhood Reinvestment Program
in 1983 and the defeat of the 1992 Chicago World's Fair in 1985.[43] These
experiences of success were important factors in providing the neighborhood movement with a sense of its own efficacy, as well as legitimacy in the
eyes of others.

The ability to mobilize support and organize around a wide range of
issues was strengthened by the ever-growing number of neighborhood organizations. The urban programs of the Carter administration provided a
temporary surge in federal resources, and under Mayor Jane Byrne neighborhood organizations involved in commercial revitalization and economic development began to receive city funding. This period, extending
into the early 1980s, also saw the birth of half a dozen coalitions and
technical assistance providers, which brought a new level of expertise, resources, and legitimacy. In addition to the Rehab Network, this included
the Center for Neighborhood Technology, the University of Illinois at
Chicago's Center for Urban Economic Development, the Chicago Association of Neighborhood Development Organizations, which initially
brought together the commercial organizations mostly working in white
neighborhoods, and the Community Workshop for Economic Development (CWED). The last of these included most of the people who
developed and ultimately helped implement Mayor Washington's neighborhood economic development policy. Several of the authors in this
volume, including Brehm, Ducharme, Gills, Mier, Moe, Kretzmann and
Wiewel, played important roles in CWED.

CWED resulted from a conference for community organizations on enterprise zones in 1982. Most organizations represented poor and minority
areas and they rejected the idea of enterprise zones as fostering competition
between neighborhoods in a "beggar thy neighbor" strategy. They also
agreed that they should formulate their own economic development program, primarily aimed at the upcoming gubernatorial elections. CWED
never achieved a strong statewide presence, and soon focused its programmatic statements on Chicago and the 1983 mayoral election. The process
of formulating the CWED platform, both before and after the conference,

was the organization's main activity prior to Washington's election. The platform's preamble presented an analysis of "The Impact of Economic Crisis on Illinois Communities" which attacked private sector disinvestment and the role of public policy in assisting selective reinvestment in high growth areas only.[44] Importantly, it was not just looking to the public sector, but argued that "Communities Know What to Do" in economic development. Its seven principles, illustrated with specific programs, were as follows:

1. Full employment in every community
2. Increasing ownership share for residents and workers
3. Community involvement in planning and administering economic development programs
4. More resources for community development projects
5. Resource allocation through open negotiation
6. Management and technical assistance
7. Allocation of resources based on affirmative action.

With some variations, these principles, along with many of the specific program ideas, were incorporated in Washington's campaign documents and subsequently in *Chicago Works Together*, the official Chicago Development Plan published in 1984.[45]

Harold Washington's Election

The chapter by Doug Gills presents detail on Washington's campaign and election. This represented the coming together of what had been building during the preceding fifteen years: the mobilization of the black community, the political reform movement of the "Lakefront liberals," and the growth of the neighborhood movement. With the gradual disappearance of the machine's traditional voting blocks, and inspired by Washington's formidable persona, this new coalition was able to take power, albeit just barely.

The campaign started with massive voter registration drives, yielding 180,000 black voter registrations, increasing the number of black registered voters by about 20 percent over the 1979 total. In the Democratic primary, Washington ran against Jane Byrne and Richard M. Daley (the former mayor's son) and won with 36 percent of the vote. In the general election, most of the remnants of the machine united behind Bernard Epton, the Republican candidate. Washington won, by 50,000 out of 1.3 million votes cast. His support was virtually unanimous in black wards, but averaged only 12 percent in white wards. Critical votes came from the

Latino wards, which he had not carried in the primary, but where he averaged 74 percent in the general election.[46] Thus, Washington started his mayoralty on the strength of a black mass movement, with critical support from white independents and from Hispanics, but faced with very strong opposition.

Our Approach in This Book

In this introductory chapter we have tried to set out a context, derived from urban theory and the broader sweep of recent city development in the United States, for what happened in Chicago under Harold Washington. This raises a number of challenging questions that it would be tempting—for us as academics—to address directly.

But while we come back to the general issues in a concluding chapter, our approach in putting together this book has been to get on paper the recollections of participants in a segment of Chicago's neighborhood movement and a part of the Washington administration, rather than a set of analyses by outsiders and academics. There is some analysis in these chapters, and some of the authors are currently academics; but at the time of the events described all were in neighborhood organization jobs or in close support roles or in city administration jobs.

Therefore the chapters that follow deal with a set of questions that have more immediacy and need to be exposed, if not fully answered, before the more theoretical questions can be addressed:

First, what experiences did the participants bring to their work during 1983–1987? Most were from a "movement" background, and it was obvious that this represented a potential contribution to government and political action different from that represented by persons involved in other types of government, such as the machine politics that had previously characterized Chicago.

Second, what was it like to be in and around the Washington administration for persons that had developed the neighborhood movement perspective represented here? The initial response we received was its intensity, and a kind of exhilaration that sustained intensity.

But this led to a third question: what was the substance that made the intensity around the events recounted in these chapters different from that involved in other intense situations like working for any new administration? The answer for these authors seemed to relate to the way Washington—and therefore those around him—touched a people who had previously not been part of the city's mainstream. This is what provided the exhilaration and intensity unique to the 1983–1987 period and motivated the work described here.

If this was true, still a fourth question arose: what did they hope to be able to do, or have the Washington administration do, and what did they attempt? From these chapters it will be clear that they invented and carried out programs that took on life from the people newly incorporated and given access. Perhaps that is the main contribution these chapters make: descriptions of what was tried.

Out of these descriptions emerges a fifth thing: a fresh sense of how the authors succeeded, what obstacles they faced, and what lessons they were beginning to draw from this. We will try to assess this in the concluding chapter. Because we feel that while Chicago is unique in many respects— its size, diversity, and particular political history—its experience with progressive government contains significant lessons for other cases. Thus we share with our authors the goals of recording history and contributing to similar efforts in the future.

NOTES

1. On the difficulties of redistribution, the key recent work is Paul E. Peterson, *City Limits* (Chicago: University of Chicago Press, 1981). Other works include Charles Murray, *Losing Ground: American Social Policy, 1950–1980* (New York: Basic Books, 1984), and William J. Wilson, *The Declining Significance of Race* (Chicago: University of Chicago Press, 1978); but see D. Thomas Boston, *Race, Class and Conservatism* (Boston: Unwin Hyman, 1988).
2. Our conception of "new political terrain" and the set of alternative policy possibilities described below comes from those of John Mollenkopf, *The Contested City* (Princeton, N.J.: Princeton University Press, 1983).
3. For this conception of "progressive" urban government see also Robert Kuttner, *The Life of the Party* (New York: Viking, 1987), p. 7, where he writes:
    I use the term "progressive populist" to describe the modern Democratic Party philosophy that began with the New Deal, which also incorporated several antecedents and resonated with the intuitively egalitarian strain in the American character. It appropriated the demand for economic justice from the populists; it embraced and enlarged several regulatory inventions from the Progressive Era. It defined the modern mixed economy. It added the idea of macroeconomic management by the federal government, as well as direct federal spending in a variety of areas dedicated to the betterment of the common American. It included a social-democratic welfare state, and a dose of economic planning. It contained a salutary whiff of class warfare whenever "economic royalists" sought to resist its forward momentum.

We are indebted to Alan DiGaetano for a manuscript that points this out and further elaborates the U.S. evidence: "The Democratic Party and City Politics in the Post-Industrial Era." Further elaboration for the case of "progressive" cities is in Pierre Clavel, *The Progressive City: Planning and Participation, 1969–1984* (New Brunswick, N.J.: Rutgers University Press, 1986).

4. Samuel Bowles, "The Post-Keynesian Capital-Labor Stalemate," *Socialist Review* 65 (September/October 1982), 45–72; Bennett Harrison and Barry Bluestone, *The Great U-Turn: Corporate Restructuring and the Polarizing of America* (New York: Basic Books, 1988); and Ira Katznelson, "Was the Great Society a Lost Opportunity?" in Steve Fraser and Gary Gerstle, eds., *The Rise and Fall of the New Deal Order, 1930–1980* (Princeton, N.J.: Princeton University Press, 1989), pp. 185–211.

5. Mollenkopf, *The Contested City*; David M. Gordon, "Capitalist Development and the History of American Cities," in W. Tabb and L. Sawers, eds., *Marxism and the Metropolis: New Perspectives in Urban Political Economy* (New York: Oxford University Press, 1978); and Susan Fainstein et al., *Restructuring the City: The Political Economy of Urban Redevelopment*, rev. ed. (New York: Longman, 1986), p. 249

6. See, for example, Kenneth Jackson, *Crabgrass Frontier: The Suburbanization of the United States* (New York: Oxford University Press, 1985), chap. 11, on the institution of "redlining"—proscribing mortgage credit in black neighborhoods— in the 1930s.

7. Mollenkopf, *Contested City*, and Stephen L. Elkin, "Cities without Power: The Transformation of American Urban Regimes," in D. Ashford, ed., *National Resources and Urban Policy* (New York: Methuen, 1980).

8. The terminolgy of "growth" is most prominent in Mollenkopf, *Contested City*, and also in Harvey Molotch, "The City as a Growth Machine," *American Journal of Sociology* 82, no. 2 (1976), 309–332. The idea is exhaustively explored in Todd Swanstrom, *The Crisis of Growth Politics: Cleveland, Kucinich, and the Challenge of Urban Populism* (Philadelphia: Temple University Press, 1985). The idea that growth coalitions are producer coalitions comes from Mollenkopf, *Contested City*; but see also the provocative critique, stressing the consumerist base of such politics, in C. B. Macpherson, *The Life and Times of Liberal Democracy* (New York: Oxford University Press, 1977).

9. See Alan Wolfe, *America's Impasse: The Rise and Fall of the Politics of Growth* (New York: Pantheon, 1981), especially chap. 4; and Marc A. Weiss, "The Origins and Legacy of Urban Renewal," in P. Clavel, J. Forester, and W. Goldsmith, eds., *Urban and Regional Planning in an Age of Austerity* (Elmsford, N.Y.: Pergamon Press, 1980), pp. 53–80. On Moses, see Robert Caro, *The Power Broker* (New York: Vintage, 1975).

10. The claim to solving race issues is at least implicit in this literature. On Philadelphia see James Reichley, *The Art of Government: Reform and Organization Politics in Philadelphia* (New York: The Fund for the Republic, 1959). On the increasing costs of federal support for the urban coalitions, see Elkin, "Cities without Power."

11. Manning Marable, *Black American Politics: From the Washington Marches to Jesse Jackson* (London: Verso, 1985)

12. Bowles, "Post-Keynesian Capital–Labor Statemate"; Thomas Ferguson and Joel Rogers, *Right Turn: The Decline of the Democrats and the Future of American Politics* (New York: Hill & Wang, 1986) see chap. 3, passim.

13. Mollenkopf, *Contested City*; see also the earlier critique by James O'Connor, *The Fiscal Crisis of the State* (New York: St. Martin's Press, 1973), and also the recent one by Ira Katznelson, "Great Society."

14. On this relaxation of federal control and its effects, see P. Clavel and N. Kleniewski, "Space for Progressive Local Policy: Examples from the U.S. and U.K," in John R. Logan and Todd Swanstrom, eds., *Beyond the City Limits: Urban Policy and Economic Restructuring in Comparative Perspective* (Philadelphia: Temple University Press, 1990).

15. Mollenkopf, *Contested City*, chap. 7; though see also Norman R. Glickman, "Emerging Urban Policies in a Slow-Growth Economy: Conservative Initiatives and Progressive Responses in the US," *International Journal of Urban and Regional Research 5*, no. 4 (1981), 492–528.

16. William W. Goldsmith and Michael Derian laid out, in some detail, the withdrawal from urban policy beginning in the 1970s: see their "Toward a National Urban Policy," *Journal of Regional Science* 19, no. 1 (1979), 93–108. On the conservative policy of the 1980s, see Ann Markusen, "The Militarized Economy," *World Policy Journal* 3 (Summer 1986), 497; and "Defensive Cities: Military Spending, High Technology and Human Settlements," in M. Castells, ed., *High Technology, Space and Society* (Beverly Hills, Calif.: Sage, 1985), p. 107, on the military buildup part of it, as well as Martin Carver, "The Second Pillar of Prosperity: The International Security Economy and the Reconstruction of Industry and State Relations in the United States" (Master's project paper, Department of City and Regional Planning, Cornell University, 1989); and for the major federal urban inititative of the 1980s, William W. Goldsmith, "Enterprise Zones: If They Work, We're in Trouble," *International Journal of Urban and Regional Research 6* (September 1982), 435–442, and Margaret Wilder and Barry Rubin, "Targeted Redevelopment Through Enterprise Zones," *Journal of Urban Affairs* 10 (1988), 1–17.

17. Houston may be a good example. See Joe Feagin, *Free Enterprise City: Houston in Political-Economic Perspective* (New Brunswick, N.J.: Rutgers University Press, 1988); and again, see Mollenkopf, *Contested City*.

18. O'Connor, *The Fiscal Crisis of the State*. The populist alternative to the existing variants of urban policy has been presented by many. In addition to Mollenkopf, see Derek Shearer, "In Search of Equal Partnerships: Prospects for Progressive Urban Policy in the 1990s," in Gregory Squires, ed., *Unequal Partnerships: The Political Economy of Urban Redevelopment in Postwar America* (New Brunswick, N.J.: Rutgers University Press, 1989), pp. 289–307; and Glickman, "Emerging Urban Policies."

19. Susan Fainstein, "Local Mobilization and Economic Discontent," in Michael Peter Smith and Joe Feagin, eds., *The Capitalist City: Global Restructuring and Community Politics* (Oxford: Blackwell, 1987), pp. 323–342.

20. For examples, see the cases of Kevin White in Boston or Edward Koch in New York. The neighborhood revolt could also come against more serious progressives. See Clavel, *The Progressive City*, on Cleveland and Hartford.

21. Manuel Castells, *The City and the Grass Roots* (Berkeley: University of California Press, 1983); Carl Boggs, "The New Populism and the Limits of Structural Reforms," *Theory and Society* 10 (1983), 343–363.

22. Bruce Stave, ed., *Socialism in the Cities* (Port Washington, N.Y.: Kennikat Press, 1975), provides a number of short accounts. See also Richard W. Judd, *Socialist Cities: Municipal Politics and the Grass Roots of American Socialism* (Albany: State University of New York Press, 1989).

23. Rod Bush, ed., *The New Black Vote: Politics and Power in Four American Cities* (San Francisco: Synthesis Publications, 1984); Doug McAdam, *Political Process and the Development of Black Insurgency, 1930–1970* (Chicago: University of Chicago Press, 1982); Abdul Alkalimat and Doug Gills, *Harold Washington and the Crisis of Black Power in Chicago* (Chicago: Twenty-first Century Books, 1989); James Green, "The Making of Mel King's Rainbow Coalition: Political Changes in Boston, 1963–1983," in James Jennings and Mel King, eds., *From Access to Power: Black Politics in Boston* (Cambridge, Mass.: Schenkman, 1986).

24. Green, "Mel King's Rainbow Coalition."

25. See Shearer, "In Search of Equal Partnerships." For case study detail on these progressive local cases, there are a number of key books and articles. For a general overview of five cases through 1984 (Hartford, Cleveland, Berkeley, Santa Monica and Burlington), see Clavel, *The Progressive City*; for a more recent and broader review see Shearer, "In Search of Equal Partnerships"; on Cleveland see Swanstrom, *Crisis of Growth Politics*; on Boston see Green, "Mel King's Rainbow Coalition"; on Berkeley see Harriet Nathan and Stanley Scott, eds., *Experiment and Change in Berkeley: Essays on City Politics, 1950–1975* (Berkeley, Calif.: Institute of Governmental Studies, 1978).

26. See Marie Kennedy and Chris Tilly, with Mauricio Gaston, "Transformative Populism and the Development of Community of Color," in Joseph Kling and Prudence Posner, eds., *Dilemmas of Activism* (Philadelphia: Temple University Press, 1990).

27. Some of the best material on this issue is in Nathan and Scott, *Experiment and Change.*

28. Eve Bach, N. Carbone, and P. Clavel, "Running the City for the People," *Social Policy* (Winter 1982), 15–23.

29. See Clavel, *The Progressive City*, p. 71.

30. Ibid., p. 83.

31. Ibid., p. 29.

32. Wim Wiewel, *The State of the Economy and Economic Development in the Chicago Metropolitan Region* (Chicago: Metropolitan Planning Council, 1988), p. 4; and John F. McDonald, *Employment Location and Industrial Land Use in Metropolitan Chicago* (Champaign, Ill.: Stipes, 1984), pp. 55–93.

33. Wiewel, *State of the Economy*, p. 44.

34. Ibid. p. 21.

35. U.S. Department of Commerce, *County and City Data Book 1988* (Washington, D.C.: Bureau of the Census, 1988), p. 644, and *Statistical Abstract of the United States 1989* (Washington, D.C.: Bureau of the Census, 1989), p. 451.

36. Wiewel, *State of the Economy*, p. 46.

37. Larry Bennet, Kathleen McCourt, Philip Nyden, and Gregory Squires, *Chicago: Race, Class, and the Response to Urban Decline* (Philadelphia: Temple University Press, 1987).

38. Mayor's Committee for Economic and Cultural Development of Chicago, *Mid-Chicago Economic Development Study*, 2 vols. (Chicago: Mayor's Committee for Economic and Cultural Development, 1966).

39. Mayor's Council of Manpower and Economic Advisors, *Unemployment–Labor Force Policy* (Chicago: The Mayor's Council of Manpower and Economic Advisors, 1976), and *Seven Year Economic Development Plan* (Chicago: The Mayor's Council of Manpower and Economic Advisors, 1978).

40. Commercial Club of Chicago, *Make No Little Plans: Jobs for Metropolitan Chicago* (Chicago: The Commercial Club of Chicago, 1984).

41. See Thomas L. Philpott, *The Slum and the Ghetto. Neighborhood Deterioration and Middle-Class Reform, Chicago, 1880–1930* (New York: Oxford University Press, 1978).

42. See, for instance, the recent biography by Sanford Horowitt, *Let Them Call Me Rebel: Saul Alinsky, His Life and Legacy.* (New York: Knopf, 1989).

43. See John Metzger and Marc Weiss, "The Role of Private Lending in Neighborhood Development: The Chicago Experience" (Evanston, Ill.: Center for Urban Affairs and Policy Research, 1988), and Robert McClory, *The Fall of the Fair: Communities Struggle for Fairness* (Chicago: Chicago 1992 Committee, 1986).

44. "Draft Platform: The Community Workshop for Economic Development" (Chicago: Community Workshop for Economic Development, September 15, 1982).

45. City of Chicago, *Chicago Development Plan: Chicago Works Together* (Chicago: Department of Economic Development, 1984). Also see Robert Mier, Wim Wiewel, and Lauri Alpern, "Decentralization of Policymaking Under Mayor Harold Washington," in Kenneth Wong and Laurence Lynn, eds., *Policy Innovation in Metropolitan Chicago* (Greenwich, Conn.: JAI Press, 1992).

46. Alkalimat and Gills, *Harold Washington.*

Chicago Politics and Community Development:
A Social Movement Perspective

Doug Gills

Harold Washington's election as Chicago's first black mayor in April 1983 was the product of unprecedented participation in the local electoral process by large segments of Chicago's racially, ethnically, and socio-economically diverse population, segments that had been previously alienated from the political mainstream. This participation was facilitated by the formation of a loosely unified coalition of reform-minded institutional elites (dubbed "insiders" herein) and progressive community activists and political insurgents ("outsiders").

There were certainly some institutionalized insider elements—members of the city council, ward committeemen and women, career city officials— who helped to effect Washington's election and to participate in governance of the city once the election was won. Their support ranged from ardently enthusiastic to plain opportunistic. Some became converts to Washington's program, as though they had always been waiting for such leadership. Others were politically ambitious careerists and political entre-preneurs who claimed to support the reform aims that Washington sym-bolized. They paid lip service to the reform program to the extent that it provided opportunities for their own self-aggrandizement or protected their political futures.

But what was most striking was the extent of organization and the painstakingly developed programmatic focus of the outsider part of the coalition. In Chicago during 1982–1987, movement politics was as impor-tant as insider maneuvering. It had its own logic and rules of organization. One can identify three main groups, loosely organized around three main ideas:

First, Mayor Washington's electoral base was overwhelmingly Black in composition, with the critical support of poor Latinos and poor whites. There was tremendous electoral mobilization of the Black community *under united black leadership*. Blacks, in the main, had endured decades of political exclusion and public neglect. Even while their numbers had increased significantly, they had received little more than symbolic participation in the economic and political life of the city. The black community organized politically, in both formal and informal ways, with a nearly single-minded purposefulness.

Second, the Harold Washington electoral coalition received the support of reform-minded liberal whites, as well as Jewish and black business elites. For these, and to some extent the other elements of the coalition, there was a consensus that the conventional practice of machine politics had to be rejected. Were Chicago to go forward into the twenty-first century, it had to shed its image of racist politics, corruption, graft, patronage, and unmerited privilege. There was a pervasive assault upon the patronage-based political machine of the regular Democratic party inherited from the era of Mayor Richard J. Daley.

Third, the movement underpinning Harold Washington's campaign and his early administration was marked by aggressive, vocal, and independent action on the part of people associated with neighborhood organizations and community action groups. These community activists had been isolated from meaningful political participation in prior regimes. Now, they pressed their demands for a neighborhood agenda that included greater effective input in decision making about the city's future and a greater share of city funds to be expended in the neighborhoods relative to the central business district, O'Hare, and the Near Loop Lakefront areas.

The other part of the story is that, among movement elements, while the most obvious thing is the mobilization of the black and allied groups— e.g., Latinos, poor whites, ethnics—a critical part of movement organization and the dominant substantive program came from the economic development initiatives that had emerged over a period of years from the community-based organizations and networks. The community-based network was critical to the larger outsider social movement and coalition, providing a large part of its organizational basis and the substance of much of its policy direction. As a result, the community-based movement was prominent in Washington administration initiatives after the 1983 election.

The purpose of this chapter is to describe how this rise to prominence of the community-based agenda came about, and how these ideas and interests fared once Washington and his immediate successor, Eugene Sawyer, were in office during 1983–1989. I treat the story as four topics: (1) a brief summary of the economic and political background out of which the larger outsider coalition emerged; (2) the twenty-year development of the community development wing of that coalition and how it contributed to the initial 1982/83 campaign; (3) the experience of that group's program in the

Washington administrative and political program after the election; and (4) some brief concluding thoughts on the future of the community development coalition.

Economic and Political Background

The history leading up to the successful election of Harold Washington as mayor of Chicago is described in many publications; in this section I review this history, but it is not purely an objective setting out of the facts. It is also an account by a participant and is, in part, a statement of a view of this history as it was seen by me and others in the community-based and black movement at the time.[1]

In some respects my own position in this history—often peripheral to the main events but in a position to observe them—has fitted me to tell this story. I came to Chicago in 1979 from North Carolina, did doctoral work in the Northwestern University political science department, then took positions as researcher and organizer in such groups as the Illinois Council for Black Studies, the Chicago Rehab Network, and most recently the Kenwood–Oakland Community Organization (KOCO). My dissertation research was on the Task Force for Black Political Empowerment, one of the central groups in the effort to mobilize support for Harold Washington's election during the fall of 1982, and I had been one of the charter members of that coalition effort. I have also been active in coalition-building activities within the reform and progressive wings of the neighborhood empowerment movement and electoral politics. I am currently on the board of directors of the Chicago Workshop for Economic Development (a group that I helped to found), the Chicago Rehab Network, and the Neighborhood Capital Budget Group. All have been important citywide coalitions having an impact upon the course of public policy reform and the resources available to the people. The following account reflects these experiences. It is as objective as I can make it; where it seems to depart from "mainstream" interpretations of this history, I try to so indicate.

Economic Crisis

The relevant history—so we believe—begins with the economy. Over several decades, major changes took place within Chicago's economy. These economic changes necessitated changes in the prevailing political system, in government policies and practices. The old political arrangement of the "machine" associated with Richard J. Daley, mayor from 1956 to 1976, and his successors (Michael Bilandic and Jane Byrne) through the 1983 election had been based upon the doling out of patronage in the form of jobs and contracts, which served to maintain personal loyalties between machine elites and their ethnic-based constituencies. This system had become increasingly inappropriate to address the needs of large numbers of African-Americans who had begun to occupy several of Chicago's neighborhoods in the period following World War I, as well as the needs of the Latinos and Asians whose numbers grew apace in the post–World War II period. In fact, the twenty years of Chicago's race relations leading up to the 1983 mayoral election were marked by a series of recurrent political confrontations, protests, and disruptions of normal patterns of urban behavior. This was due to the ever present effects of an increasingly intense urban crisis. It was essentially an economic crisis, but it manifested itself in the political arena as the heightening contradiction between declining sources of public revenues and the growing level of legitimate demands for public services and assistance.[2] In short, the ruling elites could not rule through the traditional arrangements, and vast sectors of the population grew increasingly intolerant of "business (or politics) as usual." The government thus became a contested arena of political battle.

Thus the urban crisis had several interrelated dimensions: economic, fiscal, and political. In past studies of Chicago politics many have argued the interconnectedness of these elements.[3] But what the Washington election made clear was the underlying importance of a fourth dimension—the direct mobilization of a new *social* base. Much of this new politics is noninstitutionalized (i.e., movement politics or social protest politics), involving social movements and factions that arose from fundamental shifts in the city's political economy—producing a *social crisis* marked by the inability of large segments of the population to gain income adequate to support viable households. The consequences were increased crime, deterioration of major social institutions, and the breakdown in the quality of community life.

Black Social Base and Political Solidarity

This crisis affected many groups, but a lot of it was specific to blacks. Historically, black people had long played an integral part in the political and economic life of the city, and this produced their political aspirations and motivations as well as their potential as a collective agency of sociopolitical change. First, blacks were not recent arrivals to Chicago. The town was founded by a black man, Jean Baptiste Point DuSable, and there was a permanent settlement of blacks here—albeit most were refugees from southern slavery—at the time that Chicago was incorporated in 1837. Later, a combination of southern racist terror and repression and the industrial expansion during World War I spurred blacks to migrate to Chicago in the hope of finding stable employment, good schools, and adequate housing in a less hostile environment; and the great South Side enclaves grew at increasing rates between 1920 and the 1950s.

But the peak of Chicago's industrial expansion had been reached during the 1920s. Therefore, although the early black arrivals into Chicago were proletarianized and integrated into the production side of the industrial economy, each subsequent generation of blacks and most urban-born Afro-Chicagoans were increasingly marginalized and alienated from the production side of the local economy. By the time black immigration into the Chicago area subsided, the mostly white (ethnic-based) working class had been fully proletarianized for several generations. Their progeny fully benefited as the United States became the preeminent economic and political world power after the two global wars. While white working-class families had access to open unions and the newly consolidated Democratic machine to enhance their status as a privileged stratum within a multiracial working class, blacks were excluded from full and open access to all but a few unions and they were limited in their political participation by the machine. While blacks had limited mobility within the political machine between 1930 and 1983, white ethnics used the machine as an instrument of upward social mobility.

Thus blacks were absorbed into the industrial work force in Chicago—at all levels—at lesser rates and lower pay than were whites. It is true that as the outcome of fierce struggle through the New Deal, Square Deal, New Frontier, and Great Society periods blacks were more or less completely absorbed into the public economy, mainly on the social consumption side, and integrated into civic relations (i.e., civil rights gains, increased voter registration, the Fair Housing Act, etc.), while making gains in political office holding as their numbers increased in given political jurisdictions. But even at the beginning of the 1980s black integration into the mainstream of the urban political economy remained tediously incomplete. It was slowed by the new conservatism in U.S. politics ushered in by the Reagan administration, and by the precarious position of the vast majority of the black middle class whose income, status, and occupations were overwhelmingly tied to the welfare state and to public employment (i.e., teachers, public administrators, civil servants, government-regulated affirmative action contracts, and employment in social service programs). As recently as 1985 a survey found that more than 67 percent of black middle-class income earners were dependent on public sector jobs. Moreover, the heavy dependence of poor black families on public assistance had become a cause for national alarm, if not action.[4]

In contrast, a smaller percentage of the white middle-class and poor whites in Chicago were tied to the public sector for employment and/or transfer payments. A higher percentage of whites derived income from the production side of the economy. This accounts for a significant amount of the conservatism on the part of whites who perceive their taxes as support-ing black welfare recipients.

The black middle class had aspirations and interests similar to those of their white counterparts. On the consumption side, many middle-class blacks aped the tastes of the white middle class in order to escape their so-cietal identification with the lifestyles of most blacks and were pained by the perceptions of the black masses held by most whites. Thus, there was not only the growing gap between most whites and most blacks but also a growing class differentiation among blacks. This reality and the relative di-vergence of interests among blacks along class lines had important ramifications for unifying and coalition building in the black political com-munity.

However, their precarious position in the social structure forced the black middle class into alliances with the black masses in defense of their status and in defense of public sector expansion of human and social ser-vices. Moreover, race and racism were constant forces contributing to black solidarity. Particularly among blacks when there was a threat of racist attack, the political community united. In 1983 there was the widespread perception that interests of importance to blacks as a whole were being threatened. Unity was possible. For a magical moment, there was the oc-currence of all-class unity among blacks—with the united leadership scurrying frantically to stay out in front of the masses. This unity, initially defensive in nature, was transformed into an offensive to capture city hall through a black candidate whose campaign was fueled by an unprece-dented political solidarity among blacks and supported by most Latinos and significant numbers of whites.

The Machine from Daley Through Byrne

It is important to understand Mayor Richard J. Daley's role (1955–1976). On the one hand we know him as a national figure, even a folk hero, or folk antagonist, in American political literature. But as a "machine boss" he played a significant role in presiding over the political and eco-nomic transformation of Chicago from an industrial city to an urban metropolis. Under his leadership, Chicago experienced the first signs of ur-ban crisis, as cracks appeared in the political arena resulting from the transformation of the economy. Daley continued to do business as usual, but he was also caught up in the management of crisis and he needed to figure out ways to keep his patronage base intact.

During his long reign as mayor of the city and chairman of the Cook

County Democratic party, Daley was in fact becoming more and more vulnerable with each passing election. His electoral coalition and his support base got more tenuous. This was in part because the machine only turned out as many people as it needed to win. It was also partly due to a growing antimachine vote. That antimachine vote was registered initially in several local ward elections where certain independents would win election in one term (such as in the 6th, 44th and 16th wards) only to lose in a subsequent election. They were not able to sustain or consolidate power. After Daley's death in 1976 a new independent trend was able to emerge, particularly in the Lakefront wards and the West Side predominantly black wards by 1979.

In black political terms, an understanding of the role of Daley was important in this period. By 1971 black political representation in the city council reached a point where it was proportional to the percentage of blacks in the population. Blacks were 28.1 percent of the population base in the 1970 census, and in 1971, 14 of the 50 ward aldermen (council members) were blacks. So you could say that in empirical terms blacks had "maxed-out" on their "power batting average" in terms of achieving proportional representation.[5]

The thrust of black politics shifted from participation to power politics. The antimachine sentiment gained momentum in the period after Daley's death. His demise precipitated a succession controversy that pitted the machine against the black community in a symbolic struggle of major proportions. At the center of the conflict was Alderman Wilson Frost of the 34th ward, legally in direct line to replace Daley. Frost, the mayor pro tem, was not allowed (at gunpoint) entrance into the mayor's office to assume the duties of the mayor until Daley's successor could be appointed. Blacks were incensed. As part of the compromise that made Michael Bilandic mayor for 1976–1979, Frost was offered the chair of the powerful Finance Committee of the city council, which he secretly accepted while thousands of blacks ringed city hall demanding his installation as mayor. Now the black insult level had truly "maxed-out."

Another factor was that Daley's coalition among the ethnic neighborhoods began to deteriorate. The Polish community resented the Irish lock on public patronage. But they fared better than blacks, so they were told. Daley also had other troubles. He had long been able to secure support of the unions. But there developed a split between the union bureaucratic leadership and the rank and file, particularly within locals that had large black memberships. Over the years a union leadership endorsement began to carry less political weight, while racism was the political measuring stick in union halls' relationships to city hall.

A further factor in the weakening of the machine was the growth of the same type of nationality movements among blacks, Latinos, and other groups in Chicago that became prominent in other cities. This was consistent with that whole thrust toward community control and empowerment that came out of the Black Power movement. Residents who lived and worked in areas of the city targeted for redevelopment desired and exerted greater input over the course of economic development in their communities. They had to be convinced that development proposals were not just good for the city but were compatible with retaining the stability of their neighborhood areas.

For instance, the Community Development Block Grant (CDBG) process, established under the Housing and Community Development Act of 1974, became an arena of struggle. From 1974 until Daley died (and under Mayor Bilandic, who succeeded him) the Community Development Advisory Committee (CDAC) was a rubber stamp. It was mandated by the federal legislation, which required maximum feasible participation of local funding districts—the key word here being *feasible*. From the standpoint of the Daley and Bilandic regimes the CDAC process was little more than a perfunctory obligation. But by the early 1980s the CDBG budgetary, regulatory, and evaluative process had evolved into a significantly altered form with many democratic features. Under Mayor Washington it would become a peer review mechanism that effectively interacted with the city administration to set priories and make CDBG allocation decisions.

Thus, the weakening of the machine had already started under Daley, but it became very clear with Jane Byrne's election in 1979. Her maverick campaign, which ousted Bilandic, and her subsequent governance period provided new lessons. We can summarize these lessons quickly as representing four things:

First, neighborhoods provided her the basis for victory (at least, activists claimed that, whether they did so or not).

Second, there was the antimachine character of the vote. Byrne won because she was viewed as being in opposition to "business as usual." There was a real democratic sentiment within the city among alienated segments that could be mobilized into the electorate. Byrne was able to tap this sentiment, although she did not consolidate it.

Third, Byrne's election represented a palace revolt of sorts within the fragmented party that was exploitable. There was a power struggle within the machine. Almost immediately after taking office she abandoned the neighborhood agenda and closed ranks with the Vrdolyak faction of the party against George Dunne, president of the county board, and the Daley family. (It was the Daley family that had Byrne fired as commissioner of consumer affairs under Bilandic. This dismissal led to a political blood feud between the Daleys and Jane Byrne.)

Fourth, the deepening political/fiscal crisis is key to understanding Byrne. The fact is that *she had to do something*. This increased the likelihood of the series of tactical errors in handling the crisis that sealed her doom and downfall. If they had not come in 1982, they certainly would have by 1987. She speeded up the process of her own loss of credibility by committing political blunders like destabilizing black political representation on boards and committees, and misuse of funds that were allocated under the CDBG process to go into low-income areas. She reprogrammed those funds into purchasing snow removal equipment and into paying the pension funds of teachers. This provided a rallying point for opposition on her own CDAC, which became more independent and assertive. Groups like the Rehab Network began to expose Byrne's misuse of the funds in other areas in which she had abandoned the neighborhood agenda. The Rehab Network, the Chicago 1992 Committee, and the newly formed CWED (Community Workshop for Economic Development) coalition began to popularize a critique of Byrne's development policies and practices. Meanwhile, groups like Operation PUSH, the Urban League, and Chicago Black United Communities (CBUC)—groups whose leaders had not sat collectively for years—began to meet. This coalescing of diverse black interest groups led to the formation of the Task Force for Black Political Empowerment in November 1982, following Washington's announcement of his candidacy for mayor.

Development of Community Organizations Through the 1983 Election

The economic changes in Chicago increased the differences between the older white ethnic neighborhoods and the newer neighborhoods occupied by peoples of color. The former were ethnic based; the latter were communities based upon socioeconomic and political conditions of exclusion from the mainstream. There is the tradition of Chicago as a city of diverse neighborhoods organized around institutions of cohesion such as church, school, or union meeting hall. These traditional neighborhoods were thought to possess a positive sense of cultural (ethnic) identity. On the other hand, the new "neighborhoods" were a postindustrial, post-1960s phenomenon. These new neighborhoods were demarcated by the common condition of their residents—homogeneously black or brown, homogeneously poor and depressed, homogeneously identified by the prevalence of deteriorated housing and commercial districts and by public sector neglect.

In these types of neighborhoods there also emerged new types of community organizations. The new community organizations were concerned about *change, survival, and redevelopment* as opposed to the older organizations, which focused upon the preservation of the neighborhood character. The first group of neighborhood organizations appeared in the 1930s and 1940s. The second emerged during the 1960s and thereafter under the influence of the civil rights movement and its tactics of direct action.

The traditional type of neighborhood organization was improvement oriented, exclusivist and conservationist. The more recent form of organization typically emerged around the need for defense from racist attacks and for resistance to withdrawal of public services, and mobilized around demands for improvement in the standard of living and quality of life. Rather than resulting from concerns about preservation of status, the new neighborhood organizations were instruments of the community enabling it to fight back and to achieve reform. They often produced leadership with more radical or progressive orientations than their predecessors.

These organizations in the new period were characterized initially by protest. They went through several phases. An example is the Kenwood–Oakland Community Organization (KOCO), which was formed in 1965. KOCO was organized mainly around tenants and other dislocated or alienated groups whose membership was essentially tenant based. While they took up other issues like unemployment, the struggle for representation in the unions, welfare rights, and union work, they were essentially struggling to get in the system or to get more out of it. They sought reform by opening up access, shaping government policy and practice, or fighting for constituent representation on public boards and commissions.

There were many groups that fit somewhere in between KOCO and the traditional type of neighborhood organization. The Midwest Community Council (MCC), for example, was organized almost exclusively around block clubs. Block clubs tend to be conservationist. There are certain parallels between the old-style groups and MCC. A group like The Woodlawn Organization (TWO), however, is representative of community organizations that are hybrid, including both block clubs and tenants. There were also some church-based community organizations that relied less on protest and more on development initiatives.

By the end of the 1960s and through the mid-1970s, the tendency was toward self-help activities. The orientation was also toward more isolationist activities based on the nationalism that emerged in the late 1960s. Organizations began to talk about "doing-for-self" under the influence of the Nation of Islam (and to a certain extent from the Black Panther party organization) with its self-help education and breakfast programs. This represented a trend towards cultural or political autonomy and self-determination. "Black is beautiful," when translated into the social context, implied a certain kind of isolationism. "Turf" concerns became a major characteristic of that kind of community organization.

By the end of the 1970s, a shift occurred toward "developmentalism" and policy "advocacy." This shift toward power politics and away from protest was based on the reality that blacks, Latinos, and poor whites constituted the new majority in Chicago. Most community organizations found this shift acceptable. There occurred a sort of synthetic organizational development where many of the organizations either were aligned with a "protest" organization or advocacy group; or they would spin off a community development organization as Northwest Community Organization had done with Bickerdike or as KOCO had done. KOCO did the social services and advocacy work on behalf of tenant constituencies, parents, or youth. On the other side of the shop, they created a specially designed Kenwood–Oakland Development Corporation (KODC). The development corporation was under the control of the parent organization but had people on the board who brought a certain technical expertise—making possible rehabilitation and new construction projects in housing and commercial development. While they differed in style and capacity, these groups all had one thing in common: they had emerged in struggles against the local political system in some form or another. And they had some level of connection to constituents most affected by the urban crisis through their outreach efforts.

These organizations tended to be anticorporate, antiunion, antimachine, mass oriented, and the source of an emergent indigenous leadership. They became alternative paths for political leadership to emerge, particularly in the late 1970s and through the 1980s. Thus community-based organization (CBO) leaders like alderpersons Danny Davis, Ed Smith, Dorothy Tillman, Helen Schiller, Percy Giles, Marlene Carter, and Bobby Rush developed from within community struggles. They went into the institutionalized political structure. They went into the electoral arena and won election onto the city council as they defeated machine-backed incumbents, while numerous community activists went into major administrative positions within city government—particularly under Harold Washington and his successor, Eugene Sawyer.

On the other hand, most community organizations were not indigenously led, mass-led organizations. Their (indigenous) boards might enact policy. However, most were staff driven. Even among the few that were board driven, the central character of their leadership was middle class by function, orientation, accumulated experience, and training. The staff became more professionalized and bureaucratized. (This development was accelerated after 1983 through the capacity-building strategies of city administrative policymakers under Mayor Washington.)

This staff development resulted in a new complexion. On the one hand, the staff and much of the board leadership in most community organizations represented a militant, radicalized wing of the community-based movement. But there was also the dominance of bureaucratic and legal relations that the community organizations had with their private and public sources of funding. These relations set limits upon the range of options open to most community-based actors. To be a "delegate agency" of the state was to become credentialed by the government to act on its behalf. To some extent they were constrained by these legal relations; their independence and initiative were circumscribed, limited, and therefore controlled.

Nevertheless, the community organizations of the new type were more open to coalition building, networking, and sharing and pooling resources than were the older traditional organizations. While they still adhered to the principle of mutual respect for each group's "local agenda," they were open to establishing ad hoc committees of their peers to work on single issues. An example was opposition of many activists to the so-called Chicago 21 Plan, which had been promoted by the Chicago Central Area Committee in 1971. The Chicago 21 Plan (or the "Master Plan") proposed the use of public dollars to promote massive private redevelopment of the new Loop South, West, and Northwest crescent as part of a large-scale urban renewal plan.

Such single-issue coalition building among black, brown, and white reform or progressive community-based groups remained the dominant type of associational network. In the mid-1970s networks with formal memberships began to emerge. One such group was the Chicago Rehab Network, which was formed in about 1976. Part of the impetus for it was the Housing and Community Development Act of 1974. This legislation provided resources through the Community Development Block Grant (CDBG) process, for the city to delegate to certain community-based actors a role in administering city-funded programs—federally funded programs with the city as the lead agency. A number of those groups came together in 1975, and over the next couple of years they formed the Rehab Network to provide technical assistance to community-based actors doing housing rehabilitation. The other motivation on the part of the founders of the Rehab Network was the desire to provide an advocacy front, to speak for and with its affiliates rather than having the "downtown" civic organizations—with no community constituencies—speak for the neighborhoods, co-opting their agendas and brokering resources for them.

Following that successful experience with the Rehab Network, other coalitions of community-based actors and organizations began to appear. During the summer of 1982 two simultaneous coalitions emerged: The Chicago 1992 Committee and the Community Workshop on Economic Development. The 1992 Committee concentrated its efforts on opposing the proposed Chicago World's Fair and exposing it as a veiled attempt at economic development that sought to use public resources to promote massive gentrification and wholesale displacement on the Near West and South sides. The Community Workshop on Economic Development (CWED, pronounced "see-wed") emerged in response to the Reagan-supported "enterprise zone" concept and Job Training Partnership Act. In both cases the fear among community activists was that the private sector would receive large inducements and incentive benefits without significant resources being recaptured by actors seeking control over the economic development process in their respective communities. These proposals were rejected because they were "top–down" rather than emerging on the basis of community initiative and reflecting the needs of local communities.

Politicization

The CBO social policy movement was converted into a political movement and steered into the electoral process through (1) broadening the base of the coalition by identifying the new allies on a mass scale, and (2) a process of agenda building and popularization of a new emerging consensus that Byrne and the machine could not/would not deliver on this agenda.[6]

Political organizing through the electoral process broadened the base of the movement. It provided the opportunity to dismantle the political machine and set the stage for social and public policy reform under the leadership of Harold Washington. Both CWED and the Chicago 1992 Committee were composed of people who were exercising leadership within the Chicago Rehab Network. However, each group was successful because it was able to attract membership and participation from a more diverse range of community groups doing development or engaged in community-specific struggles.

I cite the Rehab Network because I think it was a central forum and one of the leading agencies promoting community-based coalition building. It was a harbinger of various kinds of groups that came on the scene in the period from 1981 to 1983. It led to a proliferation of networks. Groups emerged like the Illinois Coalition Against Reagan Economics (I-CARE); and following that, during the summer of 1982, more mass-based militant groups like POWER, the People's Organization for Welfare Economic Reform. POWER was the successor to I-CARE, as a coalition of grass-roots participants. The Rehab Network/CWED model, and the I-CARE/ POWER model emerged as two of the predominant types that formed in this period. They attempted to bring neighborhood-based activists across the city in black, brown and low-income white communities into the political process through policy advocacy and through electoral participation.

Groups like the Rehab Network and CWED provided forums for the exchange of experiences and ideas across race lines and across sectors of the community. I-CARE and POWER represented more insurgent protest and were less institutionalized. While there were differences between them, I-CARE and POWER were clearly oriented more toward mass pro-test/resistance, while the Rehab Network and CWED represented a forum for the leadership of formally organized CBOs with specific agendas, under essentially middle-class leadership. I-CARE was also under middle-class leadership, but it had a mass base among some labor unions, public service recipients, and civil service employers. POWER represented an attempt to fuse unemployed workers and welfare recipients with community activists and progressives who had a long term interest in promoting radical social change.

POWER—at least temporarily—demonstrated what the potential for such organizational work could be when leadership was provided by a group of radicalized, militant community activists with roots in mass community struggles among poor people. POWER tended to be more democratic; I-CARE was more elitist. The I-CARE/POWER groups were composed essentially of the direct or indirect recipients of social services and neighborhood-based programs. The CWED and the Rehab Network groups were composed of public-assisted CBOs that coalesced and hired staff who provided some technical expertise.

By 1982 the more mass-based coalitions like POWER had moved to another level. They urged their constituents and activists to escape the limitations of "turfism." They were "anti-turf" organizations in the sense that black, Latino, and low-income white community constituents were encouraged to view development threats to their communities in the context of the entire city of which they were a part. They mobilized support with the argument that certain megadevelopment projects proposed by big developers and the machine, as well as antiurban federal and state policies, would be devastating for individual neighborhoods and for the overall public economy of Chicago. In this sense these groups were broad class coalitions that represented the vast majority of the city's population in contention with the policies supported by the corporate elites and their cronies in city government.

Finally, it must be made clear that middle-class professional activists penetrated and assumed important positions of leadership and influence within these citywide advocacy coalitions—of both types. These were not merely spontaneous, purposeless coalitional efforts. Moreover, the activists' associations existed prior to Harold Washington's campaign bid in 1982. In each instance the organizations were implicitly, if not explicitly, opposed to the machine in power. Many activists at the local and coalition level had been involved in antimachine electoral campaigns and pubic policy struggles over the previous 10–20 years dating back to the early 1960s. Some had been involved in struggles against Mayor Daley in 1963,

1966, and in 1968.[7] Others had opposed the city's handling of the infamous Fred Hampton—Mark Clark assassinations.[8] Most of the Chicago
Rehab Network early membership had worked with each other in opposition to the redlining practices of banks and insurance companies and in the
citywide resistance to the Chicago 21 Plan to redevelop the South Loop
and the Near North and West Sides as gentrified middle-class
communities.

Coalition Agenda Setting

The Chicago Rehab Network and the Community Workshop on Economic Development both drew upon the common experiences of their
diverse member groups in order to shape a neighborhood agenda, particularly around housing, land use, economic development, and resource
allocation for depressed neighborhoods. The 1981/82 period in Chicago
was replete with numerous protest struggles within pubic institutions as
the crisis deepened. Perhaps the most significant development for our current discussion was the struggle to prevent Chicago from sponsoring a
World's Fair in 1992. The World's Fair proposal entailed much more than
merely an opportunity for Chicago to have a good time or to host a big
party. At the core of the issues surrounding it was a plan for the economic
redevelopment of the Near South Side. It was viewed by many activists as a
resurrection of the old Chicago 21 Plan. It was derisively referred to as
"Master Plan Number Two." It called for the redevelopment of the area
from 13th Street south all the way down to 31st Street and over as far as the
Pilsen community. Parts of Pilsen and Chinatown were scheduled to be
razed and made into parking lots for visitors to the fair. More importantly,
there were designs to build a new residential development with mini—
shopping centers and malls that would have housed or employed as many
as 300,000 people on the air rights over the Illinois Central Gulf Railroad
tracks just south of the Loop. It would thus open the land use market to
middle- and upper-income groups who desired access to the nearby
Lakefront.

The city had a history of using public infrastructure resources to support
private economic development: 65–80 percent of the capital improvement
dollars allotted by the city had been expended within the Loop and O'Hare
areas during recent administrations. What about the other 48 wards? Or
what about the other 73 or 74 community areas? And who would pay for
this? Under Mayor Byrne the city used its bond capacity to support Near
Loop real estate development while the neighborhoods were neglected.
Moreover, developers received substantial tax incentives to build projects
that could have been developed without public support. Advocates of

neighborhood development wanted to see more balance and linkage in return for local city support. The first issue was whether or not community development resources should be tied up around this engine for development, which could be supported by private investment. Some questioned whether the private developers of the World's Fair should be allowed essentially to walk away with no risk while the public would bear most of the risk if the fair was not successful. Others hammered away at the notion that the World's Fair site should contribute to strengthening existing communities rather than facilitating their destruction and the displacement of existing residents and businesses. There was an operative consensus that the fair was ill designed, whether or not it should be held at all. Similarly, it was argued that other developers who used city capital development dollars should provide revenues to support housing, economic development, and job generation in the neighborhoods. Individuals and groups networking around CWED, the Chicago Jobs Council, Chicago 1992 Committee, the Rehab Network, and the Center for Neighborhood Technology began to advocate for a comprehensive urban development policy with the following key components:

a. Housing and commercial development should not displace indigenous residents and businesses.

b. Community-directed economic and housing development should secure the interests of local groups and include the input of CBOs in the planning, implementation, and benefits of private–public development ventures.

c. The city should encourage "balanced growth" between the business district and depressed neighborhoods and linkage between large developments using public resources and the need for reinvestment in the neighborhoods.

d. When developers wanted to do business with the city, they should expect to hire Chicagoans first, respect affirmative action and minority set-aside agreements, and support community-based initiatives in economic development by providing technical and financial assistance.

e. Banks and other lending institutions holding city funds or city employee pension funds should be pressured to support community-based redevelopment projects by reinvesting in depressed neighborhoods and by lending to public–private partnership ventures.

f. The city should view community-based nonprofit development organizations as legitimate partners in community redevelopment projects.

g. The city should shift a larger share of its CDBG dollars into direct support of housing, commercial and community redevelopment initiatives, and direct staff development and capacity building among neighborhood development organizations and agencies.

The Community-based Network in the 1983 Election

The same forces that came together to support Jane Byrne and to defeat Michael Bilandic in 1979 were at the front lines of the movement to defeat Byrne and elect Harold Washington in 1983 and again in 1987. The associational networks with linkages into the black, brown, poor white, and liberal Lakefront communities made possible the transformation of mass social protest into a massive political mobilization inside the electoral arena.

How was this possible? On the surface it could be characterized as a black nationalist movement. But beneath this was a long-building set of forces and linkages. Many of the most active representatives of CBOs in coalitions like the Rehab Network, CWED, and the Chicago 1992 Committee on the one hand and POWER on the other were active militants in civil rights, black empowerment, and affirmative action movements among the black and Latino communities. These broad associational linkages made possible deep and extensive outreach to constituents who could be politicized and steered into the electoral arena.

When Jane Byrne refused to act on a neighborhood agenda emerging out of low-income communities, it was a rejection of the black and Latino activists who also became discouraged as a result of the racist effects of her policies with respect to nationality representation and the continuance of business as usual at city hall. When these groups and their leaders criticized her policies, she reacted viciously and revoked their public service contracts. Not only did this further incense these organizations, but it destroyed her credibility with reform-minded liberals and the media as well.

Meanwhile the community-based networks had developed an ability to work in concert. The Rehab Network demonstrated that multinational coalitions could be built on a permanent basis and could provide more than protest leadership. This kind of coalition could be proactive and develop a progressive reform agenda, particularly around housing development. CWED, which shared an overlapping constituency with the Rehab Network, differentiated itself by focusing on community economic development issues and CBO-initiated commercial development projects.

Groups like I-CARE and POWER proved that multinational coalitions could be built by reform and progressive leadership that mobilized and organized among the masses. These groups forged unity and brought grassroots actors and other ordinary citizens into motion around substantive and politically symbolic issues of struggle important to both neighborhood-based groups and their constituents among the working poor and unemployed across the city.

Thus there was a coincidence between this reform neighborhood development agenda and the core demands of the black empowerment movement for fairness, open government, and ethical practices. When stripped of its ideological and rhetorical symbolism, the neighborhood development agenda was compatible with the short-term aims of the black and Latino empowerment movements. The neighborhood movement demanded equitable resource allocation to black and Latino communities, enforcement of affirmative action and minority set-aside mandates, access to government policymaking, to information, and to public officeholders, along with the elimination of patronage with respect to public employment, contracts, and provision of public service. One reason for this compatibility of interest was that the community development movement originated out of these nationality movements among Black and Latino community activists and developed alongside of them.

This was the case of the Task Force for Black Political Empowerment, the informal arm of the Harold Washington campaign within the black community. Some of the same actors in the community-based movement were instrumental in its formation: Nancy Jefferson, Joe Banks, Dorothy Tillman, Marian Stamps, Robert Lucas, and others played leading roles in both formations. A similar development took place among Puerto Ricans and Mexicans who formed a Latino Empowerment Task Force.

The agendas emerging within the nationality movements and within the community-based development movement among housing and economic development activists were convergent and interdependent. The basic point of convergence turned out to be the need for a reform agenda, the targeting of public policymakers for public policy changes, and the support for an alliance between the working poor and community development actors in the neighborhoods. They brought black, Latino, white, and other leaders to the table and provided a context within which a black-led empowerment movement could find legitimacy and acceptance outside the black political community. This convergence in the campaign was able to take place because a *high level of sociopolitical networking and associational linkages was in existence prior to the Washington campaign.* The movement underpinning Harold Washington was not just spontaneous, although indeed there was spontaneity at the grass-roots level and much innovativeness. That such creativeness did come out of the grass-roots movement certainly charged up the campaign organization and kept it alive. But to say that it was purely a spontaneous thing—all resistance and no plan—would be incorrect.

As early as 1981, in the black community, Harold Washington had been identified as a potential candidate; in the white community progressives like Slim Coleman had put him on their circuit, speaking to CBOs at their annual conventions. Citywide organizations did the same. So in that sense it was a deliberate effort to build a neighborhood agenda. Of course Harold Washington addressed their concerns. This agenda building culminated in the late summer of 1982 in what was called the All-Chicago Community Summer Congress, which brought activists from community organizations and independent political organizations together to unite around a neighborhood (or community-based) agenda for economic development, housing development, health care, education, etc. It had certain planks in it that were similar to most of the things that community organizations fight for today—affordable housing, affordable health care, the idea of linked development or balanced growth in terms of the city's allocation of resources.

So there was also planning by a conscious leadership element. They had gained experience in successful coalition building and positioned themselves at critical vantage points on the political landscape that represented Chicago in the 1980–1983 period. The willingness to network, reach out, and develop common agendas and resistance efforts was a positive contribution of these early, fragile coalition efforts. They survived because the local agenda was respected and the membership was tolerant of divergence from the generally accepted principles guiding local practices and because serious attempts were made to work out differences in healthy internal debate.

This movement, then, fed into the three main social bases within Harold Washington's coalition. There was the nationality vote: most blacks, a majority of Latinos, and a significant number of reform-minded whites. The Latino and progressive white vote was very critical to his election. In the primary election of 1983, the critical ingredient was progressive whites. Although Washington received 80 pecent of the black vote, 17 percent of his coalition was white, and that provided him with the margin of victory. In the general election, Latinos provided the critical margin of victory. He was able to improve from 25 percent of the Latino vote in the primary to about 65 percent of the Latino vote in the general election. Washington garnered 75 percent of the Puerto Rican vote, 62 percent of the Mexican vote, and 52 percent of the Cuban vote.

The second basis of support underpinning his coalition consisted of CBOs and community activists. The third was his ability to gain at least the nominal support of many of the locals in the Chicago Federation of Labor, and in the general election he got the nominal support of the Chicago Federation of Labor and the active support of many of the locals.

Harold Washington in Office 1983–1987:
Limitations on Reform Gains

Once in office, the Washington governance coalition found three sources of support: First was the unity of black, brown, and white forces as underscored by the presence of community activists. Community-based actors played roles not only in Washington's election organization but in the transition team; and some went on to play important roles in his administration. This set the stage for a new division of public resources in favor of a shift toward neighborhood-based expenditures—more so than in the preceding administrations.

Then there were the much publicized "council wars." These "wars" represented the initial (1983–1986) division in the 50-member city council between the weaker Washington forces and the majority bloc of white aldermen, consisting of the old guard ward bosses—or the "Vrdolyak 29," as they were called. However, the "council wars" enabled Mayor Washington to keep the community-based coalition and his primary social base—which was largely black and Latino—intact.

Third, within this unity-from-below, Washington was able to maintain the support of the black political elites and machine veterans—particularly black city council members and party committeemen and -women—because he had carried their wards. Washington outpolled each of the black machine aldermen and made possible the election of a number of antimachine candidates.[9]

Inside of this development we witnessed a certain fragmentation beginning in 1983. The first signs of division appeared very early in the black community in the struggle over who was going to succeed Washington in his vacated seat in the first congressional district. Lu Palmer was supported by the nationalists in the black community. They saw it as very important, symbolically, to be able to name the successor to Harold. But fragmentation was evident in that not less than eight candidates campaigned for the seat. Each claimed to be a staunch supporter of Washington's reform agenda. Washington endorsed Charles Hayes, a noted labor leader, who easily defeated Palmer in a low-turnout election and subsequent runoff.

The rift between Washington and the black nationalists then grew wider. It became apparent within the nationalist forces in the Task Force for Black Political Empowerment (e.g., in their concern over Lu Palmer's failed congressional bid and over the inability of nationalists to cash in on their support for Harold Washington and win primacy for the "black nationalist agenda"). Unity continued to unravel around issues of black–Latino middle-class access to scarce public sector jobs and contracts. The split was couched in nationalist terms, however.

What Washington Delivered

For the most part, Washington's administration made major steps toward delivery on the neighborhood agenda. This was necessary, but it was insufficient for addressing the tremendous substantive problems facing the low-income communities in the city. Moreover, Washington was surrounded by numerous persons at all levels of influence in government—formal and informal—who did not share his agenda of concerns nor that of the neighborhood development interests. Yet, these five years were dramatically distinctive from any period of city government in Chicago's history.

I think that the Washington victory and the consolidation of his administration resulted in the institutionalization of a new base of power in opposition to the machine. It is not clear if it functioned any differently, but it was not the machine as we knew it. In fact, I remember Washington speaking at a rally in front of Daley Plaza during the 1983 campaign, when he said that "The machine, as we now know it, is dead." At subsequent times he would speak of the machine and patronage in the same terms. Most people only focused on the fact that the machine was dead, as opposed to the notion that only the machine *as we knew it* was dead.

The need to institutionalize a base of power is something that is central to American politics and to any regime. Even if we assume that patronage is dead, you need to have a political organization that functions in the same way. If privilege is dead, then what is the incentive for political involvement—unless there are some direct or indirect payoffs? Perhaps a new morality that transcends the politics of individualism is required.[10]

The CBO provided an excellent alternative form for that. It did not provide direct patronage, but it was possible to build up a patronage-type army, a machine army, without the individual (privilege) payoff. It was possible to use the new neighborhood agenda as a framework within which access was given to neighborhood-based actors without the corruption that is associated with the under-the-table deals of the previous ward bosses. KOCO, for example, had its staff increased by four or five people in a five-year period; and other organizations emerged and had city-funded staff positions. The city did substantially increase its delegate agencies. The shift in spending from downtown to the neighborhoods represented a shift in resources allocation. It assumed that the bureaucracy could function better to deliver services if it were at the street level. So we witnessed the expansion of a street-level bureaucracy without a street level government (i.e., democracy). About $13 million of CDBG funding for staff positions were taken out of the city government and put in the neighborhood agencies. That represented a change to the extent that neighborhood-based organizations were in control of staff people who were supposed to be delivering the services to the constituencies in the neighborhoods. Presumably, this would lead to better service and more direct accountability.[11]

Yet some would have questioned whether or not that was a critical improvement. If the effect was to have better control at the local level over people who were providing services, then this change was a significant gain only if it led to more effective service delivery. But the effect was merely to contain and control the community activists through co-optation, then we had made a tragic mistake. The effect in either case seemed to reduce the independence of CBOs.

There were a number of more immediate results for the neighborhood organizations as well. *We got greater access to decision making*, implementation and evaluation, and just plain old information. It was now possible to find out what was happening in the city to a far greater extent (with respect to city expenditures and city planning) than ever happened before. It made sense from a community activist standpoint to be able to walk into Harold's office (to some folks this was the ultimate example of access). It made sense to be able to pick up the phone and talk to the commissioner of economic development, as opposed to having to write a letter, and maybe you would get an answer to in two weeks, and maybe you would get a meeting in two months.

There was *more equitable resource distribution* across Chicago. Partnerships were created where public sector resources were used to leverage private sector investments of benefit to low-income individuals and families. CBOs were treated less like junior partners (if they had been treated as partners at all) and more like legitimate participants in the development process. This administration increased the opportunity of CBOs to bring resources to the table. The more they had resources similar to what developers were looking for, the more they were treated as equal partners in the process.

There was *more budgetary scrutiny*. For the first time we had a series of public hearings around all the major city budgets. That meant something from the standpoint of neighborhoods having input into the budgetary process. This included the CDBG and the corporate budget. And a similar process was beginning to emerge around the capital budget, the capital plan for infrastructure development, although that piece had not been consolidated when Washington died. There were some efforts underway under the Sawyer administration and within the city council under the newly formed Capital Development Committee that had been set up by Washington. Its purpose was to take a look—just as was done with the CDBG budget—to see if there was a way to set up criteria that would lead to more equitable distribution of capital resources to all the neighborhoods of the city.

Another strength of the administration was the establishment of *more representative government.* A key point here is not only that it was more democratic in terms of proportional representation of nationalities in the city council and on boards and commissions but also that there was greater inclusion of other previously excluded elements of the population. We began to see a more diverse coalition in governance than at any other time in Chicago's history.

Washington appointed people with strong neighborhood backgrounds and orientations to important positions of policymaking in his government. They had a great deal of influence in subsequent governmental neighborhood policy and strategic planning. It was radical for some people that some side streets would get snowplowed in the winter time—side streets, that is, that never got plowed before. I lived on one of those streets, and I was shocked beyond belief to see a snowplow come down my South Side street in the winter of 1984. It was outside of my experience—I couldn't imagine what that sound was. The streets got plowed on the South Side of Chicago! It was great! Some streets even got paved on the South Side of Chicago! The streets also got paved on those WPA (Works Project Administration) streets in some of the white ethnic neighborhoods, and that made a difference in Washington's image for whites in the city as well.

In attempts to reach out to all Chicago, Harold Washington moved his coalition onto a broader base. It also made it more conservative, as he included more constituents. Had Mayor Washington's tenure continued, it is conceivable that his administration would have made an even greater shift toward conservatism. By the very nature of the governance process, as more divergent elements were included into the support of the administration, more practical compromises had to be made to maintain the divergent elements within the coalition.

Limitations of the Washington Program

There was also a downside for the community organizations: to some extent and for some time there was a *loss of independence and initiative among CBOs.* We took coalition building for granted. We operated as if all that we had to do was to proclaim movement politics or profess to be a supporter of black–Latino or black–white unity and . . . Presto!—we got instant unity!—when our experience had been that solidarity is forged in struggle and then debated and tested in battle.

Community activists clamored for access. They demanded inclusion. When you have this thrust you risk a compromise of independence and initiative at the same time. You may be mesmerized by "palace intrigue," or sometimes you got tied into downtown politics. This did occur. It happened to the extent that some people overly identified with city hall, to the point where they said, "*We* are in power, *we* run it."

Second (and a parallel to the first point) is that *the movement was coopted* to the extent that such thoughts prevailed as "we can't do anything to embarrass the mayor" or "we put him there so we have to support him."

Co-optation also happened in a third way: many of our *important fighters in the trenches went to city hall.* It's not that they couldn't go to city hall to work or to serve that's at issue. The fact is that once they arrived there to serve, they quit communicating and listening to the neighborhood anymore. Or their relationship to the neighborhood became one of expediency, as opposed to being a serious and honest relationship that was built on prior experience and practice and could be sustained. This becomes an important lesson in terms of how to do progressive government work and maintain a positive progressive orientation. Some of our friends in government have to learn how to do that better.

Reflections

Why did these shortcomings occur? Why weren't they corrected? Part of the problem—and what we learned during 1983–1987—was that Harold Washington operated under severe constraints. Many of us had an uninformed view of big city mayors. We did not fully understand how much a black, progressive mayor would be limited by his constitutional role but also by the political economy in which he functioned. First, *racism persisted* under the Washington administration. We saw that in the "council wars." We saw it in the 1987 and 1989 elections. The adverse reaction of party leadership was dramatic and enduring, and was a source for racial polarization and a cause for maintenance of political narrow-mindedness within the electorate. The media continuously cast the Washington administration in a negative light and contributed to reinforcement of racial polarization.

Independent of racism, there was the *bureaucracy*, a complex web of relations, procedures, and regulatory functions that provided continuity but impeded innovation. Under Washington, not only was there a half-century-old entrenched bureaucracy, there was the patronage-laden city government that resisted innovation because change was perceived as not in the patronage workers' interest.

A third constraint was the relationship of local government to the county, other taxing bodies, and other legislative bodies at the state and federal levels. This was most significant—perhaps more than most people realize. Washington's push for an urban agenda was hampered by the Republican control at the state and federal level.

Some people looked to Harold Washington to provide an immediate relief for substantive conditions outside of his control like jobs or more affordable housing. At best, he could set the tone and encourage model programs.

And there is the question of the relationship of city hall to the banking community on LaSalle Street. It is very significant that the leading bankers went in to see Harold and shake hands with him, as opposed to picking up the phone. They did so to let him know that they could shut down the city. And that is important for any radical or progressive to understand about the urban political economy—that the banks rule the government, the mayor only *manages* it. It is significant that one of Washington's first acts (like Jane Byrne before him and Sawyer after him) was to go to the bond houses in New York in order to assure Wall Street (and LaSalle Street) that there was no problem in Chicago that could not be made manageable, that the city was bankable, and that an environment favorable to business and investment in the city was being maintained. Without these assurances the city's ability to borrow money at favorable interest rates or to sell bonds would be seriously jeopardized.

Apart from these constraints, other limitations on the gains many expected from Washington in office only became apparent after his death, in the way his governing coalition splintered and accentuated the fragmentation that had already begun. It unraveled most profoundly with the disintegration of the Washington coalition in the city council. First, the black council members with the weakest links to the progressive reform movement began to engage in acts of individual political opportunism. Feeling that they had nothing to fear from a fragmented reform movement without the powerful persona of Washington, some black council members immediately went out to cut deals with the old guard while ostensibly supporting Acting Mayor Eugene Sawyer. It is clear that they abandoned the reform agenda. Others were less daring even though they might have been tempted. These divisions had a major impact upon subsequent political developments in city politics.

Several other black and Latino council members appeared to have abandoned the reform agenda, if not the respective black and Latino nationality-specific agendas of their community in 1989, though it was not clear whether their newly formed alignments with the rejuvenated machine would enhance their political futures.

The missing factor, which had been present in 1983, was the mobilizing base that had been provided by the CBOs. How did we lose this? This question hangs over us now. It is clear that by 1987 Harold Washington was funding a number of organizations that differed markedly from the original CBO constituency: neighborhood retail and industrial retention organizations are examples. Many of these did not meet CDBG guidelines for low-income eligibility. The coalition was weaker as a result in 1987. Thus, community based participation was perhaps the most problematic aspect of the Washington administration.

Washington embraced the most salient aspects of the community-directed development framework. One current irony is that a result of Harold Washington's positive response to the neighborhood development agenda was that it placed a cap on the insurgent-oriented energies emanating from CBOs and the community development movement. But part of the problem was in our own organization and tactics. We had no organization that could maintain some discipline, an organization where people felt they had a reference group they could relate to as a source of strength. We met at lunch and we struggled around things, but there was no overarching political and organizational unity. Everyone was free to be as freewheeling and irresponsible as he or she wanted to be. On the other hand, we became so immersed in day-to-day tasks that we lost sight of the forest and the horizon.

We *did not prepare new leadership* at the grass-roots level. The source of strength of Chicago's neighborhoods is the fact that indigenous leaders emerged and matured. They articulated issues on behalf of their constituencies and there was some level of accountability, in some form—block clubs, organizations, tenant unions, welfare recipients organizations, and the like. And there was a flowering of leadership in the campaign period when new actors surfaced and in the early governance period when new voices began to be heard in pubic policy. But those voices are now old voices in the sense that no new indigenous leadership emerged in 1983–1989.

Finally, there is the question of *factionalization of the leadership*, and the reemergence of top–down leadership. This is the carryover from the Washington period, in the sense that self-proclaimed community leaders speak for the low-income communities of Chicago or the affordable housing community without consultation or accountability to their constituents. It is just assumed that these leaders came out of a neighborhood context. Given the fact that there is no organization that can force accountability, they become self-proclaimed. The surprising thing is that the most prominent figures doing this were not Johnny-come-latelies. They were veterans of movement politics who should have known that movements are products of hard work and are most successful when there is clarity of collective thought and strategy based upon hard critical thinking.

Conclusion: Toward a New Agenda

I think that there are important implications of the Washington administration at both the local and the national level. The Washington victory and subsequent governance period represented a magic moment of international importance. To say that is to say there was something beautiful about it and something that brought the dead to life. People who had been dead since the 1960s, not in a physical sense but emotionally, spiritually dead, came alive! I saw and worked with winos who put on ties and picked up their pens and clipboards and walked precincts during the Harold Washington campaign. Harold was correct when he said, "You go out of the city, you go out of the country, you go out of the continent and people will say, 'How's Harold? What's happening in Chicago?' "

There is still the sense today that people look to Chicago for innovation in terms of progressive politics and on economic development issues. The Chicago Rehab Network served as a model for other cities on how coalitions can be put together on a multinational, multiracial basis. The same thing is true with CWED. It had gained national reputation as a center of the community economic development movement. That's important, and we don't have to mention the Jesse Jackson experience at all.

Win or lose, Chicago has facilitated that sense of movement around the country among blacks and Latinos; call it coalition politics or call it the "Rainbow." More importantly, in our analysis the Rainbow has better prospects for staying alive and building at the local level than it has nationally, until the development of linkages between national and local constituencies.

But in Chicago we have fragmentation in black politics. The current crisis in political leadership in the electoral arena is only one manifestation of that. It poses grave problems for the "new democratic coalition," the so-called Rainbow.

A sense of conflict, competitiveness and rivalry also exists between blacks and Latinos. Jane Byrne tried to play off blacks and Latinos in 1980–1982, but unsuccessfully. This happened again in the fragmentation of the coalition around the "Washington 26" after 1987, and later in the split between progressive Latino aldermen—with Luis Gutierrez, on one side, and Jesús García and Raymond Figureroa, on the other. This was not good for the progressive movement in Chicago.

Now, what's the road forward? In the midst of the current crisis, I think that there are several things we need to do. First is this notion of a *mass organization*. In other words, bottom–up politics. The KOCOs, the MCCs, the Lawndale People's Planning Action are good. They are necessary but not sufficient. *We need a mass organization that can take up substantive issues on the basis of a mass common program.* Community organizations are limited: they are dependent upon external sources of funding. We need to encourage and build self-standing, independent mass organizations. Both are necessary and neither is sufficient. Existing community groups have by necessity had to form coalitions. What we need is a monolithic organization, a unifying homogeneous mass organization that can raise up a standard of struggle around class-based issues facing the vast numbers of citizens.

Why is this imperative? It is doubtful that traditional party organizations and candidates making their routine campaign appeals will continue to excite the vast majority of poor people. They will not be believable. Only an organization with mass leadership can move beyond the reform agenda.

Second, *we need independence and initiative in the movement.* We've lost some of that, and until we regain it, regardless of who is elected mayor, we are at a loss without it. Until we do this we will compromise the progressive character of our politics, whoever gets to be mayor. Harold was less effective because he didn't have a strong independent movement. He *was* the movement! He was the movement personified in city hall—to the extent that we said, "We don't want to embarrass the Mayor," and "Let's not initiate anything until we check with city hall." And so we checked—privately or publicly—with city hall in order to find out what we ought to be doing. We did this without coming up with our own initiatives.

If that initiative had been there we could have clarified the lines between who *runs* and who really *rules* Chicago. If this had been happening, then LaSalle Street would not have been able to bulldog Harold into making compromises that were not in the best interests of the city. Washington would have been able to say: "My hands are tied; my constituents are saying this is what I should do."

NOTES

1. My dissertation is on the Task Force for Black Political Empowerment, one of the central groups in the effort to mobilize support for Harold Washington's election during the fall of 1982. The Task Force has been treated by Abdul Alkalimat and myself in other publications: in Rod Bush, ed., *The New Black Vote* (San Francisco: Synthesis Publications, 1984); and Alkalimat and Gills, *The Task Force for Black Political Empowerment: Beyond the Crisis in Black Power in Chicago* (Chicago: TCB Publications, 1989).
See also Paul Kleppner, *Chicago Divided: The Making of a Black Mayor* (DeKalb: Northern Illinois University Press, 1985); Melvin Holli and Paul Green, eds., *The Making of the Mayor, Chicago 1983* (Grand Rapids, Mich.: Eerdmans, 1984); also Holli and Green, eds., *Bashing Chicago Traditions: Harold Washington's Last Campaign, Chicago 1987* (Grand Rapids, Mich.: Eerdmans, 1989); Samuel K. Gove and Louis H. Masotti, eds., *After Daley: Chicago Politics in Transition* (Urbana: University of Illinois Press, 1982), especially chapters by Rakove and Preston; and William J. Grimshaw, *Black Politics in Chicago: The Quest for*

Leadership, 1939–1979 (Chicago: Department of Political Science, Illinois Institute of Technology, 1980); and Dempsey J. Travis, *"Harold," The People's Mayor: The Authorized Biography of Harold Washington* (Chicago: Urban Research Press, 1989). At the national level see Manning Marable, *Black American Politics* (New York: Shocken Books, 1985); Michael Preston et al., *The New Black Politics: The Search for Political Power* (New York: Longmans, 1987).

2. See James O'Connor, *The Meaning of Crisis: A Theoretical Introduction* (Cambridge, Mass.: Basil Blackwell, 1987); T. Robert Gurr and Desmond King, *The State and the City* (Chicago: University of Chicago Press, 1987); Roger Friedland, *Power and Crisis in the City* (New York: Schocken Books, 1983); and Terry N. Clark and Lorna C. Ferguson, *City Money* (New York: Columbia University Press, 1983).

3. Clark and Ferguson, *City Money*; Larry Bennett, Gregory Squires, Kathleen McCourt, and Phillip Nyden, *Chicago: Race, Class, and the Response to Urban Decline* (Philadelphia: Temple University Press, 1987); and Abdul Alkalimat and Douglas Gills, *Harold Washington and the Crisis in Black Power* (Chicago: Twenty-first Century Books, 1988).

4. Daniel Fusfeld and Timothy Bates, *The Political Economy of the Urban Ghetto* (Carbondale: Southern Illinois University Press, 1984); William J. Wilson, *The Declining Significance of Race* (Chicago: University of Chicago Press, 1978); also Wilson's *The Truly Disadvantaged* (Chicago: University of Chicago Press, 1987).

5. Alkalimat and Gills, *Harold Washington*, pp. 126–131; also Michael B. Preston, "Black Politics in the Post-Daley Era," in S. Gove and L. Massotti, eds., *Politics in Chicago After Daley* (Urbana: University of Illinois Press, 1981).

6. See Alkalimat and Gills, *Harold Washington*; also Melvin Holli and Paul Green, *The Making of a Black Mayor* (DeKalb: Northern Illinois University Press, 1984).

7. In 1963 a movement called "Protest at the Polls" was launched by black activists who targeted Chicago's lack of effective civil rights policies that respected the dignity of African-Americans within the city. In 1966, the principal struggles were over desegregation of housing and the public schools and specifically the student boycotts of the notorious "Willis Wagons"—mobile classrooms ordered by General Superintendent Ben Willis to keep black students confined to overcrowded segregated schools. In 1967, Dick Gregory's insult level reached the point that he announced a new party in protest to the regular Democratic party in Cook County and launched a protest candidacy for mayor. The conditions of blacks in central cities like Chicago were the root causes of the rebellions, uprisings, and riots following the assassination of Dr. Martin Luther King, Jr. In Chicago Mayor Daley reacted by ordering the Chicago police to "shoot to kill" looters as well as arsonists. The black response was to disrupt the Democratic National Convention and embarrass the mayor, who told convention delegates that there were no slums in Chicago.

8. Some call them political assassinations; others call them murders because they were premeditated. As later evidence tends to indicate, Hampton and Clark did not resist the police who broke into their house. They were shot at although they were without guns in their hands. The community response to that was to indict the system and to intensify the efforts to resolve some of the glaring examples of police misconduct within the Black community.

9. These included Rush (2nd ward), Hutchinson (9th), Beavers (7th), Langford (16th), Tillman (3rd), W. Davis (28th), and Smith (27th). In the redistricted special ward elections of 1986, Gutierrez, Soliz, García, and Figueroa all won election along with Carter (15th) and Giles (37th), providing Washington with a new majority in the city council.

10. The idea that the community-based network was a potential *organizational* as opposed to ideological alternative to the machine was current in Chicago—as a rhetorical point in the press and from members of the "Vrdolyak 29" during the "council wars" period. Kari Moe and I discussed whether it might be a real possibility at that time. There is a whole body of Marxist and left popular literature that argues that collective goods redistribution and collective interests within constituencies can serve to motivate political activism without regard to personal material incentives. The people who supported Harold Washington as volunteers were not paid, were not promised jobs. They believed in the agenda. The issue is that there must be a political organization that functions like a party to get out the vote, to register voters, to canvass voters, to nominate and promote candidates to bear their standard. The return to such participation need not be privatized or individualized. The beauty of the Washington period was that a whole sector of the population derived symbolic and collective benefits from his victory. Thus a new politics was made possible even if some of his supporters didn't agree with it. Recall that as soon as Washington died it was the black aldermen in the city council and black committee members in the predominantly black wards who swung into motion, initiating deals and making overtures to restore the old politics of patronage—Chicago's greatest tradition of the past 60 years.

11. Community activists within the Chicago Rehab Network such as Bob Lucas, Nancy Jefferson, Slim Coleman, and Maureen Hellwig argued forcefully that the city should delegate its neighborhood service functions to nonprofit community-based groups who could be certified as legitimate contractors. In 1982, under Mayor Byrne, there were less than 50 such agencies receiving CDBG contracts. By 1987 there were nearly 350 agencies who were receiving contracts to provide various neighborhood services on behalf of the city. During Mayor Washington's first budget in 1983, he reprogrammed some $13 million to nonprofit agencies—away from the Departments of Housing, Human Services, and Economic Development into community-based "delegate agencies."

Decentralized Development: From Theory to Practice

ROBERT MIER AND KARI J. MOE

This chapter is the story of our participation in the generation and implementation of a set of urban economic development policies that evolved in Chicago from the mid-1970s through 1987. The story follows our ideas and experiences through three stages: as policy analysts and activists involved in community-based coalitions; as members of the policy apparatus of the Harold Washington mayoral campaign; and as administrators in city government. We have tried to reflect carefully about what we set out to do, what we did, and what we learned.

Our course was inextricably rooted in the history of minority and community political struggles in Chicago, which we discuss in the first part of this chapter. Its direction was enabled and informed by the clear vision and legislative record of Harold Washington. He believed that politics and government could be a force for fairness, effective service delivery, and social programs directed toward the needs of neighborhoods. As community organizers and as urban planners, we believed that our role was to apply our best efforts to implement this vision, with strategies that had to include both democratic process and good results.

On a decision-by-decision basis, guided by Washington's vision and commitment, we tried to address the desires of all neighborhoods for open, effective, and fair government. We worked to make their agenda a reality in both big and small ways. We changed budget priorities and implemented reform legislation that was dramatic for Chicago. But no detail was insignificant. For example, we took care to personally rewrite letters that senior staff had prepared for the mayor's signature to make them sound less bureaucratic and more human. We also talked to secretaries about being "Harold's voice" to the citizen who had perhaps never called city hall before.

Even with our best efforts, there is no denying the huge constraints we faced at every turn in the implementation process. Moe was fond of saying that trying to get things done was like fighting a war with someone else's army. The idea that winning an election is a cakewalk compared to governing was one that we grasped immediately. We were humbled by the extreme difficulty we encountered every single minute of every day in office.

Parallel Paths of Development

Our Personal Paths

We came to the Washington administration experience on paths that had intersected before. Moe came to Chicago in 1972 as a Carleton College student in the Associated Colleges of the Midwest Urban Studies Program. She returned in 1974 and until 1980 was employed as a social worker and teacher, while also working with several community-based organizations in the politically active Uptown community. [NB: In Chicago, Uptown (capitalized) is a distinct community area or neighborhood—unlike down-town (lower case), the central business district.] Moe met Mier in 1976 when she enrolled part-time in the School of Urban Planning and Policy (SUPP) at the University of Illinois at Chicago (UIC). She later completed a Masters of City Planning degree at the Massachusetts Institute of Technology and returned to Chicago in 1982 to become executive director of the Community Workshop on Economic Development (CWED). She had broadened her focus on social welfare and youth policy issues to include community development, employment, and economic development.

Mier arrived in Chicago in 1975 to teach community development and planning at UIC. In the preceding decade he had served in Vietnam as an advisor to the South Vietnamese navy and then been actively involved in the antiwar and community development movements in Oakland, Calif. and St. Louis, Mo. He was the founding director in 1978 of the UIC Center for Urban Economic Development (UICUED). His teaching emphasis on community economic development, pedagogical emphasis on social action as a means of learning, and technical assistance activities at UICUED brought him into close working contact with a number of community development organizations. He was a founding member of CWED, with whom he helped articulate a community development policy statement. Both authors joined Harold Washington's administration in 1983.[1]

Earlier, in 1982, when we helped put together the Washington campaign economic development platform, several large and diverse neighborhood-based organizations and coalitions engaging in community economic development had emerged. The organizations included housing and commercial development groups with a sprinkling of industrial development ones.

Community-based Organizations
Move into Economic Development

By 1975, several forces in Chicago had converged to catalyze a sharpened discussion about economic development—in addition to housing—in community development. Community leaders were seeing more clearly the need to move beyond simple protest and to create jobs, promote skill training, and link people with jobs. As Gills has discussed earlier in this volume, formal and informal networks of community organizations were emerging to facilitate strategic discussions. A critical number of community development organizations existed by the latter half of the decade, and they frequently acted for a collective purpose through formal network organizations. Viable citywide organizations had been forming that would provide support and assistance to the local community organizations and networks.

The Chicago Rehab Network, as Gills has pointed out, was a group of community organization leaders who coalesced around their commitment to rehabilitate housing in low-income neighborhoods. More importantly, they focused on the limitations of housing as a single issue and were beginning to explore broader community development approaches. Some of the Rehab Network groups were among the first to broaden their purpose, considering a direct job generation approach to community development. The Eighteenth Street Development Corporation, the Bickerdike Redevelopment Corporation, the Kenwood–Oakland Community Organization (KOCO), and the Midwest Community Council in particular began to explore job training in rehabilitation construction trades as well as direct business development.[2]

The Chicago Association of Neighborhood Development Organizations (CANDO), started in 1978, was another important community institution. Some of the advocacy groups in white working class neighborhoods earlier had taken up the issue of commercial revitalization. By 1978, there were about a dozen neighborhood commercial revitalization groups. Like the Rehab Network, they first came together as an informal network, then formally associated as CANDO.

In 1978 the graduate planning program at UIC formed the Center for Urban Economic Development (UICUED). UICUED became an important source of technical assistance to community development organizations.[3] By 1980, Mier and his colleagues in the planning program at UIC had graduated a number of people specializing in community economic development. Many had joined the staffs of community organizations. Other support organizations included the Center for Neighborhood Technology (CNT), created in 1976. It worked within these networks of community organizations, trying to bring to them alternative production technologies. Their first venture was urban greenhouses for food production. Finally, the

Associated Colleges of the Midwest Urban Studies Program proved to be an important training ground for many individuals who participated in the community organizing efforts.[4]

The downtown civic and philanthropic associations also increased their focus on housing and economic development issues in low-income communities. There was evidence of this shift in the Urban League, Community Renewal Society, the Latino Institute, T.R.U.S.T., Inc., and the Jewish Council on Urban Affairs. In the late 1970s, led by the Wieboldt Foundation, the foundations shifted some of their funding to actual development activities. Once Wieboldt moved, the Joyce Foundation, the Chicago Community Trust, the Woods Charitable Fund, and eventually the MacArthur Foundation, followed.

Downtown Planning Initiatives

During this same time, interests primarily concerned with the development of Chicago's central business district began to advocate or directly undertake development planning.[5] These downtown planning initiatives were important for what they revealed about corporate interests. They also stimulated a creative response from the neighborhoods. The "downtown vs. neighborhoods" metaphor would emerge in the Washington campaign. The Chicago 21 Plan of the late 1970s was a catalyst that defined issues, interests, and relationships which endured into the Washington administration.[6]

The Chicago 21 Plan intended to shape development of a "central area" extending to Damen Avenue on the west, south to 35th Street, and north to North Avenue. These boundaries included several low-income communities that had experienced substantial housing and commercial disinvestment. The plan envisioned those neighborhoods as extensions of the central area. To organizers and planners in those neighborhoods, it seemed as if the central area development advocates had a gentrification agenda. They began to raise questions and, through organizing efforts, formed a coalition against it.

The Chicago Central Area Committee (CCAC), the sponsors of the plan, responded by pledging matching planning grants to the affected neighborhoods. The CCAC sought input on the neighborhood components of its plan, with a pledge to incorporate them. Although there was concern about co-optation, two of the four communities raised matching funds and undertook community plans. One was done in Pilsen by the Pilsen Neighbors Community Council with Pat Wright, a SUPP graduate, as its planner. The other was done in West Town, where the Northwest Community Organization (NCO) spun off a planning group led by another of Mier's former students, Maureen Hellwig.

The planning grants may have played a co-optation role to the extent that these two groups began to focus on an agenda for their respective neighborhoods and diverted their focus from the overall approach of the Chicago 21 Plan. But the community planning processes also involved more people and organizations within each neighborhood in the debate about the future of their neighborhood.[7] Residents could not visualize their neighborhood becoming an extension of the Loop without being gentrified. Gentrification became the organizing issue for the Coalition to Stop the Chicago 21 Plan.

Other events in these communities helped keep the issue of gentrification alive. For example, in Pilsen at that time, local developer John Podmajersky promoted a grandiose plan for renovating the historic Schoenhoffen Brewery as an upscale boutique development to be called Bathhouse Square. In addition, small colonies of artists emerged both in Pilsen and in West Town. Local groups perceived such artists' colonies as beachheads for gentrification.[8]

Issues similar to those provoked by the Chicago 21 Plan were emerging in other neighborhoods. For example, a major low-income housing displacement battle was being fought in Uptown in the late 1970s. On the West Side, there was community conflict over the operations of a major hospital complex. People with specific experiences in their own neighborhood found common cause with people in other neighborhoods: whites on the north side, Hispanics in West Town and Pilsen, and blacks on the West Side were experiencing the same organizing challenges and beginning to speak a common language of experience.[9]

During this time period, a parallel set of community-based organizations and networks developed around health, human services, and education issues. These organizations were similar to the development organizations in their philosophy, personnel, and networking, and in the way they visualized downtown impact on the neighborhoods. The Alternative Schools Network, within which Moe worked from 1977 to 1980, was a parallel organization to the Rehab Network. In a lot of individual neighborhoods, the local alternative school worked directly with the local housing development group to train young people in carpentry. Where Moe worked in Uptown, her students trained at The Voice of the People, the local housing rehabilitation group. This represented one example of the multiple kinds of cross fertilization going on within and among neighborhoods.

Business Alienation

A second countervailing force evolved through the 1970s. Businesses located out of the central area felt ignored by city hall. This stimulated the formation of local chambers of commerce, business development groups, industrial councils, and eventually the CANDO network. In 1977, Mier and some of his students worked with the Economic Development Commission (EDC) doing a survey of manufacturing firms in the Pilsen–Little Village area.[10] These firms were very disenchanted with city hall. This dissatisfaction led to their creation of the Pilsen Industrial Council. This council began to work with the Eighteenth Street Development Corporation. This networking between businessmen's groups and local constituency-based development groups was occurring in many neighborhoods.

Minority Political Empowerment

A third countervailing force also emerged beginning in the 1960s—that of increased independence and assertiveness within Chicago's black community. This history of rising minority dissatisfaction is well documented earlier in this volume by Gills. This movement was reinforced by the steady growth of Chicago's population of blacks and other minorities, and the verification of that growth in the 1980 census. This occurred in the national context of dramatic increases in the numbers of minority-group mayors throughout the country.[11] Finally, contributing to all of this concern and protest was the cutback of social programs under the Reagan presidency as well as its overt attack on civil rights policies.

The Paths Converge: 1982

Formation of the Community Workshop on Economic Development

The Community Workshop on Economic Development (CWED) emerged from a 1982 conference sponsored by the Community Renewal Society (CRS) to critique enterprise zones, the central Republican urban development initiative, and to focus the local urban development policy debate.[12] The participating community organizations were frustrated with President Reagan's budget cutbacks and the dismantling of urban programs. In addition, the specter of a World's Fair in Chicago loomed, an event threatening to absorb for the next decade all available discretionary public development resources. But they also understood that the times required strategies that moved beyond statements of opposition to enterprise zones and the World's Fair. The groups decided to coalesce in order to prepare a proactive policy and program statement which could undergrid their fight for dollars and their critique of programs at the city and state levels. They also wanted a statement that would reflect the experience they had been gaining over several years of delivering community development projects.

The Chicago participants felt a sense, early on, that there was an opportunity, given a hotly contested governor's race underway in Illinois, to produce a significant statewide policy statement. The state also became the focus because Reagan was transferring the control of significant urban development programs from the federal government to the states. State governments would be designating enterprise zones. This launched the effort to put together CWED as a statewide organization.[13] CWED's formation was an acknowledgement that it was time for community based organizations to get political at the state level and represented an awareness of common interests with similar groups in smaller cities.

The actual CWED policy statement, a codification of the decisions of two statewide meetings, was written in August 1982. The platform was subsequently modified based on feedback from CWED members and then ratified. At the time of its drafting, the significance of the policy-defining effort was not fully appreciated. In fact, it failed in terms of being a political organizing device to influence the governor's race because it was completed too late.

By November CWED was in transition. It had started as an ad hoc, short term effort. There was a decision by the Chicago members to continue the organization as the *Chicago* Workshop on Economic Development because of their belief that an advocacy organization focusing on development policy was essential.[14]

Harold Washington Decides to Run for Mayor

Chicago's black community was alive with political activity during the summer and fall of 1982. Operation PUSH was leading a boycott of Chicagofest, and Chicago Black United Communities (CBUC) sponsored a straw poll to identify leading black candidates for mayor.[15] The census data revealed that the mayoralty was in reach. The traditional powers of the machine wanted to defeat Jane Byrne by supporting Richard M. Daley, son of the former mayor. Ed Gardner, owner of Soft Sheen Products, supported a voter registration drive called "Come Alive, October 5." Harold Washington, clearly the favored candidate of the black community, said he would run if the registration challenge he established was achieved. Finally, as Gills has discussed, with Washington's agreement to run, many community organizations like PUSH and CBUC coalesced, for the sake of the campaign, into the Task Force on Black Political Empowerment.

Campaign Issues Development

Moe received a call from Hal Baron in early November 1982. Congressman Washington had asked Baron to cochair, with Vince Bakeman, his Research and Issues Committee for the campaign. Baron asked Moe to be the staff director of the Research and Issues Committee, should Washington ultimately decide to run.[16] By November 15, Washington had made his decision and had approved Moe's hiring, and Moe left CWED for the campaign.

In the second half of November, Baron wrote a memo to Washington suggesting alternative approaches to issues development. His favored suggestion was the formation of issues teams to bring together diverse viewpoints and constituencies and to produce a popularly generated platform. The second, more traditional alternative was to assemble a few "experts" for a short, intensive effort to shape the campaign issues. Baron suggested to Washington that he would probably end up with the same policy papers, but the first approach would develop constituencies. Washington chose the broad-based issues teams approach. Baron, Bakeman, and Moe started to organize the teams in late November and early December. Each issue team was to represent the class, race, and neighborhood diversity of the city.

Washington's approach to issues development for the campaign was significant in that it later characterized his approach to issues development in government. The approach also reflected his tendency as a legislator to "hear all views" and replicated the committee structure of his congressional district.

By early January, about fifteen issues teams had started working on topics including energy, housing, jobs, senior citizens, women, fiscal policy, transportation, neighborhoods, and economic development (which was chaired by Mier). Washington appointed an oversight body, the Research and Issues Committee, to report to him regarding policy directions and to advise him routinely regarding work progress and schedule. Each issues team produced policy papers, specific briefing papers for speeches, endorsement sessions and debates, and campaign literature. The policy papers were published in the central policy document of the campaign, *The Washington Papers*.[17]

We are still impressed by the incredible energy and effort put forth by the more than 150 volunteers on these issues teams. On their own initiative, they gathered documents, conducted interviews, held substantive debates at their meetings, and worked under extremely tight deadlines to produce written documents for the campaign. In addition, the campaign Research Office coordinated another ten to fifteen volunteers per day who prepared the candidate's daily briefing packets for all his scheduled events. Along with every other aspect of the campaign operation, the core staff worked fourteen hours per day, seven days per week, from December to April. Resources were so sparse that there frequently were not enough chairs for all the people who wanted to work.

Given all that had to be done for his campaign, Washington must be credited for allocating resources, talent, time, and status to the issues operation. He remained committed to a campaign of substance, even though often not covered by the media. He carried this concern for issues into city government.

The Campaign Trail

On the actual campaign trail, Harold Washington consistently transcended his written material. He embellished his briefing notes with history and a rich rhetorical flourish. The fact that Harold Washington was able to elevate issues in the campaign provides an important insight into his history. This point is particularly significant because of the way in which the mainstream media and the political opposition characterized him as an exciting orator but not a serious or substantive candidate. They ignored and misunderstood the content of his speeches.

Important dimensions of Harold Washington's personal history, such as his political learning within the Daley machine, his break in the late 1960s, and his successful resistance to machine attempts at his political annihilation, are well known.[18] Less well recognized by the general public at the time of his campaign was the quality of his record as an elected official.

He had always been, even as a regular Democrat, a strong issues politician. His state legislative record of accomplishments included currency exchange reform, education, promotion of minority and female business participation in government contracting (M/FBE), the Martin Luther King holiday, and funding for minority-owned and operated Provident Hospital on Chicago's South Side. His expertise on each issue was broad and deep in a way surpassed by few state elected officials. He maintained this pattern in the U.S. Congress, where he continued to score consistently high ratings from labor, women's organizations, and good government groups. He organized a variety of citizen-staffed issues committees in his congressional district. In a short time as a congressman, he became one of the leading spokespersons for the Voting Rights Act renewal.[19]

This record had not escaped the black community. In their eyes, he had become a powerful symbol. He represented, at once, liberation, strength of convictions, achievement against the odds, and substance. He was seen as a giant intellect who possessed the humility and common sense to stay in close contact with his constituency. He was respected as a leader who could lead and listen. He was seen not only as a charismatic orator but as an elected official with a pragmatic, grounded agenda.

As a candidate, Harold Washington had a rare ability to integrate the emotional, political, and content aspects of all issues and to relate to any audience with whom he was talking. One of Moe's typical daily experiences when traveling with him in his car to brief him during the 1983 general election was going from the West Side El (elevated railroad) stops to the top floor of the First National Bank building to talk to bankers. Then they went to the North Side to discuss human rights with a predominantly gay audience, then to South Side housing projects, then to the steel mills in southeast Chicago, and finally back to West Town to meet with Puerto Rican businessmen. There wasn't an audience that he didn't move. He molded each issue into a message that connected with the disenchantment and desire for leadership of these diverse audiences.

The Transition Team

After the primary victory in February 1983, the base of support needed to be broadened. Because it was too late for significant additions to the campaign steering or issues committees, Washington needed other vehicles to involve additional supporters. In addition, it was time to establish his ability to work with the broader networks that would be required in order for him to govern after the April general election and inauguration. In March 1983, he launched a Transition Committee, cochaired by Bill Berry, former longtime director of the Chicago Urban League, and James O'Connor, chairman of Commonwealth Edison. There was an Oversight Committee, dominated by chief executive officers of Chicago corporations, but it also included substantial community representation, a fact that was to become a Washington trademark. Sixteen individual issues teams were established, paralleling the structure of the campaign issues committees.

While the structure of the transition team was similar to the campaign issues structure, and in some cases membership overlapped, many actors were included who changed the nature of the committee debate. As Gills discussed earlier, many of these debates foreshadowed subsequent discussions and controversies in the administration between varying interest groups.

Some of the teams, most notably economic development, were used by business leadership to advocate a particular policy position. In a pattern common to virtually every major city that had elected a minority-group mayor, the business leadership began a campaign to move the public development functions from under the control of the mayor into a quasi-public development corporation. They argued that this would provide development with "immunity from politics," but it was in fact a much deeper struggle over the control of development priorities and resources.[20]

In addition to generating policy recommendations, the staff of each Transition Issues Committee went to the city departments during April and May 1983, to conduct interviews and collect documents. The Washington team wanted to have as much information as possible. The final transition report was released to the public in September 1983. The recommendations of the *Washington Papers* and the transition report subsequently served as an explicit reference point for the administration's review of its progress up through the 1987 election.[21]

Taking Over and Starting Up

With the election victory, many of Harold Washington's supporters from the community and economic development networks and organizations—like us—began to think of taking roles in the new administration. To each of us, working for Harold Washington was an opportunity to implement the campaign agenda. It was clear that Moe was moving from the car into the Mayor's Office. From the transition experience, the importance of getting someone who was committed to community-oriented development policies appointed commissioner of economic development was clear. In the month after the election, Mier decided to make a push for it. Eventually, seven members of the economic development issues group would join the administration.[22]

Reflections on What Lay Before Us

Until the time we joined the city administration, we were both "outsiders" to local government, with our feet firmly rooted in community work. We knew the transition from outside to inside was significant, but it was not possible at the time to anticipate all of the consequences. We vowed not to become "bureaucrats." Contemplating the choice to join Mayor Harold Washington in government service, we attempted to be explicit about the major issues and our values and understandings toward them.[23]

A lot of this was a matter of the way we viewed local government. We thought several local government functions presented both opportunities and constraints in the achievement of our objectives.[24] One such function of the local government was service provision. We recognized we had little ability to impact the larger economy but were optimistic about our ability to improve the basic quality and distribution of service. We realized that the credibility of Harold Washington's ability to govern rested on his ability to deliver such things as garbage pickup and snow removal, and to deliver them fairly. Of course, basic economic development services were included in this calculus.

We also believed that local government, by virtue of its proximity to local residents, provided the potential to be a laboratory of democracy wherein city residents who had been alienated from government could experience a different relationship with it. We believed this could be done through freedom of information policies, community forums, citizen task forces, or major speeches. We wanted to raise the local citizenry's expectations and have them set a standard to which they would hold the administrators accountable. With Chicago's history of having a dominant mayor who could command media, corporate, and business attention, we thought that Mayor Washington had a unique opportunity to influence the terms of the public policy debate at the local, state, and national levels.

We recognized the tendency of government to co-opt challenging social movements as a way of maintaining consent for the basic structures of society. We knew there was the danger that we might defuse the community actions that brought the mayor into office. We saw the opportunity, on the other hand, to use the co-optive power of government to broaden the base of support, both within and outside of government, for our goals. Thus, while we believed that local government was, more often than not, exploited by its relationship to "growth coalitions," we believed that we could alter this relationship through "public return on public investment" policies, like betting on basic industry.[25] We thought these policies would have a longer term impact on the macroeconomy. We wanted to test the ability of local government to enlist the growth coalition's support for a broader public policy agenda.

We also had a social issue agenda. We believed that the two central social issues before us were poverty and race relations. We knew that local government, especially in Illinois, where the welfare system is essentially state managed, had only a limited capacity to address poverty. Notwithstanding, we felt that we would have to keep the issue of poverty at the forefront of everything we would undertake. Similarly, we knew the racial divisiveness within Chicago would face us every day, even within the ranks of the Harold Washington coalition. But we believed that local government, because of its closeness to people's lives, played an important role in mediating social relations across race, class, and neighborhood lines. We believed that, by bringing people of diverse backgrounds and perspectives together, local government could promote at least understanding and perhaps decreased hostility among different interest groups. We were unsure about the ability of local government to develop consensus, except on a personal, issue-specific basis.

We hoped to bring our personal commitments to social justice into the government and to make it operational in our day-to-day decision making. In this regard, following the theories of John Rawls and the practice of Norman Krumholz, we hoped to be able to focus attention on the least advantaged in any public decision making situation and to give their circumstances priority attention.[26] We also thought that an economic development agenda that opened job opportunities to the most work-needy Chicagoans was a major means of achieving justice.

In addressing the issues of poverty and race, we knew that neighborhood-based organizations were a needed ally.[27] We anticipated actively opening government decision processes to wide public participation. We believed that neighborhood organizations could be supportive of a broader social justice agenda, beyond their individual neighborhood concerns. To do this, we anticipated that much of the informal networking in which we had engaged as activists would still play an important role.

Economic Development: From Activism to Administration

The Department of Economic Development (DED) was an essential department to control. Although it had a relatively modest budget of $35 million, it had important legal authority and it carried out community development functions that could be significantly enhanced. It was a central department for reaching the mayor's neighborhood and small business constituencies. DED was a platform from which to set the terms of the economic development debate. For example, the Playskool plant closing case of 1984 dramatized a new direction for government–business relations that had national impact.[28] A paradox of DED's role was its limited spending authority vs. its significant "setting the terms of the debate" authority.

There were a number of objectives we started with that were based upon our experience, *the Washington Papers*, the transition report, and the mayor's leadership:

1. *Direct Community Development Block Grant (CDBG) and infrastructure funds to support neighborhood development.* This objective was central to Mayor Washington's priority of neighborhood revitalization. The need for these program dollars

was obvious, especially in minority areas that had been traditionally neglected. Mayor Byrne's concentration of CDBG funds and infrastructure programs on downtown projects and favored wards had been the subject of community protest.

2. *Enhance business retention programs focusing on small- to medium-sized businesses constituting the bulk of Chicago's employment base.* In this regard, we envisioned community development and businessmen's groups as a potential first point of contact with the more than 100,000 businesses scattered throughout Chicago.

3. *Develop and implement an overall program that is sensitive to the idiosyncracies of particular economic sectors and can identify and seize strategic opportunities.* This challenge required understanding the enormous diversity of Chicago's local economy and recognizing that city government, with limited resources, had to invest carefully. We believed that we would find low-cost, high-return projects by looking within specific sectors such as the steel industry.

4. *Increase the participation of small and minority-owned businesses in city loan and procurement programs.* These programs had been structured to favor large businesses or contractors, making it difficult for the vast majority of Chicago businesses to either get help or do business with the city. One consequence, for example, was that more than 60 percent of the City's $400 million annual purchase of goods and services was going to non-Chicago suppliers, thus resulting in the loss of a significant opportunity to stimulate local job generation.

5. *Advocate an urban agenda at the state and national levels.* Given his rich experience in the state legislature and Congress, the historic political strength of the Chicago mayor's office, and a national leadership vacuum on urban issues, Mayor Washington felt that he could play a role in focusing public attention on such issues as housing for low-income and homeless people or jobs and training for the work needy.

6. *Better coordinate economic development, employment and training, and education efforts.* Our goal was to change the public perception that training programs were little more than disguised welfare and to make training and education central to business development. Beyond that, the goal was for the mayor to focus on the education bureaucracy, relating education to development. This objective, although certainly as pressing as all the others in the early debate, was overwhelmed by the day-to-day realities and did not surface as a strong agenda item until Mayor Washington's second term.[29]

7. *Improve government operations.* We knew that little attention
had been paid to fundamental facets of management such as the
development of personnel and information systems. We sought to
modernize operations.

The overarching goal of all these objectives was the need to provide jobs
for Chicagoans needing work. As a result of the virtual hemorrhage of the
city's manufacturing base during the 1960s and 1970s, combined with the
severe recession of the early 1980s, Chicago's unemployment rate exceeded
12 percent—with a substantial concentration among minorities in general
and minority youth in particular. We knew that there were substantial
limits to the impact a local government could have on that, but were determined to gauge everything we did by the standard of providing jobs for
work-needy people.

Assessing the Department

Virtually all the departments in the government inherited by Harold
Washington operated as if they were part of a 1950s organization. For example, there were no computers in DED when we walked in. None of the
financial staff was using electronic spreadsheets; everything was being
done by hand. Department staff were calling on 3000 businesses a year
with paper records that were virtually inaccessible. This backwardness
held for all city government systems, as diverse as the personnel system and
the check-writing system.

DED was a young organization, having been created in 1982. It succeeded the Economic Development Commission, which then had been
vested with some line authority. The new department was created by
adding some units from the Departments of Planning and Neighborhoods
to those in the Economic Development Commission.[30]

When Mier started, a large amount of DED's $35 million budget was for
infrastructure development. The city had received counterrecession federal
Economic Development Administration (EDA) funds, so it was rebuilding
industrial streets and undertaking some commercial area improvements.
DED also had a $1 million EDA revolving loan fund and was packaging
federal Urban Development Action Grants (UDAGs). There was a business
contact program with ten or twelve people in the field knocking on doors.
DED supported chambers of commerce to implement marketing programs
for their neighborhood commercial strips. There were about thirty-
five community business organizations annually receiving about $1 mil-
lion in grants. A staff of about ten people managed the commercial strip
program.

DED lacked a clear mission and identity, partly owing to its newness. There was no marketing program. There was no program designed to provide comprehensive services to small businesses. There was only a limited industrial policy focus.[31]

While DED lacked a clear mission, it had an organizational culture. This departmental culture accepted that significant projects went through an essentially political decision process. Favored nongovernmental deal brokers handled the major projects or programs. Therefore, the department staff was relegated to less significant work.

Staff accepted that they didn't have the resources or authority to commit the bureaucracy. This paradox fostered an individual behavior, on the one hand, of trying to sound responsive while, on the other, not being able to deliver. Bureaucratic procedures existed to shove away problems while pretending to take them seriously. If anything, this problem was exacerbated with the election of Harold Washington. His campaign promise to make government accessible to everyone had raised expectations. The scarcity of resources and the overwhelming nature of many problems lead to enormous "queuing" problems.

Another problematic aspect of organization culture was a serious lack of information and knowledge across departmental divisions. For example, there were about ten people who contacted businesses through field calls. These ten people had received no training regarding the loan programs of the department. If a business person wanted financial assistance, he or she couldn't find out about it from the DED agents who were the first point of information. The business person had to go through the deal brokers. We identified several similar problems in this early analysis.

Organizing the Department

Mier took office in August 1983. By mid-October, several division heads who were sensitive to and capable of managing the Harold Washington agenda were in place.[32] But Mier was still troubled by the presence of many staff people who were set in their ways. These staff ranged from apolitical bureaucrats who had been stuck in a job for years to political appointees who were allied with the mayor's opposition. The consequences of this included low productivity, bad morale, and—in the worse cases—sabotage.

We knew that changing organizational culture and staff behavior throughout DED would take two to three years. This was too long a time frame to achieve organizational effectiveness. We wanted the ability, at a moment's notice, to seize opportunities to implement concrete projects that embodied the Washington agenda.

In order to provide a stimulus for innovation and to keep a focus on larger strategy questions, Mier formulated the idea of a new Research and Development (R&D) Division within DED. In November, 1983, we drafted the functions of the division. It would provide staff resources to line divisions when they engaged in entrepreneurial activities, work with community based organizations engaged in policy research and development, improve information systems within the department, and manage special projects. The R&D Division, described more fully later in this volume in Giloth's chapter, was launched in January 1984, when Moe transferred to DED from the Mayor's Office.

Redefining Culture

With his key managers in place, Mier knew that he needed to foster a different organizational culture. The components of the desired culture were in some cases linked directly to the mayoral campaign. One theme was respect for the processes of community empowerment. This required creating a different attitude in the bureaucracy, one that respected and responded to external initiative instead of being exclusively internally driven, or driven by the political apparatus.

Consistent with themes of openness and democracy, he wanted to minimize bureaucratic boundaries and to create a climate of problem solving based on point to point communication and teamwork. Mier recognized and rewarded this kind of initiative. This discomforted the division heads, even ones he had appointed. Like Washington, Mier would symbolically reinforce his emphasis on point-to-point communication by doing it himself.

A major obstacle, which cannot be overemphasized, impeding the creation of a different culture was the predominant administrative rules and norms of the bureaucracy. DED was subject to personnel regulations, hiring rules, and fiscal control systems that slowed everything down and frustrated employee morale significantly. In spite of this context, we also promoted culture change through traditional, formal approaches. We implemented orientation and training sessions for the staff regarding the new directions of the department. We revised operational procedures, emphasizing the need for openness and accessibility. We symbolically reinforced these actions with, for example, new marketing paraphernalia. Over time, we underscored all this by introducing performance evaluations and tying them to achievement of our departmental objectives.

Within months we began to have quarterly all-department meetings, where Mier would reward people for actions that best exemplified the new goals. When someone undertook an initiative supportive of the new directions, he would share the episode with the entire department, emphasizing how it fit into the big picture, and then reward the employee with office memorabilia such as calling card cases or pen sets. High performers were also promoted whenever possible.

We placed a strong emphasis on the goal of equal opportunity. We were probably one of the earliest departments that made substantial inroads into equal employment opportunity (EEO) hiring. A key was Mier's personal involvement. He wouldn't let people hire unless he was satisfied that they had really done an EEO search. Moe developed the departmental procedures for such a search. Mier set goals for divisions, sections of divisions, and occupational hierarchies. When the Latino Commission did an evaluation of departments' EEO hiring efforts, they acknowledged DED as an model for other departments in terms of pursuing an EEO hiring program.[33]

Part of what we were doing was along the classical lines of good government reform—creating an organization that was responsible to the mayor, yet operating along lines that were clear and accountable to the public.[34] Mayor Washington wanted the departments to be accessible to the public and to constituencies directly, as distinct from having citizens go through their city council representatives (aldermen) or consultants. For example, Commissioner of Streets and Sanitation, John Halpin made himself available directly to community groups so they could get their streets cleaned by talking to him directly.

As soon as Mier started in August 1983, then Chief of Staff Bill Ware asked him to form a subcabinet of commissioners from the development departments. Two were carryovers—Tom Kapsalis of Aviation and Jerry Butler of Public Works. The majority were Washington appointees: Brenda Gaines, Housing; Liz Hollander, Planning; Maria Cerda, MET (the Mayor's Office of Employment and Training); and Fred Fine, Cultural Affairs. Common to all of them was minimal or no involvement in the campaign. They were professionals in their fields.

The development subcabinet was the first such grouping established in the government. The mayor wanted a forum for information transfer both up and down through the hierarchy, as well as a forum for policy debate and coordination of programs and projects. He did not want department heads running their operations as fiefdoms, which had too often occurred in the past.

Mier had a large task on his hands and recruited Moe to staff the development subcabinet even prior to her joining the department. The early meetings consisted of gathering information, defining an agenda, and attempting to get all the commissioners on board with *The Washington Papers*. The subcabinet became focused when we undertook production of "Chicago Works Together: The 1984 Development Plan" (CWT).

The effort began when Mier woke up one morning in January to hear on the news that the mayor had announced the release of his development plan in about sixty days. So Mier walked into Washington's office that morning and asked, "What's this development plan you were talking about?" The mayor quietly beamed with the smile he wore when he was about to ask for something impossible with the complete confidence it would somehow get done. He said, "I figured you'd fill in the blanks." We had sixty days to produce a development plan.

We met his goal with the highly acclaimed plan.[35] CWT was a policy plan that laid out five broad goals (job development, neighborhood development, balanced growth, efficiency, and a state legislative commitment) that set the framework for more than 45 specific policies. Finally, the policies were to be implemented with more than 200 specific projects.

The R&D Division of DED was by then directed by Moe, and in the course of preparing the development plan she emerged as the chief of staff for the development subcabinet. All the departments contributed staff to support the effort, and it turned out to be a great device to motivate the rest of the departments in the development cluster. Because the matters of the development subcabinet closely involved DED, they served to reinforce the goals and directions of the department. With the completion of the development plan, it was reasonable to expect a clearer sense of purpose and more pointed output from DED.

Managing DED Programs

Once the policy agenda was set, we were faced with the task of implementation. By the spring of 1984, DED had been reorganized into five operating divisions: business services, neighborhood development, real estate development, international business development, and R&D. These divisions together were responsible for managing a wide variety of programs and projects.

Within each of these divisions we faced a number of common problems. Staff capacity was limited, and the bureaucracy continued to move too slowly. We had too little money for everything, from computers and books to loan program dollars. We faced intransigent historical and institutional obstacles, such as trying to initiate development planning in neighborhoods where no new development had occurred for several years. We experienced covert and overt political opposition within our ranks. The media was uninformed, hostile, and disinclined to cover neighborhood development stories. Finally, we experienced disagreements about strategic directions. Any two or three of these factors operating at once would make management in any organization challenging. All six together made it extremely difficult.

Each division and its programs could be the object of considerable analysis and evaluation. Instead of focusing on all of them, we will highlight one program area: neighborhood development through community-based organizations, as this was central to the Washington development agenda. One division had major responsibility for this program area, but it touched the work of all the operating divisions. In addition, we will describe a number of large projects that we managed during the second half of the mayor's tenure.

Neighborhood Development Program

In 1983, DED supported 35 community based business development organizations, known to the bureaucracy as "delegate agencies." They provided a variety of services in their local neighborhood. This arrangement was politically controversial because in some respects it circumvented the political ward organizations. It was also a system that put Washington directly in touch with his grass-roots constituency, which was also why previous mayors supported the concept to some degree.

Up until 1983 there was little oversight of the delegate agency program. The thirty five groups receiving money were subject to few requirements, although some were performing quite admirably. To the extent there was an evaluation system, it was superficial. Funding was based on a three-year cycle, at which point the departments wished groups to be "self-sufficient." In reality, the criteria were unclear and few groups were ever defunded.

Based on campaign commitments and our philosophy of neighborhood development, we wanted to expand and improve the delegate agency program. We wanted to demonstrate that development services could be effectively delivered through community-based organizations. Within two years, the number of neighborhood-based organizations or citywide groups supporting the neighborhood effort receiving direct funding from DED had grown to more than 100.

The expansion involved four types of groups. First, there were new local businessmen's organizations being created, often encouraged by one of the major network organizations like CANDO or CWED. Second, there were groups in other functional areas, most often housing rehabilitation, who were broadening their work to include direct business assistance or development. Third, there were particular efforts to encourage business organization development in low-income areas such as within public housing projects. Finally, there were service groups brought in to provide technical assistance to new or growing neighborhood based organizations. For example, the League of Women Voters received a DED grant to conduct board training.

DED rewarded groups that developed business service capacity both by giving them more money and letting them carry on a greater load of the work. When they evolved to what DED considered the most complete stage of development, they were given twice the amount of money any group had been given in the past. DED staff were then pulled out of that community. The local organization would become the city's first line of contact with businesses outside of the central area. This final stage of development was called the Local Industrial Retention Initiative (LIRI).[36]

The LIRI program originated in the field operations division of DED, run by Arturo Vázquez. It evolved from an identification of the half dozen local industrial councils or community organizations among those routinely working with DED that had the highest organizational capacity to step up their industrial retention efforts. DED and these groups tried to formulate a systematic and strategic methodology for dealing with industrial retention: what businesses should be approached; what should they be asked; what could be done to give them more confidence in the city; and, most importantly, what concrete problems could the city realistically tackle?

In varying degrees, other departments of the city that worked with neighborhood-based organizations were trying the same thing. The Department of Housing was supporting groups to rehabilitate housing for low- to moderate-income tenants. The Department of Human Services supported neighborhood-based social service providers. The Departments of Health and of Aging and Disability and the Mayor's Office of Employment and Training similarly were developing networks of neighborhood based service providers.

Evaluation of the Neighborhood Development Program

The program of support to more than 100 community development organizations made programmatic sense, policy sense, and political sense. But is was always a very tough program to manage because of the varying levels of capacity and performance from the groups.

Performance evaluation was very difficult and labor intensive. It exposed the uneven skills of our staff and their varying capacity to assist the groups and assess their performance. We needed an evaluation system that could minimize the risk associated with widely divergent groups and widely divergent staff skills. By supplementing our staff with outside evaluators drawn from local technical assistance providers, we developed a workable system. However, evaluations continued to generate discomfort among groups being reviewed. This process was essential both for our own internal purposes, and for the public and the city council.

Frequently, when we went before the city council, some delegate agency contract was the object of council members saying "That group in my neighborhood isn't doing anything." We had to prove that they were doing something worthwhile. We were constantly risking being attacked for just dumping money on groups for political purposes. They really wanted to attack us on that and make the case that this was a political operation, not a professional operation.

Our critics could not make their case. In four years, they could not find a case to demonstrate that a group we proposed to fund was not performing adequately. This standard required accountability from groups, and every year we defunded five or six groups for nonperformance. These actions were often protested, but we held our ground. Opposition council members could never find a nonperforming group that we hadn't already found and were planning to defund.

The U.S. Department of Housing and Urban Development (HUD), which provided most of DED's funds through the CBDG, was auditing DED on a case-by-case basis. They investigated every group we were supporting and asked whether it met the HUD national standards. During the four years, HUD evaluated 100 percent of the DED projects. This close scrutiny created an atmosphere both within our staff and among business and community groups working with us that HUD was not supportive of what we were trying to do.

Large-Scale Development Initiatives

Several development initiatives were of such scale and importance that they transcended the capacity of any one department to direct. Examples include projects such as the renovation or replacement of professional sports stadiums, the construction of the new central library, the development of new transit stations and adjacent land, and the development of surplus land at the city's airports. Each of these projects involved tended to involve multiple departments from the development subcabinet, the city's legal and financial staff, departments with specific technical responsibilities like Public Works, and departments holding key assets such as land owned by Aviation or Public Works.

Since DED chaired the development subcabinet, and since the mayor wanted economic development considerations to be preeminent in these projects, its top management was expected to play a part in these projects. In addition, the mayor had gained confidence in our individual abilities to respond quickly and thoroughly to projects with complex requirements. Over time, Mier assumed major responsibility for many of them, and their dictates were superimposed over the normal functions of the department.

To a degree, Mayor Washington undertook such projects reluctantly. They were not consistent with his development philosophy of small, widely dispersed projects with lots of opportunities for community involvement. The large projects risked activating the urban growth coalitions and having them again run roughshod over neighborhood interests. As Hollander also shows elsewhere in this volume, the mayor found he had little choice.

His first problem was that he had not been able to effectively market a "small is beautiful" development metaphor. This image never really took hold. Second, the media held him to a standard that would not have been placed on a white mayor. Reluctance to deliver megaprojects, the mayor increasingly feared, would be seen as fundamental evidence of his inability to govern, where it would be judged as strategic choice for a white mayor. Early in stadium deliberations, Washington told Mier that he believed if he lost a professional sports team, even to the suburbs, neither he nor any other black candidate for mayor could win the next election.

None of this was consolation to his community constituency, and these projects generated controversy. Neighborhood groups' views about the correct development course were clearly defined by their own interests. They tended not to prioritize projects with a citywide impact or benefit. Harold Washington's track record on major projects was not their concern. We will illustrate these dilemmas by means of the stadium projects and the new Central Public Library, projects for which one or the other of us had major responsibility.

The White Sox

There were three stadium projects that surfaced during Mayor Washington's tenure. Since the Bears and the White Sox wanted new stadiums, the initial efforts were focused on finding a site that could accommodate a new stadium complex. After some early consideration of a domed stadium, it became apparent that neither team wanted to play indoors or on artificial surfaces. Further, they had vastly different needs in terms of stadium size, with football seeking a 75,000-person stadium and baseball a 45,000-person one.

Other issues eroded the idea of a stadium complex. One team owner was reluctant to enter into any cooperative management arrangement with the other and was not confident that scheduling conflicts could be amicably handled. Also, the Bears wanted to own their own stadium, whereas the White Sox wanted a publicly built one.

By July 1986, any prospects for a stadium complex with two teams as tenants evaporated. The White Sox then announced that they were going to leave Chicago to play in west suburban Addison, Ill. Needless to say, a community outcry erupted.

The ensuing "Save Our Sox" campaign was dominated by community activists who were more baseball fans than they were connected to the neighborhoods around Comiskey Park. Their organizing efforts were complemented by political activists seeking to build an organizational base in the communities adjoining the baseball park. They focused their attention narrowly—on keeping the White Sox in Chicago and retaining historic Comiskey Park. They built grass-roots support among White Sox fans. They did not really entertain the possibility that keeping the White Sox in Chicago might mean building a new stadium for them.

Importantly, we failed to expand the issue into a broad community context. This was the first of the big projects with a direct community impact. Further, it did not really "fit" in any department. As such, the team appointed to negotiate with the White Sox and the state, led by Mier and one of the mayor's key private sector advisors, Al Johnson, was always trying to borrow resources from departments.[37] City departments responded by trying to minimize staff effort.

By midfall 1986, support for the White Sox in Addison had eroded, and in early November they lost by a close vote in a local referendum. The White Sox were being quietly courted by St. Petersburg, Fla., and Denver, Colo. With the Illinois state legislature due to convene for a brief session in late November, a window of opportunity for the mayor to "Save Our Sox" opened. He seized the opportunity.

Things moved very quickly. In a matter of forty-eight hours after Thanksgiving, a deal got put together that kept the White Sox in Chicago but called for a new stadium to be built in the vicinity of the current Sox stadium. That choice was totally driven by costs—reusing existing infrastructure would save $30–50 million. Within five working days, it was passed by the Illinois General Assembly. The new stadium would be financed by rent paid by the team, supplemented with a new tax on hotel and motel rooms, a tax base that would not have been available for uses other than those seen as benefiting the "visitor industry."

In the short run, there was widespread euphoria. After Mayor Washington's death, much controversy erupted that warrants exposition elsewhere. In a nutshell, the White Sox walked away from the deal, raised the stakes, and forced another $150 million of public subsidy into the deal. Also, the Illinois Sports Facilities Authority, empowered with building the stadium, was accused of running roughshod over the community and, in so doing, exposed the lack of community roots in the original community organizing and city planning efforts.

The Bears

After the collapse of the stadium complex idea, the focus also shifted to the Bears. Two forces shaped the direction that deliberations with the Bears took. The Chicago Central Area Committee (CCAC) became a strong advocate for a privately financed stadium and stood poised to organize the business community to purchase the luxury seating that could make such a venture feasible. A West Side grass-roots organization, the Midwest Community Council (MCC), organized a campaign in 1986 to bring any new Bears stadium to their neighborhood.

Mayor Washington was initially reluctant to consider the West Side. Although there was considerable vacant land in the area being advocated by the MCC, there also remained a significant number of occupied housing units. In late 1986, he proposed a site immediately north of existing Soldier Field. To complement the privately financed stadium, he proposed demolition of Soldier Field, moving parking off the Lakefront to open up the space, and creation of a museum complex to segregate football fans from visitors to the Museum of Natural History, the Aquarium, and the Planetarium immediately north of Soldier Field.

His proposal was immediately scorned by Lakefront protection interests, and taken up as a major mayoral campaign issue by his opponents. Together, they captured the support of the *Chicago Tribune*, and the mayor reluctantly backed down. He created a site location committee with a goal of deflecting the issue until after the election.

We were reluctant to include the West Side site in the committee's deliberations, but a strong group of organizations in that area demanded its consideration. In mid-1987, the committee recommended the West Side site. In the course of the committee's deliberations, strong local opposition to the site also emerged.

The city project management team, again led by Mier and Al Johnson, initiated and managed a broader community planning process around the proposed Bears Stadium, one that should have occurred with the Sox. We realized the magnitude of the relocation problem on the West Side. We encouraged community debate and, working with both proponents and opponents, facilitated a process of community dialogue. We made a continual effort to reconcile community differences.[38]

As the community dialogue ensued, the cost of the community demands, although quite reasonable, began to mount. We pledged to address the community needs and decided to subsidize community improvements with tax revenues from the luxury seating that would exist in a new stadium. We saw this as an opportunity to implement development policies of balanced growth and linkages between large and small projects.

In the end, we proposed guaranteeing any dislocated household the option of physically moving and improving their home or building a new one of greater value. Further, we proposed holding them harmless for any increased costs they might encounter, such as increased taxes. We proposed a number of community facilities, like a library and park. Most of this would be paid from tax revenues derived from the luxury seating.

Pate Phillips, the conservative Republican leader of the Illinois State Senate gave the best testimony on the Bears deal. He looked at it and said, "This deal is dangerous. If we pass this it's going to set up a precedent that we can't live with elsewhere." After Mayor Washington's death, the General Assembly rejected the deal.

The Cubs

A 1982 proposal by the Chicago Cubs had aroused a firestorm of controversy in the neighborhood surrounding Wrigley Field. The well-organized, highly educated and articulate upper-middle-income community had engineered local and state legislation prohibiting lights. In 1984, the Cubs joined the chorus of dissident teams and proposed moving to the suburbs.

Mayor Washington agreed to take up the lights issue. He was partially motivated by a reluctance to avoid a thorny sports team issue affecting an upper-income white neighborhood when he was facing up to similar issues in poorer, largely black neighborhoods. Also, he saw the issue as a classic land use conflict and felt it had strong similarities to ones he faced in attempting to retain industry in Chicago.

He directed that an open, public process be undertaken to find a way to partially accommodate the Cubs, enough to make it difficult for them to leave the city. The process consisted of creating a negotiating committee comprising neighborhood residents, business leaders, and the Cubs. Their meetings were professionally facilitated, supported by considerable information gathering including the use of survey sampling, and a number of community meetings. A compromise resulted, hammered out over an almost two-year period, which placed severe limitations on the number of night games (eighteen) and which specified starting times, a curfew for alcohol sales, and stringent neighborhood parking restrictions. By all accounts, including those of the main "no lights" advocates, the solution has worked quite well.

Central Public Library

The possibility of a new Central Public Library was another such large public development. This was a project that had been on the agendas of at least two previous mayors. Byrne's approach had been to put the new facility in a renovated department store on State Street—Goldblatt's. The site was subject to intense controversy, and the issue of the library project moved on to the mayor's large project development agenda by late 1985, around the time Moe moved back to the Mayor's Office. In a series of "midcourse correction" meetings during this time to critically assess what essential work was yet to be done, the central library emerged as a priority for three of the five subcabinets. This was largely due to the realization that the Washington administration had to demonstrate its capacity to effectively implement large-scale development projects. This was against the background of the administration's rejection of the World's Fair and inability to move the Navy Pier project in the face of opposition by the city council's opposition majority.

Because of the time pressure to deliver this project and in light of the controversy surrounding cost overruns at such other projects as the State of Illinois Center and at McCormick Place, the mayor was searching for an approach that would deliver this project on time and within the budget. It was also more subtle: we all understood the way large projects were done to enhance the functioning of traditional development networks, with featherbedding of consultant costs, inflated change orders, etc. We wanted to change this process. There was also a desire to change the process in a different way, by including a greater degree of public involvement.

The mayor established a Central Library Advisory Committee to counsel him on the specifics of the development approach, in particular, completing the library as "design-build" project. Using this technique, which Hollander describes in more detail later in this volume, bids would be solicited to design and build the library within a specific cost. The developer would be selected based on both design and cost criteria. And significantly, the developer would be selected by a committee following extensive public debate on the designs themselves. In this case the designs of the competing teams were on display at the Cultural Center and were the subject of extensive public hearings.

This approach was a fundamentally important departure from traditional approaches to development of such projects, not only in Chicago but in the nation. In choosing the design-build approach, the mayor clearly understood that he was authorizing a procedure that was completely insulated from political influence in the development process, even influence that might work to his advantage.

The process worked beyond our imagination. Thirty thousand people viewed the design entries at the Cultural Center. In effect a constituency for the new Central Public Library was developed through the process. Construction began in 1988.

Assessment of Large Projects

Our involvement with large scale projects convinces us that it is both necessary and possible for a progressive local government to undertake them. To a degree, community attitudes toward large projects have been conditioned by decades-old "downtown vs. the neighborhoods" community-organizing emphases. These emphases were given teeth by the paternalistic tendency of old-fashioned politics, exemplified by the handling of the World's Fair by the Byrne administration, to treat large projects as too important to involve common people.

But by 1987, the large-scale projects were being undertaken as if community people mattered. The Central Public Library, fittingly named for the mayor after his death, may best exemplify this change in attitude. People throughout the city seem to claim ownership and, through it, can see a public interest that transcends local, community interests. Finally, this public interest had been given teeth during the tenures of Mayors Washington and Sawyer by tight fiscal management and vigorous pursuit through contracting and purchasing of equal opportunity goals.

Conclusion: What Did We Accomplish?

An action-based view of planning requires ongoing self criticism. During 1983–1987, we continually assessed what we were doing, and we would like to share some of our observations.

On the whole we are comfortable in saying that we achieved a lot of what we set out to do. This included substantial work with and in neighborhoods, most involving concrete projects: facilitating community-based development, helping smaller businesses, and encouraging housing construction and rehabilitation. We also made headway on the large projects—Southwest Rapid Transit, the stadium deals, and the Central Public Library—but believe we undertook them in ways to make them less onerous to neighborhood people.

We emerged from our experience with a powerful sense of the importance of basic service delivery. Despite our emphasis on process and planning, we spent the majority of our time trying to deliver projects and programs. Yet, in thinking about accomplishments, it is important to reflect again on the environment within which we were working. Harold Washington took office in the trough of the 1981–1983 recession, and the so-called Reagan recovery was slow to reach Chicago. Unlike previous

Chicago mayors, he did not enjoy the confidence and support of the Democratic political establishment at either the national or local level. In a pattern quite dissimilar to that of other cities undertaking government management reform, he received only limited business community support until after the 1986 special aldermanic elections that gave him control over the city council. Finally, he inherited a bureaucracy dominated by political appointees of his local opposition who hardly saw it in their interest for Harold Washington to succeed.

We came to appreciate that the structure of local power was more complex than we realized in 1983. The entrenched machine the mayor sought to dissolve had substantial influence, if not outright control, over most of the major local public and private institutions. These included the sister local governments: the Housing Authority, the Transit Authority, the city colleges, the Board of Education, and the Park District. The machine's influence reached deep into major financial and legal establishments, the unions, and even the Catholic church. In fact, the metaphor of a machine is quite misleading. A machine operates in a consistent and predictable way. A weed, with its ever-spreading roots and tenacity, is a better metaphor.

The idea of a "power elite" had always been abstract to us, but our experience in government brought it to life. In Chicago, it is not a small, tightly knit club, but a large, multilayered, informal network bound together by corporatist ideology. It was an ideology that had a difficult time accommodating the notion of a strong black mayor.

In addition to these obstacles, Mayor Washington faced enormous fiscal constraints. He inherited a $168 million current operating deficit, and in his first term saw federal revenue sharing decrease by a total of almost $200 million. He found little slack in the local budget, with almost 70 percent of the resources committed to provision of police, fire, and sanitation services. These areas of increasing public demand for expansion were virtually immune to efficiency improvements.[39]

In light of these realities, Mayor Washington had to reach beyond usual constituencies for support and encouragement. He found it both in the base that elected him and in some new places. Within the base, the black churches and black talk radio continued to provide important forums to exchange ideas and solicit support.[40] Within the white community, civic groups like the League of Women Voters afforded him the respect they traditionally showed all Chicago mayors. Within the Hispanic community, local business groups became important connecting points. Across all parts of the city, community-based organizations played a crucial support role, including areas of the city, like the Northwest and Southwest Sides, which had voted overwhelmingly against Washington in 1983. Given the historical connection between the community development movement and

Washington's election, community-based organizations became an essential constituency supporting the mayor's development agenda.

From the perspective of efforts within government at policy and program development and implementation, support of community-based organizations was a powerful countervailing force with which the mayor could face entrenched political or bureaucratic interests. In some cases, the quality of the support was so rich that the mayor could move boldly. Examples include the Playskool suit, the shutdown of Community Development−funded departments in 1985, and pursuit of Planned Manufacturing District designation.

We constantly were aware of the fragility of relations with community-based organizations: many of our staff felt them to be alien and hostile, and the community organizations themselves were walking fine lines between being helpful and feeling co-opted. This led to a growing frustration on their part. The large-scale projects placed a particular strain on the relationship. Nonetheless, the continued capacity development of community-based organizations and their sophistication at agenda setting may be one important legacy of the Washington years.[41]

With the backing of community-based organizations, we were able to do many things differently. Most important among them was to attack discrimination and to vigorously pursue equal opportunity programs. For example, in the ten years prior to Washington taking office, the Department of Economic Development and its predecessor, the Economic Development Commission, had concluded nine financial deals involving minority firms; within three years of Harold Washington's inauguration, we concluded sixty.

This achievement had multiple roots. Most important were the development of a small business lending program, which previously the city didn't have, and the recruitment of black and Hispanic professionals to the staff so applicants could talk to people more understanding of their situation. With these and comparable accomplishments, we believe we significantly changed the nature and distribution of the outcomes of government development efforts.

Our initial expectation that local government could play an substantial role in illuminating issues was borne out. It had capacity to focus attention, shape debate, endorse or invent language, and influence forums. In the context of promoting participatory decision making, this is a powerful conception of planning's role.[42]

Only history will judge whether the changes we implemented will stand the test of time. Certainly we were aware that a progressive local government in Chicago would likely be temporary, and we constantly tried to institutionalize our progress. Three means stand out. First, we recruited talented and politically progressive people into the bureaucracy. Many of them are still there, we're glad to note. Second, we tried to fix with tradition and law means of opening up government information to ordinary citizens. An example is the Freedom of Information executive order. Finally, by bringing all interested parties to the tables of discussion and debate, we hoped to build both capacity and expectation in citizens to participate in government decision making. Harold Washington was a great believer in democracy, and these means were vital to him. Ultimately, their stability and significance, we believe, will hinge on the state of race relations in Chicago.

We came away with a humbling sense of the enormity of the issues of poverty and race. Poverty seems an overwhelming issue. Partially, we feel this because we had little chance to address it without control of vital service institutions like the schools and the Housing Authority. In Chicago, the racial issue is possibly even more intractable. Because poverty and race are so intertwined in this society, the inability to deal with race is a major cause of the inability to deal with poverty.

We hope that our enthusiasm and commitment has come through on these pages. What is probably less clear is the raw intensity of the effort demanded. For example, the amount of time and effort necessary to effect public dialogue across races and classes while also managing a large public bureaucracy is almost beyond description. We found ourselves working some 80–100 hours a week, year in, year out; Harold Washington seldom put in less than a 120-hour workweek. We found a constant need to network with reform-minded individuals outside government to check our progress, solicit new ideas, and garner support. Like the mayor, we liberally handed out our office and home phone numbers to everyone who wanted to share an opinion, favorable or otherwise, about our progress. We constantly struggled to find language and metaphors, like the development logo "Chicago Works Together," that could ease our work in a multirace, multiclass development environment.

In the flush of election victory, we joined the Washington administration believing a lot of the hard work had been done. We felt that relative to the demands of implementing an agenda, the hard tasks had been policy planning, program development, and political mobilization. Our priorities are now reversed: we believe that organizational development and program implementation is the most difficult job.

But we have faith and remain inspired by our great mentor, Harold Washington. Shortly before his death, in his annual State of the City address to the League of Women Voters, he said in reflecting on his accomplishments:

In years past, through some of the healthiest and happiest periods in our country's life, there was an active federal–urban partnership that flourished and nourished not only our cities, but the suburbs around them. But the spirit of those bright days has been eclipsed by a new ethic of sink-or-swim, a mean-spirited myopia that can focus only on the bottom line, blind to the crisis we are creating at our lowest income levels—or the growing sense of dread among those with fixed incomes—or the creeping anxieties of our middle classes.

We must counter that specter of despair with the New Spirit of Chicago. We have proven to ourselves that change is possible in our own city. And we have taken the national leadership among cities, in working for change in Washington, D.C. The federal budget is our business. Our country's foreign trade policy is our business. Our country's economic policy is our business. Every policy that affects jobs, education, housing, is our business. We have a direct interest in federal policies toward the poor, the homeless, the aging, the disabled, mothers and children, and all those others who have been thrown at our doorstep by a federal administration in retreat from reality.

And so I ask for your hand and for your voice. Lend a hand to help your city, in our efforts to "do for ourselves." And let your voice be heard as we make our case at the federal level, where the responsibility for our cities must ultimately lie. Working together, we can build on the progress of the past four years, to meet challenges of the years ahead.[43]

NOTES

1. See Robert Mier, "Academe and the Community: Some Impediments to Professional Practice," *Journal of Planning Education and Research* 6, no. 1 (1986), 66–70.
2. Several authors of chapters in this book have played prominent roles with several of these organizations. Bob Giloth directed Eighteenth Street Development Corporation, Bob Brehm directed Bickerdike Redevelopment Corporation, and Doug Gills has worked for KOCO.
3. A founding staff member and the director since Mier went to the city is Wim Wiewel, coeditor of this book.
4. Moe and Donna Ducharme were students, and Jody Kretzmann, Hal Baron, and Lu Palmer were professors. Ducharme and Kretzmann are authors of other chapters in this book. Baron was Washington's chief policy advisor. Palmer headed an organization, Chicago United Black Communities (CBUC), that played an important role in Washington's candidacy.

5. These interests included the Chicago Central Area Committee (CCAC), the Metropolitan Planning Council, and later the Commercial Club. The *Chicago Tribune*, a long-standing growth advocate, did a critical series that examined the city's Economic Development Commission and its lack of a comprehensive game plan; see Richard Longworth, "City on the Brink," *Chicago Tribune* (May 10–14, 1981).

6. For example, the coalition to stop the Chicago 21 Plan proved to be a training ground for some of the key leaders of the coalition that fought the World's Fair; see Anne B. Shlay and Robert P. Giloth, "Social Organization of a Land Based Elite: The Case of the Failed Chicago 1992 World's Fair," *Journal of Urban Affairs* 9, no. 4, (1987) 305–324. The plan was prepared for the CCAC by the architectural firm of Skidmore, Owings and Merrill; see Chicago Central Area Committee, *Chicago 21: A Plan for Chicago's Central Area Communities* (Chicago: 1973). The CCAC historically has been composed of the major central area property interests—real estate developers, banks, utility companies, the newspapers, etc.

7. New organizations emerged as a consequence of that broadened debate. In Pilsen, the Pilsen Housing and Business Alliance (PHBA), led by Arturo Vázquez, was created to focus on the gentrification issues of east Pilsen, the area closest to the central area.

8. See Robert Mier, "City Official Rebuts *Tribune's* Development Series," *Chicago Tribune* (October 16, 1986), Sec. 4, p. 1ff.

9. See John Forester, *Planning in the Face of Power* (Berkeley: University of California Press, 1989), for a more general treatment of this phenomenon.

10. The team included Giloth, Greg Longhini, currently the assistant to the commissioner of planning at the city, Joel Werth, former deputy press secretary to Acting Mayor Eugene Sawyer, and John-Jairo Betancur, currently a research assistant professor in UICUED. See Marianne Nealon, "Factors Related to the Intention of Chicago Manufacturers to Relocate from Their Sites" (Master's project, School of Urban Planning and Policy, University of Illinois at Chicago, 1977).

11. See, for instance, Robert Mier, Joan Fitzgerald, and Lewis A. Randolph, "African-American Elected Officials and the Future of Progressive Elected Movements," in David Fasenfest, ed., *Economic Development Policy Formation: Experiences in the United States and the United Kingdom* (New York: St Martin's Press; London: Macmillan, forthcoming).

12. CRS is a civic organization sponsored by the United Church of Christ. Its mission throughout its 100-year history in Chicago has been the care for and development of low-income communities.

13. CWED was chaired by Arturo Vázquez of PHBA and Squire Lance of the Englewood Businessmen's Association. Vázquez would subsequently become a deputy commissioner of economic development, then the director of MET (the Mayor's Office of Employment and Training) under Acting Mayor Sawyer. Lance was a former executive director of The Woodlawn Organization (TWO).

14. Its incorporation papers were signed by Mier, Gills, and Vázquez. Moe stopped working for CWED in November and was replaced by Tom Carlson. Carlson, an ordained United Church of Christ minister, had previously worked at CRS, CWED's original sponsor, where he had undertaken a variety of community development projects.

15.   In an effort to broaden the base of support for the boycott beyond the black community, the "Committee of 500" was formed of white, Latino community, and labor leaders. It was cochaired by Vázquez and Uptown activist Slim Coleman. On this and the straw poll see Abdul Alkalimat and Douglas Gills, *Harold Washington and the Crisis of Black Power in Chicago* (Chicago: Twenty-first Century Books, 1989).

16.   Baron was a former research director for the Chicago Urban League and was a faculty member of the Urban Studies Program of the Associated Colleges of the Midwest when Moe was a student there. He coordinated program development for Washington during his unsuccessful 1977 run for mayor. Baron later joined the Washington administration as the chief policy advisor. Bakeman was the president of a social service consulting agency, a faculty member of Kennedy–King College, and chair of the coordinating body of Washington's issues teams in the 1st Congressional District. He also served as an ad hoc advisor to the Mayor's Policy Advisory Council (MPAC).

17.   See Committee to Elect Harold Washington, *The Washington Papers* (Chicago, 1983).

18.   See Alton B. Miller, *Harold Washington: The Mayor, The Man* (Chicago, Bonus Books, 1989); and Dempsey Travis, *"Harold," The People's Mayor: An Authorized Biography of Mayor Harold Washington* (Chicago: Urban Research Press, 1989).

19.   Washington had clearly impressed the members of the Congressional Black Caucus. To his credit, several of them campaigned and raised funds for him during the primary and general elections. Beyond the Black Caucus, leaders such as the late Congressman Claude Pepper of Florida campaigned for Washington because of his commitment to the issues.

20.   See Washington Transition Committee, *Toward a Prosperous, Compassionate and Efficient Chicago* (Chicago, 1983), pp. 129–152; and Alkalimat and Gills, *Harold Washington*, pp. 128–141.

21.   Moe served as the keeper of the "Washington record" from the beginning through the 1987 election. Much to his credit, Washington supported the generation of both internal and external reports on the Washington record in comparison to his campaign commitments in years two, three, and four. We know of no other elected officials who were so willing to be held accountable. Moreover, the public release of this information helped him create a constituency to hold his own cabinet members accountable.

22.   Mier, Ros Paaswell as first deputy commissioner of economic development, Milam Fitts, Rodrigo Del Canto, and Steve Alexander as deputy commissioners of economic development, Wayne Robinson as first deputy corporation counsel and then chairman of the Plan Commission, and the late Winston Mecurius as director of research in MET.

23.   We are laying the foundation for an interpretative approach to evaluation in the spirit developed in Peter Marris, *Meaning and Action: Community Planning and Conceptions of Change* (London: Routledge & Kegan Paul, 1987); and Peter Marris and Martin Rein, *Dilemmas of Social Reform: Poverty and Community Action in the United States* (Chicago: University of Chicago Press, 1982).

24.   In fact, like James O'Connor, *The Fiscal Crisis of the State* (New York: St.

Martin's Press, 1973), we believe that some of those functions are inherently contradictory.

25. See Ann Markusen, "City on the Skids," *Reader* (November 24, 1989), 1ff.; Robert Mier and Irene Sherr, "A Review of *The Contested City*," *Journal of the American Planning Association* 50, no. 4 (1984), 542–543; and Robert Mier, Kari J. Moe, and Irene Sherr, "Strategic Planning and the Pursuit of Reform, Economic Development, and Equity," *Journal of the American Planning Association* 52, no. 3 (1986), 299–309.

26. See Robert Mier and Howard McGary, "Social Justice and Public Policy," *Educational Studies* 8 (1977), 383–393.

27. We say this fully aware that the history of neighborhood organizations in Chicago contains a strand that is built on institutionalizing racism. Philpot reports that Chicago's first neighborhood organization was a "conservation association" organized to fight for restrictive property title covenants; see Thomas Philpot, *The Slum and the Ghetto* (New York: Oxford University Press, 1975).

28. See Brehm's chapter, as well as Robert Giloth and Robert Mier, "Democratic Populism in the U.S.: The Case of Playskool and Chicago," *Cities: The International Quarterly on Urban Policy* 3, no. 1 (1986) 72–74.

29. At the beginning, getting control of the core city departments was extremely difficult; getting even the most basic information out of the other local governments (the Board of Education, Chicago Transportation Authority (CTA), Chicago Housing Authority (CHA), the city colleges, and the Park District) was next to impossible. The city council effectively blocked the mayor's appointees to these boards until two and a half years into the first term.

30. The unit in the Department of Neighborhoods that was transferred to DED had itself been created in 1979 when some units out of the Department of Human Services had been transferred to Neighborhoods.

31. DED extensively used industrial revenue bonds, and considered this almost singular tool an industrial policy. See Robert Giloth, "Industrial Development Bonds in Chicago, 1977–1987: Subsidies for What?" (Ph.D. dissertation, Department of City and Regional Planning, Cornell University, 1989).

32. This was a major problem for the entire Washington administration. Most of the mayor's supporters did not have experience in government. We needed people who were committed to the agenda, loyal to Washington, and technically competent. This proved to be extremely difficult for all five years.

33. See Mayor's Commission on Latino Affairs, *Chicago Hiring Update* (Chicago, 1984).

34. An important distinction from classical reform efforts was Washington's emphasis on accountability to *all* citizens rather than some form of elite accountability. See Samuel P. Hays, "Reform in Municipal Government," in Allen M. Wakestein, ed., *The Urbanization of America: An Historical Anthology* (Boston: Houghton Mifflin, 1970), pp. 288–314.

35. In reviewing the development plan, Krumholz et. al. say: "The *Chicago Development Plan 1984* is the strongest indication thus far that American cities are willing to harness economic development for their disadvantaged residents. It is virtually certain to be the forerunner of similar plans, especially in cities where the political power of blacks and Hispanics is on the rise." See Norman Krumholz,

Patrick Kostigan, and Dennis Keating, "A Review of *Chicago Works Together: 1984 Development Plan*," *Journal of the American Planning Association* 51, no. 3 (1985) 395–396.

36. We acknowledge this is a form of "privatization," although one with substantially more community control than is normally associated with the term. We also note our emphasis on "industrial" over "commercial."

37. Johnson was one of the more prominent black businessmen in Chicago. A former hospital administrator, he acquired the nation's first minority owned automobile dealership in the late 1960s. He became an important financial supporter of Operation PUSH and was the chairman of the Political Action Conference of Illinois (PACI). PACI played a major role in advancing the Illinois congressional, legislative, and aldermanic redistricting suits. Johnson was a significant financial backer of Harold Washington's 1983 and 1987 campaigns, and served Washington as an ad hoc special assistant on business affairs and a member of MPAC.

38. The group leading the opposition was the Interfaith Organizing Project (IOP). IOP now is representing the community in negotiations with the owners of the Chicago Bulls and the Chicago Blackhawks to build an indoor arena at the same West Side site.

39. To be blunt, the white neighborhoods felt unsafe with a black mayor, and Washington's opposition exploited those fears. For example, in 1984, Washington attempted to reduce the police force by 500 uniformed personnel, from 12,000 to 11,500. He argued that Chicago's force was one of the largest, on a per capita basis, in the country. By the time the city council opposition had fanned the flames, the police force was *expanded* to 12,500.

40. See Miller, *Harold Washington*.

41. See Robert Mier, Wim Wiewel, and Lauri Alpern, "Decentralization of Policy Making under Mayor Harold Washington," in Kenneth Wong and Laurence Lynn, eds., *Policy Innovation in Metropolitan Chicago* (Greenwich, Conn.: JAI Press, 1992).

42. See Forester, *Planning*.

43. Reprinted in Alton Miller, *Climbing a Great Mountain: Selected Speeches of Mayor Harold Washington* (Chicago: Bonus Books, 1989), p. 186.

Making Policy with Communities: Research and Development in the Department of Economic Development

ROBERT GILOTH

The mayoral administration of Harold Washington was at once more diverse and more narrow than his electoral campaign movement. It included ex-HUD (U.S. Department of Housing and Urban Development) bureaucrats, civic planners, community activists, dollar-a-day business consultants, fiscal conservatives, leftist sectarians, and instant converts or long-time progressive moles from within the previous administration of Mayor Jane Byrne. Amid this ideological crazy quilt emerged several centers of progressive innovation in the Washington administration: for example, parts of the Mayor's Office, the Strategic Planning Group in the Mayor's Office of Employment and Training (MET), and the Research and Development (R&D) Division of the Department of Economic Development (DED). Activists in these centers promoted neighborhood participation in municipal government affairs and advocated for the equity and community agenda of the Harold Washington movement.

In this chapter I examine one of these outposts of innovation—the R&D Division of DED. I describe the division, its roles and activities, exemplary cases, and what worked and what did not work. In particular, this chapter focuses on R&D's pursuit of collaborative, special projects with community organizations, what I have termed joint problem solving.[1] The R&D Division also played other salient roles: it developed models of administrative reform and strategic planning that the Washington administration adopted; it helped Robert Mier, commissioner of economic development, become a key intellectual leader in the administration; and it attracted a quality, professional staff that performed policy, planning and development tasks in a manner new to Chicago's government.

I returned to Chicago in March 1984 to work for the Washington administration and the R&D Division. It was a difficult choice: my wife and I juggled jobs and locations, and I put off a doctoral dissertation. But it was an irresistable opportunity for someone who had worked in Chicago community organizations in the 1970s: Harold Washington momentarily healed the animosities and unified the fiefdoms that had fragmented Chicago's liberal/progressive community.

In the 1970s, I had been executive director of the Eighteenth Street Development Corporation—a community-based organization in the Pilsen neighborhood on Chicago's Near Southwest Side. Pilsen was an activist neighborhood—a training ground for many people and a place where experimentation, controversy, and infighting flourished. I first became involved in Pilsen as a planning intern with Pilsen Neighbors Community Council, working on its alternative plan to the Chicago 21 Plan—a master plan developed by corporate elites to remake Chicago's central area. At Eighteenth Street Development Corporation we trained young people in the building trades, renovated abandoned buildings, counseled homeowners, and worked on projects as diverse as park renovation and solar greenhouses. We also started the Pilsen Housing and Business Alliance— an advocacy group that fought the high-income renovation plans for the Schoenhofen Brewery—a complex of old industrial buildings that contained manufacturing firms employing more than 150 workers, many of whom lived in the neighborhood.

Working at the Eighteenth Street Development Corporation also involved me in citywide affairs. I was a founding member of the Chicago Rehab Network and collaborated with the Center for Neighborhood Technology, the Center for Urban Economic Development, and the Jewish Council on Urban Affairs. These relationships, networks, and experiences would come alive again for me under Harold Washington.[2]

Returning to Chicago to work for a mayor who articulated a neighborhood agenda was all that I could hope for. What better arena to test my skills and commitment? Yet, my community organizer instincts also read caution: Could community-based interests really take over city hall? What about the powers-that-be that had promoted the Chicago 21 Plan and the Chicago 1992 World's Fair? Friends from community organization days counseled that I keep my eyes open.

What Was the R&D Division?

In late fall 1983 Commissioner Mier hired the first staff person for R&D, and in January 1984 brought Kari Moe—the issues coordinator on Washington's campaign—from the Mayor's Office to head up R&D as assistant commissioner. Mier established R&D as the only DED division that reported directly to him: its purpose was strategic planning, policy research, and special projects and demonstrations. In retrospect I think one of Mier's strengths as a leader was that he created a division that would help him advocate policy innovation within the Washington administration and the broader community. Mier joined a small research unit with the marketing unit of the Administration Division and consolidated a number of unfilled positions to create R&D.

Much of the R&D agenda had been set in the jobs platform of *The Washington Papers*, which itself had evolved from the work of a number of neighborhood networks.[3] As a result, by 1984 R&D had a mandate that had legitimate political currency and a list of specific projects to undertake. Washington's jobs platform recommended initiatives for distressed industries, small business development, resource recycling, early warning for plant closings, community loan funds, and neighborhood planning.

R&D eventually had ten professional staff with backgrounds in neighborhood organizing, labor, independent politics, and academia; they had training as planners, economists, teachers, and historians and brought a wide range of community experiences and networks to government. Three of the initial R&D staff had worked on the Employment and Economic Development Research Group with Mier, a policy group that was formed during the first Washington campaign. From the outset, interns from University of Illinois at Chicago, University of Chicago, Northwestern University, and the Associated Colleges of the Midwest supplemented this staff.

R&D was far enough away from the immediacy and political groupthink of the Mayor's Office so that it had organizational space to pursue early stage work on controversial issues. At the same time, it was very close to the mayor because Mier chaired and Moe staffed the development subcabinet (i.e., the cluster of development departments), Mier and Moe played important roles on the Mayor's Policy Council, and Mier was perhaps the most articulate advocate of neighborhood-oriented policies in the Washington administration. Harold Washington also backed Mier and Moe.

Three people directed the R&D Division between 1983 and 1987: Kari Moe, myself, and Kenneth O'Hare. Moe and I had worked with Mier as city planning students and as neighborhood activists since the 1970s. O'Hare had worked with Mier and Moe on the campaign and with Mier and me when he was with MET under Mayor Michael Bilandic. Professional ties commingled with long-time friendships and social networks to create the foundations of teamwork and a "free space" for innovation within a bureaucracy.[4] For example, Mier and I had worked together in the 1970s on a number of projects in Pilsen, including the Schoenhofen Brewery. Other R&D staff shared similar relationships.

R&D Theory and Practice

What did the R&D Division do, and what was its theory of problem solving? An early metaphor for the R&D Division's work was "let a thousand flowers bloom," which often meant that R&D responded to evolving opportunities. But the R&D Division also had an intentional structure; it evolved five functions that combined the routine and the nonroutine: economic research; marketing and public relations; R&D special projects; legislation; and commissioner staff work.

There were three overlapping R&D phases during the Washington administration. From Washington's election until summer 1985 was a period of administrative consolidation, R&D strategic planning, and communicating the Washington agenda. Moe ran R&D during this period. R&D provided staff for the 1984 "Chicago Works Together" development plans during this phase, for example. A second phase from summer 1985 to summer 1987, coinciding with my period as director, emphasized special projects, big project planning, and the Washington reelection effort. Projects ranged from promoting Planned Manufacturing Districts (PMDs) to sports stadium planning. The period from summer 1987 through Washington's death and the relatively short administration of Eugene Sawyer was one of implementation and keeping the Washington agenda alive. Kenneth O'Hare oversaw the R&D Division during this period of transition.

This chapter focuses almost exclusively on the second phase of the R&D Division's history—collaborative special projects and problem solving with community groups to design and implement loan funds, resource recycling demonstrations, plant closing responses, business incubators, worker buyouts, and industry plans. I was most involved and interested in this phase, so this is the story that I can tell best. However, in the minds of Mier and others, strategic planning, administration-wide innovation, implementation, and communicating the Washington message were the most important R&D functions.[5]

R&D's theory of how to pursue special projects changed dramatically during the course of the Washington administration. At first, under Moe, R&D worked closely with other DED divisions on special project teams assigned to work on issues such as first source hiring, new loan programs for small businesses (i.e., microloans), minority- and female-owned business development, enterprise zones, and industry marketing and visitation. R&D typically cochaired the special project teams with line division personnel.

That approach ultimately did not work for a number of reasons despite the design of several new policies and programs. First, line divisions often were not committed to the special project teams because they did not have enough qualified staff early in the Washington administration. At the same time, they perceived that Mier valued policy innovation and they resented R&D interference that upstaged their potential to be innovative on issues that were arguably on their turf. Second, most of the R&D staff wanted to make their mark and felt that they represented the best of the Washington administration's progressive spirit. In their minds, having to work with line divisions diverted R&D's energy. Third, there was a conceptual and bureaucratic difference between R&D as experimental work and R&D as program design support for line divisions: line divisions wanted R&D to design parking program evaluations and program application forms; R&D wanted to launch demonstration projects or to study business needs. Fourth, although personality conflicts played their part, Mier did not build a department-wide management team or a common vision among diverse managers about the mission of the department. That freed the R&D Division to set its own agenda but constrained its ability to implement projects or to institutionalize its approach.

In this context, the R&D Division evolved a theory and practice of special projects that did not depend upon the resources or participation of the line divisions and that became more externally focused. This practice developed in all R&D phases. R&D's audience was Mier, the mayor, other DED divisions, other city departments, foundations, the media, the business community, and community coalitions. The R&D method of developing special projects was to work with community-oriented research groups to nurture, package, and publicize alternative ideas and practices of economic development, whether new policy initiatives or project feasibility studies. R&D engaged in all phases of the policy cycle—from goal setting to policy experiments, demonstrations, knowledge utilization, and evaluation. Without knowing it, community-oriented planners in an organizational setting supportive of innovation produced a practice of joint problem solving. Later they would begin to outline a theory.

R&D pursued special projects using this method. Six R&D methods, summarized below, illustrate how R&D approached policy and planning issues from many directions. There were many accomplishments. Nevertheless, one cost of these successes at the organizational level was the alienation of most of the DED. It was predictable that when Mier and I left the department in the summer of 1987, R&D was gradually stripped of positions, functions, and status.

1.   R&D had Community Development Block Grant funds (about $150,000 a year plus demonstration project funds) that it allocated for special projects, demonstrations, and research and feasibility studies. Table 1 categorizes the more than 40 projects that R&D

TABLE 1.
R&D Contracts and Demonstrations, 1984–1987

Category	No. of projects	Amount ($)
Chicago Capital Fund (e.g. equity capital)	1	83,700
Feasibility studies (e.g., worker buyouts, incubators, facility reuse)	11	95,525
Business incubators	3	500,000
Labor/neighborhood studies	2	27,000
Minority/female business research (e.g., Latino business, women's self-employment)	7	119,860
Resource Recycling (e.g., curbside, buy-backs)	11	287,380
Industry studies and task forces (e.g., steel, apparel, printing)	5	75,700
Miscellaneous policy and economic research (e.g., inventor's guidebook)	5	26,680
Total	44	1,215,845

SOURCE: "Summary of R&D Projects" (Chicago: Department of Economic Development, 1987).
NOTE: This list does not include projects that R&D supervised but did not directly fund.

funded from 1984 to 1987, including worker buyout feasibility studies, steel research, the design of a women's self-employment program, a directory of Hispanic businesses in Chicago, and policy research on first source hiring. Research sponsors included the Midwest Center for Labor Research, the Resource Center, the Chicago Jobs Council, and the Center for Urban Economic Development at the University of Illinois at Chicago (UICUED).[6] R&D identified projects and research sponsors based upon *The Washington Papers* and its own internal goal setting. It also responded to queries by different groups, including other divisions of the DED and other city departments such as Housing and MET. Developing R&D contracts often took a year or more because time was needed to refine the project concepts.

R&D funding was in the form of professional service contracts that purchased specific research and demonstration products. In short, research contractors were not free to go their way; R&D negotiated research designs, established community advisory boards, promoted publicity, and conducted evaluations.

2. R&D deployed its staff to work on special task forces and on community projects. The best example of the first is the two industry task forces—Steel and Apparel—that R&D staffed.[7] The best example of the second is that R&D staff worked on a Plant Closing Early Warning Demonstration with the West Side Jobs Network and researched and designed solutions to the problem of industrial displacement in conjunction with the Local Employment and Economic Development Council of the New City YMCA.[8]

3. R&D used printing, publication, and media resources to give special projects public exposure. Indeed, R&D was preoccupied with coming up with the appropriate "words" almost to distraction, as it published a working paper series of ten documents that made available the results of R&D research and demonstrations and cosponsored public release events with the Capital Base Task Force, the Local Inititives Support Corporation (LISC), the Midwest Women's Center, and the Resource Center. R&D also promoted its research and demonstrations with the media. For example, R&D released its work to *The Neighborhood Works*, a Chicago-based magazine of the Center for Neighborhood Technology.

4. R&D conducted its own policy research and evaluation studies. R&D monitored the employment outcomes of business incentive programs such as Industrial Revenue Bonds (IRBs), assessed the impacts of industrial displacement in the River North and Goose Island/Clybourn industrial corridors, and researched particular aspects of Chicago's steel complex.[9] In addition, short-turnaround research projects included investigating defense production in Chicago and the employment and investment impacts of enterprise zones.

5. R&D served as an advocate, thorn, and educator within DED and across the Washington administration on issues such as resource recycling and industrial displacement. Several examples stand out. R&D urged researchers at the Center for Urban Economic Development at the University of Illinois at Chicago to study the location and impacts of Chicago's Urban Development Action Grants and provided them with access to information. R&D advised the Coalition on Alternative Waste Disposal about how they should advocate for recycling with the Department of Streets and Sanitation as well as to startup a Recycling Industry Development Corporation. Finally, several R&D staff worked with Chicago White Sox fans to

lobby to keep the White Sox baseball team in Chicago and then to save Comiskey Park. That effort combined formal assignment and the personal interest and commitment of individual R&D staff.

Above all R&D provided access: to the corridors and conference rooms of DED; to file cabinets and data archives; to the design of public hearings and briefings; to decision makers such as Mier; to gossip and inside dope about administration thinking. In short, many community groups became insiders through R&D's efforts, an experience new for community groups in Chicago.

6. Finally, R&D performed standard research, policy and project planning, and legislative functions. It gathered basic employment, economic, and business information and made this information available to the public and DED. R&D staff pushed the department toward computerization, a difficult and late-in-coming project. R&D provided the core staff for the 1984 "Chicago Works Together" development plans, promoted legislative initiatives such as a Chicago Nuclear Free Zone and Illinois Development Action Grants, and produced business retention and attraction materials, including proposals for the Saturn Plant, the Lutheran Church merger, and Firestone's administrative offices.[10]

R&D Management Style

R&D developed its own organizational method for performing high-quality, experimental, short-turnaround work. During its first year under Moe, there was an uneasy combination of top–down planning and accountability sessions called "drill and grill" and participatory initiative. In part, this style was necessary to cope with a number of incompetent and politically hostile leftover staff and to function within the most turbulent period of the Washington administration. Indeed, city council opponents lambasted the R&D Division as "political hacks."

Management became more participatory in the subsequent three years when I directed R&D. R&D staff needed teamwork to share information about overlapping projects. R&D held weekly staff meetings that included outside speakers, debates, videos, readings, and discussions, the purpose of which was to keep R&D staff up-to-date on Chicago and national community economic development practice and to motivate a common dialogue among staff that would carry over into project groups. R&D's four unit managers (i.e., for economic research, R&D, legislation/marketing, and the development subcabinet) met weekly to solve coordination problems and to focus the divisional agenda. Those units also held their own staff meetings.

At least once a year, R&D conducted its own internal evaluation and strategic planning exercise. As a part of this process, R&D convened focus groups of R&D contractors and researchers to review R&D projects and to make suggestions for R&D's future agenda.

R&D Cases

The R&D Division had a rich agenda that produced many projects worthy of case studies. Several of these projects, such as Playskool and Industrial Protection, have received national attention. Six additional cases illustrate the breadth of the R&D agenda, different R&D methods, and the limitations of R&D's practice. The cases are: the Chicago Capital Fund; Resource Recycling; Business Incubators; the Playskool aftermath; Industrial Revenue Bonds (IRBs); and Chicago Electroplaters.

In particular, these cases illustrate how the R&D Division and, more generally, the Washington administration promoted a new "culture of interaction" among community, civic, business, labor, and public officials. Such collaborative efforts demanded new roles, flexibility, and understanding among diverse groups. This experience expanded conventional notions of how to build civic participation and partnerships.

Early Warning Plant Closing Responses

R&D experimented with different types of plant closing responses between 1983 and 1987. It worked collaboratively with the Midwest Center for Labor Research, the UICUED and other community and labor groups. In many cases, R&D worked in conjunction with the commissioner of the Department of Economic Development, other city departments, the corporation counsel, and the Mayor's Office.

Lack of public standing to intervene in plant closures and the variety of plant closing causes made R&D's efforts strategic and experimental.[11] R&D pursued joint problem solving in search of organizing, development, or public relations initiatives that would enable public action on some ten to fifteen plant closing cases.

Playskool and Bankers Print represent two relative successes. The West Side Jobs Network, which DED funded and the Midwest Center for Labor Research staffed, raised public awareness of Playskool's breach of trust in relocating from Chicago after obtaining public subsidies. Joint strategizing between the city administration and community groups produced a Playskool toy boycott and the City of Chicago lawsuit. A joint city and community/labor committee reviewed settlement offers.

Workers purchased Bankers Print in 1987 to form a worker cooperative. Bankers Print was a commercial printer with fifteen to twenty employees that was threatened with closure because the individual owner was quite sick and had no successor. R&D funded two phases of prefeasibility studies before the buyout was finally negotiated, using a variety of public, private, and philanthropic dollars. Bankers Print initially increased sales and added new employees, but ultimately failed because of a poor choice of company manager.

Less successful plant closing interventions resulted because of bad timing, owner intransigence, a lack of organizing potential, unsuccessful community organizing, and city reluctance. These cases ranged from the Ludwig Drum Factory to Wisconsin Steel and the LTV Steelworks. Although much was learned from these cases, they stressed all participants; in the heat of action, parties strenuously and often narrowly pressed their individual points of view. A major point of controversy was whether the city should automatically take the "position" that all shutdowns resulted from unjustified owner disinvestment and therefore could be turned around by worker buyouts or municipal eminent domain.

Two outgrowths of this work made long-term impacts. R&D funded the Midwest Center for Labor Research to identify viable worker buyout opportunities. The center staff studied small manufacturers on Chicago's West Side and showed that lack of successorship in family-owned firms was a major cause of shutdowns. The project also brought attention to worker ownership as one answer to the successorship problem by having Mayor Washington declare Employee Ownership Day in March 1987, conduct a tour of employee-owned businesses in Chicago, and hold a public forum. Two outcomes of this effort, in addition to Bankers Print, have been other worker buyout opportunities and the design of a program to promote minority leveraged buyouts of firms without successors by the Midwest Center for Labor Research, Chicago United, and DED.

A second outgrowth was the formation of the Coalition to Keep Stewart Warner Open. Stewart Warner is an auto parts manufacturer on Chicago's North Side that employs more than 1500 workers. The union and nearby community groups formed the coalition with help from the Midwest Center for Labor Research and the UICUED. R&D played a minimal role, providing a small amount of funding and initially maintaining liason with the coalition. Today, as expected, the company has been sold and the absentee owners are considering relocation. City and state officials, after years of early warning, wrung their hands and offered incentives to keep Stewart Warner in Chicago. Community and labor groups supported the passage of local legislation that would enable the use of eminent domain when absentee owners disinvested in local firms.

Industrial Protection

Perhaps R&D's most sustained and successful experiment in joint problem solving involved the issue of industrial protection and displacement, especially as it occurred in the Goose Island/Clybourn Corridor.[12] While R&D quickly recognized the importance of the issue, Mier, the Planning Department, and the Mayor's Office were slower getting on board.

The essence of this joint problem solving was to get the public to recognize a "problem." In so doing, the public had to confront the fact that manufacturing was not dead, that the benefits of manufacturing were at least as important as those resulting from commercial real estate development, that industrial displacement was a problem that local government could do something about, and that contradictory public policy was part of the problem. Getting the problem recognized as a problem required research, unusual city interventions, media coverage, aldermanic involvement, mayoral attention, and time.

Was this joint problem solving successful? The city council passed a Planned Manufacturing District (PMD) enabling ordinance and several specific planned manufacturing districts in 1988, protecting 5000 jobs. Negotiations on several industrial displacement cases resulted in design or scale changes, linkage agreements, and local employment commitments. A North Side industrial plan has been completed that calls for additional planned manufacturing districts. A broad coalition of community groups, business, labor, and government has come together around the issue of industrial protection that hopefully will stand fast against attempts to turn back industrial protection policies. Initially soft on industrial protection, Chicago's new mayor, Richard M. Daley, came out in support of PMDs in spring 1990 and two more districts are in the process of designation. On the other hand, a major business supporter—Procter & Gamble—has decided to close its Clybourn plant employing 275 workers and occupying a larger strategic parcel of land.

Chicago Capital Fund

One of the first research and program design contracts funded by R&D was with the Capital Base Task Force. By 1988, a $10 million fund had been established to provide equity capital and management assistance to neighborhood manufacturers. Ten firms had obtained capital investments, although the fund was experiencing some difficulty in identifying viable businesses for investment.

R&D played the role of resource provider and friendly critic for this project. The idea for an alternative capital fund originated in the neighborhood small business community before Harold Washington became mayor. A group of some twenty-five economic and neighborhood development professionals established the Capital Base Task Force.

The Chicago Capital Fund answered the Washington campaign's promise to establish a quasi-public authority to invest in economic development. R&D provided $80,000 of research and design funds over three years and helped to secure foundation funding. It pushed the task force to include more black and Hispanic representatives, critiqued research designs, published a working paper, cosponsored a public-release event, and helped convince the business community that small businesses needed capital as well as management assistance. In 1987, R&D finally convinced DED to invest $500,000 in the Chicago Capital Fund and persuaded the commissioner of economic development to serve on its board.[13]

Resource Recycling

Like many cities, Chicago faced a landfill crisis in 1983 and still faces it today. Upon assuming office, Harold Washington instituted a moratorium on new landfills, established a goal of 25 percent recycling by 1995, and convened a Solid Waste Task Force. In addition, the jobs platform of *The Washington Papers* called for innovative, community-based recycling initiatives that would create neighborhood jobs.

In this context, R&D funded recycling initiatives for a total of $350,000 over four years. Initiatives included three recycling buy-back centers, two curbside pick-up demonstrations, and three research projects on markets, intermediate industries, and demonstration evaluations. Most of the funding went to the Resource Center, a long-established nonprofit recycling organization in Chicago. In 1986, the Resource Center collected 8000 tons of recyclables, $460,000 went to community alley entrepreneurs, and their programs generated $300,000 for project support.[14]

In addition, R&D became the chief advocate of recycling within the Washington administration, often finding itself a lone voice against the bureaucrats of the Department of Planning and the Department of Streets and Sanitation. R&D published working papers on its recycling demonstrations, funded evaluation studies, helped promote recycling days, and on occasion even went on recycling pick-up routes. R&D also counseled the Coalition for Alternative Waste Disposal on the importance of organizing a power base to force action from the city and to consider organizing a Recycling Industry Development Corporation that involved private as well as community interests.

By 1988, the city administration was still moving slowly on recycling, although another successful curbside pick-up program had been launched in a South Side neighborhood. Chicago recyclers had established the Recycling Industry Development Corporation and had obtained $1 million for new recycling demonstrations.

Business Incubators

The theory of business incubators is that environments can be created that increase the chances for small business survival and success. Supportive business environments include low rents, flexible spaces, shared services, access to management assistance and seed capital, and synergistic interaction with other tenant firms. A public policy rationale for business incubators is that small businesses are believed to create the most new jobs.

R&D obtained a special allocation of $900,000 of Community Development Block Grant monies in 1984 to implement a business incubator demonstration. R&D pursued that demonstration largely because of Commissioner Mier's experience in helping to design the Fulton–Carroll Incubator of the Industrial Council of Northwest Chicago, an incubator in a rundown industrial corridor that had received national attention.

R&D designed the demonstration to cast a broad net for the best ideas and variations on the incubator theme. R&D decided only to solicit ideas from nonprofit sponsors, although these groups were encouraged to join in partnerships with private incubator developers. In the summer of 1984, R&D received 30 short incubator proposals after having collected more than 70 inquiries. After evaluating these proposals, R&D asked 11 sponsors to submit detailed project proposals.

Nonprofit sponsors submitted six final incubator proposals. R&D set up a review panel that included outside architects and industrial real estate agents that visited sites and reviewed project designs. In the end, Mier decided to make preliminary commitments to five projects of different types and locations throughout the city instead of going with the one or two best projects. He felt that project diversity would help get final incubator projects approved by a hostile city council.[15] The incubator projects each had distinctive target markets: small manufacturers and service businesses, high-technology computer firms, minority suppliers, or combined employment training and small-business start-ups.

After three years, only one of the original incubators had gone foward successfully. Two sponsors failed to secure viable sites. One sponsor never submitted a final proposal even with R&D's provision of a part-time development consultant. One promising project obtained funds from the City of Chicago, the State of Illinois, and major Chicago corporations but fell apart when its director entered a drug rehabilitation program and the organization that sponsored the project was found to have misappropriated funds.[16] In response to these failures, R&D went back to groups that originally expressed interest in developing business incubators and found the Neighborhood Institute's plan to develop an incubator for small service businesses. Ultimately, DED invested $150,000 in this incubator. The Industrial Council of the Northwest sponsored the most successful incubator, the same group that had already established a national reputation as an incubator developer. Even this success, however, ended up serving small service-oriented businesses that provided little employment for job-needy Chicago residents.

Many community groups that participated in R&D's incubator demonstration felt let down. On the one hand, groups felt they did not have enough time to develop legitimate proposals. On the other, several organizations felt that DED changed the rules in midcourse—initially conveying the idea that the incubator funds were to be on a grant basis but later requiring payback arrangements based upon the economic strength of the projects. Finally, some groups felt that DED's finance people really did not understand community economic development and were intentionally making the processing of incubator loans more difficult than necessary.

The Playskool Aftermath

Mayor Washington decided that the city would have to sue Hasbro Industries in December 1984 for reneging on its promise to create 400 jobs and for relocating its Playskool facility to Massachusetts. Playskool had received a $1 million Industrial Revenue Bond (IRB) from the City of Chicago in 1981. The City of Chicago lawsuit resulted because of the community uproar ·about this breach of public trust. (Also see the chapter by Brehm).

A negotiated settlement saved 100 jobs for a year, established a $50,000 emergency fund, launched a job placement program for dislocated workers, and commited Hasbro Industries to work with the city government for one year to find an acceptable reuse for the Playskool property that would reemploy Playskool workers. It was a modest victory at best, but inspired other creative plant closing responses in Chicago and around the country.

Two aspects of the Playskool case have received less attention. First, did the city government tighten up its agreements with other firms or developers that had obtained business incentives? The answer is no. Immediately after the Playskool suit, R&D drafted a set of restrictions aimed at tightening up the loan negotiation process, strengthening business reporting requirements, and imposing penalties for relocation, nonreporting, or failure to meet job creation promises. That step was taken in part because the city council, in the political heat of the Playskool suit, had passed a resolution calling for tighter IRB agreements.

R&D circulated the draft of proposed restrictions to the city's corporation counsel, other DED divisions, and to several prominent bond counsel firms. The last-named group, in particular, stated point-blank that more restrictions would make Chicago's bond program noncompetitive; firms were already turning to the State of Illinois rather than the City of Chicago because of quicker application processing. In addition, IRBs were on the way out because of national legislation. Not surprisingly, city officials dropped the discussion about restrictions on City of Chicago loans except as it related to First Source Hiring. By 1988, twelve firms that had received Chicago Industrial Revenue Bonds had closed their doors.

Second, did the city government enforce the agreement with Hasbro Industries to the fullest possible extent? Again, the answer is no. Within several months, for instance, it was clear that the job placement program at Playskool was not reaching those most in need: low-income, Hispanic and black women.[17] By this stage, however, part of the problem had become the inadequacy of the city's own employment and training programs for dislocated workers.

R&D, in conjunction with other DED divisions, attempted to find a developer to develop a reuse plan for the Playskool facilities. R&D funded the Greater North Pulaski Development Corporation to complete a quick and dirty market analysis of the potential for the Playskool facility. Most experts agreed that the 750,000-square-foot site should be subdivided for small manufacturing and distribution companies.

A prominent developer was found who put together a proposal that required $3 million of public investment. R&D kept community advocates at bay while the proposal was put together, including a proposal for $500,000 to the federal government from Greater North Pulaski Development Corporation. Eventually, however, the developer backed out. Hasbro sold the Playskool property to a private partnership that did not require public monies; they planned to subdivide the site for industry.

During this period, R&D had convened a working group of government officials, community advocates, and technical assistance providers to devise a marketing, social service, and negotiating strategy for the Playskool property that would maximize benefits for dislocated Playskool workers. They identified the miscellaneous plastic products industry as a growing industry in Chicago that contained occupations that were close to the skill levels of Playskool workers. They explored what incentives might attract such firms and what services workers would need on site.[18]

That design effort fell apart soon after the Playskool property was sold. DED would not advocate it, and activism in the community around Playskool had dwindled or splintered into organizing and development factions. By 1988, the Playskool site was occupied by 15 companies employing 400 people; unfortunately, few of those employees were dislocated Playskool workers. An attempt in 1988 to establish day-care and employment training facilities at the Playskool site was stopped by MET.

Evaluating Industrial Revenue Bonds

IRBs are one of the most popular and widespread low-interest loans, and are relatively costless to municipal governments. IRBs require a public purpose to justify their exemption from federal income taxes such as creating and retaining jobs. Congress has extended the tax exemption for IRBs as of September 30, 1990.

In 1984, the City of Chicago had an IRB portfolio of more than 100 loans for over $200 million. Chicago's IRBs were targeted to manufacturers, including firms like Playskool. Increasingly during the early 1980s, community advocates had raised questions about Chicago's IRB program as to the disclosure of recipients, job creation performance, and the appropriateness of specific loans. Their concern was that the availability of publicly-funded incentives should be tied to job opportunities for those most in need.

The primary development goal of the Washington administration, according to Chicago's 1984 Development Plan, was jobs. Not surprisingly, an early project for the R&D Division was to evaluate the job performance of the City of Chicago's IRB program. R&D's evaluation design called for a survey of IRB recipients, with particular attention to job creation and retention experience, and an analysis of a control group of Chicago manufacturers that had not received IRBs.

Results from the survey, available beginning in November 1984, showed two disturbing facts. First, firms in Chicago's IRB portfolio had lost jobs overall rather than creating jobs. Second, nine loan recipients had closed their doors, including Playskool. IRBs were hardly the job creation tool that job projections led the public to believe.[19]

Those findings created problems for the City of Chicago. They were embarassing facts in a politically volatile time: a mayor promising jobs lost jobs. It also upset the DED finance staff by making their efforts look futile. The DED's response to these troubling facts was threefold: IRBs *retain* jobs and industries, but they do not *create* jobs; IRBs lost fewer jobs and firms than overall manufacturing in Chicago or Illinois; and IRB applicants should be discouraged from overestimating their job creation projections.

The second part of R&D's evaluation design, completed in 1988, showed that a select group of large, healthy firms in declining manufacturing sectors obtained Chicago's IRBs. Those firms created jobs before they obtained IRBs but had no better job creation record than similar manufacturers that invested without them. IRBs at best helped healthy firms that were starved for capital.[20]

Despite these evaluation results, there was no bureaucratic response other than a retooling of rhetoric. Community reaction was minimal. R&D had not established a collaborative process to review the appropriateness of business incentives as tools for job creation and industrial retention and whether the jobs measure was the proper one for evaluating economic development programs.

Chicago Electroplators

Some manufacturers that discharge production wastes cannot afford to install environmentally sound waste treatment technologies because of their small size. Such industries include food processing and electroplating. Impending implementation of the Clean Water Act of 1971 and other environmental regulations promised to drive many of these small manufactuers out of business in the mid-1980s. In fact, the Environmental Protection Agency (EPA) developed closure prediction rates for different types and sizes of business once their regulations came into effect.

The Center for Neighborhood Technology (CNT) requested R&D funding in the spring of 1984 to conduct an impact study of the implementation of environmental regulations on small manufacturers in Chicago. R&D provided $5000, critiques of CNT's research design and draft reports as well as copyediting, and published the final report as a working paper.[21]

That rather small investment of R&D dollars has made quite an impact. CNT has raised more than $1 million for technical assistance to businesses. In addition, CNT helped to complete a feasibility study for a cooperative waste disposal program for small electroplators and has effectively lobbied to have state finance programs changed to allow the financing of waste disposal technologies. This project assisted seventy-five businesses that employed more than 1000 workers.

Conclusion

This chapter has argued that outposts of innovation in the Washington administration developed a new style of joint problem solving with community groups that broke ground in terms of citizen participation, encouraging grass-roots initiatives, and using city powers. The history of the R&D Division of the DED presents the record of one such outpost.

I left the Washington administration and Chicago in August 1987. My goal had been to help get Washington reelected and then to move to Baltimore to be with my wife. I organized Loop precincts for the campaign and collaborated on the campaign platform: having missed the first campaign, I felt as though I was paying my dues.

I was also weary of balancing community groups, the bureaucracy, and the Washington agenda. Indeed, they seemed less balanced and more weighted toward the center at the time of Washington's reelection than when I arrived in 1984. There were a number of dimensions to this transformation: modest participation of community activists in the second campaign compared to city workers; a growing cynicism on the part of bureaucrats toward the community; and a growing preoccupation with delivering "big bang" projects.

In my last year, I was increasingly drawn into big development issues: lights for Wrigley Field, the White Sox retention, and the Bears Stadium controversy. It was ironic that so many of us became embroiled in these issues: the mayor, in a speech to his policy cabinet that was reproduced for all senior staff, promised that he did not want to be remembered for building Taj Mahals. And yet one Friday evening I found myself with the mayor's sports czars at the Metropolitan Club in Sears Tower. Drinks in hand we circled our private dining room, gazing down upon Chicago, wisely considering the pros and cons of alternative stadium sites on Chicago's South, West, and Northwest Sides.

I felt at an intellectual and political impasse. Harold Washington, like all mayors, needed big projects to stay alive politically (or those around him thought so), and the scale of potential benefits from these projects seemed to hold real promise for communities in need. Wasn't this the cutting edge for a progressive municipal administration: if anyone could cut good development deals, it was the Washington administration. That was our hubris. Everything from my experience cast doubt on the likelihood of success of such an approach. Community groups refused to become believers. Yet the scrawny, often infeasible but politically correct projects of community groups increasingly fell short as credible alternatives. It was definitely time to leave.

Despite my eventual burnout, I think the R&D Division showed how joint problem solving between a city administration and the grass roots enabled communities to advocate innovation more effectively while making city government more open and responsive to change. Our collaboration helped to overcome the barriers to organizing and innovation that confronted communities and bureaucracies on a daily basis. The strategic use of media, dollars, staff, and simply paying attention influenced public policy problems, actors, and solutions.

Many lasting benefits resulted from the R&D Division's activities. Despite its modest successes, R&D as an administrative innovation existed at the margins of municipal government: R&D failed to make significant inroads into the line divisions of its own department or other departments; and it applied its methods to a specialized set of issues and communities. In the end, R&D's creativity depended upon a blend of personalities, a mayoral mandate, an unusual degree of organizational discretion, and heightened community expectations—not the stuff that easily institutionalizes new government functions.

I think our experience of joint problem solving has potential to inform a broad arena of policymaking in addition to helping progressive municipal administrations achieve their visions. It demonstrated innovation, participation, and collaboration, in which government and the grass roots reinforced each other's strengths—often achieving outcomes that could not have been accomplished alone. In this sense, the administration of Harold Washington made a major contribution to the conceptualization and practice of collaboration between a municipal administration and the grass roots. That legacy will, I hope, inspire other experiments that bridge communities and municipal government.

NOTES

1.   Working for Harold Washington was a rare opportunity. Many other people made this experience important for me: Rob Mier, Kari Moe, Ken O'Hare, Toni Preckwinkle, Steve Alexander, Margie Gonwa, Greg Longhini, Wendy Wintermute, Roz Paaswell, Josh Lerner, Diana Robinson, Gwen Clemons, Judy Waitz, Donna Ducharme, Susan Rosenblum, David Ranney, Patricia Wright, and Bob Brehm. Many of these coworkers also gave me valuable comments on this chapter, in particular catching me when I was tempted to simply rewrite the history of R&D as my personal projects. Pierre Clavel encouraged me to tell the R&D story and save the theorizing for another occasion. I want to thank Anne Shlay for her perseverance when we were trying to find two jobs in one location.

2.   These networks included many people whom I would work with when I joined the administration of Harold Washington: Bob Brehm, Tom Carlson, Tom Clark, Slim Coleman, Doug Gills, Bob Lucas, Nancy Jefferson, Lew Kreinberg, and Arturo Vázquez, to name a few.

3.   See Committee to Elect Harold Washington, *The Washington Papers* (Chicago, 1983); and Robert Mier, "Your Jobs Policy" (memo to Harold Washington from the Employment and Economic Development Research Group, Chicago, 1983).

4. See Sara Evans and Harry Boyte, *Free Spaces* (New York: Basic Books, 1985).

5. Robert Mier, Kari Moe, and Irene Sherr, "Strategic Planning and the Pursuit of Reform, Economic Development, and Equity," *Journal of the American Planning Association* 52, no. 2 (Summer 1986), 277–289.

6. These documents may be found in the Municipal Reference Library of the City of Chicago, the Harold Washington Archives at the Chicago Historical Society, and in the contractual files of the DED.

7. See Steve Alexander, Robert Giloth, and Joshua Lerner, "Chicago's Industry Task Forces: Joint Problem-solving for Economic Development," *Economic Development Quarterly* 1, no. 4 (November 1987), 352–357; also City of Chicago, *Building on the Basics: The Final Report of the Mayor's Task Force on Steel and Southeast Chicago* (Chicago: City of Chicago, 1986), and City of Chicago, *Cooperation for Survival and Growth: New Designs for Apparel Manufacturing in Chicago* (Chicago: City of Chicago, 1987).

8. See Robert Giloth and John Betancur, "Where Downtown Meets Neighborhood: Industrial Displacement in Chicago, 1983–1987," *Journal of the American Planning Association* 54, no. 3 (Summer 1988), 279–290; and Robert Giloth and Susan Rosenblum, "How to Fight Plant Closings," *Social Policy* 17, no. 3, (Winter 1987), 20–26.

9. Gwendolyn Clemons, Robert Giloth, and Ricardo Tostado, *Monitoring Chicago's Industrial Revenue Bond Performance, 1977–1984* (Chicago: Department of Economic Development, 1985); and Donna Ducharme, Robert Giloth, and Lynn McCormick, *Business Loss or Balanced Growth: Industrial Displacement in Chicago, 1977–1984* (Chicago: Department of Economic Development, 1985).

10. City of Chicago, *1984 Development Plan: Chicago Works Together*, (Chicago: City of Chicago, 1984); and City of Chicago, *Cooperation for Survival and Growth*.

11. See Giloth and Rosenblum, "How to Fight Plant Closings."

12. See Ducharme et al., *Business Loss or Balanced Growth;* and Giloth and Betancur, "Where Downtown Meets Neighborhood."

13. James Patterson and Cathy Sieros, *Plan of Action: Community Equity Corporation of Chicago* (Chicago: Department of Economic Development, 1985).

14. Patrick Barry, *Recycling: An Economic Development Opportunity* (Chicago: Department of Economic Development, 1987).

15. Judy Waitz, "Business Incubators as an Economic Development Tool" (Master's project, University of North Carolina, 1986).

16. Merrill Goozner, "Did Dream Have to Die: Distress Signals Ignored on Incubator Plan?" *Chicago Tribune* (November 15, 1987), 1, 6–7.

17. See Carol Kleiman, "Stereotypes Plaguing Blue-Collar Women, Too" *Chicago Tribune* (February 29, 1988); West Side Jobs Network, "Union and Jobs Network Survey Finds Playskool Job Center Efforts Inadequate" (West Side Jobs Network, Chicago, February 15, 1985).

18. David Ranney, "Playskool Work History Analysis and First Source Hiring Agreement" (memo to the Playskool Project Team, Center for Urban Economic Development at the University of Illinois, 1986); and Wendy Wintermute, "Playskool Team Report and Recommendations" (memo to Robert Mier, commissioner of economic development, (Chicago, January 7, 1987).

19.   Clemons et al., *Monitoring Chicago's IRB Performance.*

20.   See Robert Giloth, "Industrial Revenue Bonds in Chicago, 1977–1987: Subsidies for What?" (Doctoral dissertation, Cornell University, 1989).

21.   Steve Basler and M. Kitwana, *The Impact of Environmental Regulations on Small Manufacturers in Chicago* (Chicago: Department of Economic Development, 1986).

The Department of Planning Under Harold Washington

ELIZABETH HOLLANDER

Why I Was Chosen, and Who the Mayor Chose

When Harold Washington was elected he sent out signals early on that he would be assembling a cabinet reflecting the city's racial diversity. He also made it clear that he was very interested in recruiting women to key posts and he was turning to not-for-profit groups as a source of recruitment. I was then with the Metropolitan Housing and Planning Council (a fifty-year-old civic group now called the Metropolitan Planning Council (MPC).

MPC had a history of major housing initiatives, but when I got there the leaders in housing were in other organizations and the MPC was seen as a rather middle-of-the-road, somewhat business-oriented partner. To increase MPC's visibility on housing issues, we published a report in 1980 on housing conditions in the city. It documented housing demolition, rehabilitation, and new construction in each of the city's seventy-seven community areas. It was used by every community to rally around the need to do something about housing. It was one of the activities for which I was known in Harold's base. The other projects that I initiated at MPC, related to reform of the Regional Transportation Authority and the condition of the city's infrastructure, made me highly visible but primarily in the business community.

My interest in planning, which began much earlier in my career, was generated out of two major concerns: a social justice view of urban and racial conditions, and an aesthetic interest in urban life. As a political science major at Bryn Mawr College in the early 1960s, I had been the leader of the civil rights group on campus and wrote my senior honors paper on the condition of the black community on the suburban Philadelphia "mainline." After college, I started my career working for the federal government on urban renewal programs in the Philadelphia and Chicago regional offices. Then, after a decade of child raising and private consulting, I eventually made a key association with Ira Bach, city planner and development director for four Chicago mayors. Ira was an important mentor. He walked the city enjoying its landmarks, sculpture, architecture, old and new. He had only friends, never enemies, and kept his focus on making the city a handsome and thriving place, sidestepping politics along the way.

Ira awakened in me the interest in aesthetics and devotion for urban living that was also my family's legacy. I grew up in New York City, and both of my parents had art history training. I was taught early on to look at my surroundings with an appreciative and critical eye.

My standard for city life was New York's Upper East Side in the 1950s. On my block on East 84th Street, German hausfraus leaned on their pillows in the windows of five-story tenements and watched us play on the sidewalk (including the kids like me who lived in townhouses). All needs could be purchased at nearby shops, movies were two blocks away, and the city never slept. A short bus or subway ride took us to the delights of the zoo, the museum, or Radio City Music Hall. Cars were only useful to leave town.

In 1963 when I came to Chicago it was not like New York. The center of the city was dead after six, Wacker Drive had many handsome buildings and nowhere to stop for a cup of coffee. The carefully replanned Hyde Park neighborhood eliminated interesting tiny shops in the name of renewal and replaced them with shopping centers surrounded by parking lots. The politics and the racism appalled me. Not only was the city dominated by Mayor Richard J. Daley and his machine, the liberal forces seemed to have been shaped by Daley so all of their activities were anti-Daley, not really independent. When I expressed an interest in racial integration at work everyone said, "Oh, you must live in Hyde Park."

It was this background, rather than a planning degree, that I brought to the Metropolitan Planning Council and eventually to city government. I learned later that I brought three other key characteristics: I was female, Jewish, and backed by the Chicago business community.

When Harold Washington was elected, it occurred to me that as a visible female good-government leader in planning I might be considered for employment but I quite consciously did not chase the job. Several feelers were sent out, though, and in June 1983 I received a call asking me to come talk to Harold Washington.

I can still remember that I was wearing a big red straw hat. The red hat later became a trademark that allowed Harold to find me in any crowd. I walked into his office and he said, "I hear you want to be my commissioner of planning." And I said, "I think you've asked me to be your commissioner of planning." He held up his hand with his inimitable grin and said, "Let's talk." We talked for an hour. We discussed the members of the

Planning Commission, who they were, how I felt about them. I asked him about objectives for the Planning Department. David Schultz, the budget director had, a month before, taken all the Community Development Block Grant funds out of the Department of Planning budget, which reduced the staff by a third. So I asked, "Are you serious about planning? There is no point in running a planning department if you are not serious about it. What are you going to do with it?" He said he cared more about development than I might want, especially neighborhood development. I told him that I was professional and not a political person and that what I could bring to him was professional objectivity. He told me Alderman Larry Bloom had recommended me for exactly those qualities.[1]

I also told Harold that I had no degree in city planning. He held up my résumé and said, "Your whole résumé says planning." As I was leaving, he said to me, "You know my wife was a union organizer, and I am used to dealing with aggressive women." It really took me aback, since I had not thought of myself as an aggressive woman. I started the job in August 1983.

During the next five years, the Washington administration moved from a general interest in fairness, openness, and concern for every Chicago citizen (especially those traditionally "cut out") into a coherent planning and development strategy. My own vision was also expanded. This chapter is one account of how the development strategy evolved from the chaos and confrontation of the early days. My subtext is the story of the convert to a citywide investment strategy who never lost contact with the business constituency. I insisted on professional management and on keeping downtown aesthetics and amenities on the agenda. However, my vision for enhancing the city's built environment in an open and participatory way was stretched to the city's limits.

The perspective of Harold Washington and his closest confidants on development (such as Rob Mier and others) was that the strength of the downtown area allowed scarce public resources to be strategically invested in leveraging private investment in Chicago neighborhoods. This was feasible even in traditionally neglected black and Hispanic areas and could be done with full neighborhood participation. The "postindustrial" cliche overlooked the continuing importance of the manufacturing sector as a source of well paid jobs. In fact, the jobs measure, not real estate investment, was the best indicator of economic development.

Initially I did not share these beliefs. I was skeptical about the prospects for investment in poor communities, and impatient with the antigentrification forces. I had no subtle understanding of the city's industrial base, and I measured economic development by real estate investments rather than jobs. By the end of my tenure I not only understood but championed these ideas.

Framing Development Policy

In August 1983 the Plan Commission had not met for four months because of conflicts with the city council. Thirty percent of the staff of the Department of Planning had been eliminated as a cost control measure. There had been no full staff meeting since 1968. The Planning Department's major substantive policy document was a hastily written comprehensive plan produced at the end of the Byrne administration. It was a rationale to justify the five-year capital investment program, then driven by the investment needs of the proposed 1992 World's Fair.

The state of the Planning Department was characteristic of the overall challenge of the new administration to bridge the gap between rising expectations and declining resources. Minority poor Chicagoans expected jobs and affordable housing to be more available, but in fact federal budgets were being drastically cut and the city had a deficit of more than $100 million, declining bond ratings, and a bloated and unresponsive bureaucracy. When Harold Washington became mayor in 1983, Chicago garbage trucks still had four man crews. Washington became what Terry Clark has called a "fiscal populist" mayor, that is a chief executive officer (CEO) elected by a populist constituency who had to institute fundamental fiscal reforms and severe budgetary control. During the first two years Washington cut 8000 employees from the city's labor force of some 42,000. GAAP (Generally Accepted Accounting Principles) were instituted along with management by objectives. Each budget year brought more emphasis on "doing more with less."

The development departments handled these constraints through a combination of symbolism, sharing of realities and decision making with affected constituencies, and redirection of resources from the downtown area to the neighborhoods and from the bureaucracy to neighborhood groups. There was also a great emphasis on minority participation, whether in government employment, development opportunities, boards and commissions, or contracts. Under the leadership of Rob Mier, then commissioner of economic development and intimately involved in the mayor's development agenda, the development departments were organized early on (fall 1983) into a subcabinet. The group of departments that included Economic Development (DED), Employment and Training, Housing, Planning, and Cultural Affairs were pulled together to articulate the mayor's policy. Mier organized a retreat in the first week of January 1984 to review *The Washington Papers* and transition reports and evaluate the many large projects in process. We placed sheets of paper on the wall and set priorities for jobs, housing, and other goals along one axis and the large, ongoing projects along another.

The North Loop project, the city's largest downtown commercial renewal program, was a Department of Planning responsibility. It survived the tests of policy because a tax increment financing plan was underway to avoid diverting any additional general obligations bonds to it and also because we made commitments to negotiating minority and female participation in all of our agreements.

The other major downtown projects that stayed on the list were renovation of the old Goldblatt's Department Store for a central library and the expansion of the McCormick Place convention center. Both were additions to the city center's strength as a cultural and trade center. Neither would happen without public funding. They were also opportunities to deliver projects as well as process. The pressure for projects was coming from developers, the press, and the business community. None of these constituencies had any tolerance for innovative policies and strategic redirection of resources.

Our next step was to provide a public statement of our policy. The Development Plan, produced in May 1984, articulated not only our policy but our intended actions. That plan was the development policy document for the first term. It was unlike any traditional comprehensive plan. There was only the briefest of situational analyses, and it included no maps, charts, or pictures. Instead it contained a series of development policies followed by lists of programs and measurable achievements such as the number of houses to be rehabilitated and jobs to be created. The most central policy was "balanced growth," and the most central idea that economic development was not measured by real estate development but by job retention and expansion.

The underlying assumption of the plan was that the private investment in downtown Chicago had so much market strength we could target most of our limited public resources on neighborhood development where new opportunities for housing, commercial and even industrial investment were apparent. Downtown Chicago was in the midst of an explosive growth period that never abated during Harold Washington's term. Commercial office space grew by 41 percent in the City Center between 1979 and 1989; downtown residential space increased by 30 percent. A pause in the construction of new hotel rooms was changed by our decision to expand McCormick Place. An additional 3000 hotel rooms were announced between 1983 and 1989.

We didn't neglect the symbolic importance of the Development Plan; in fact, we hired someone to develop a logo and motto for it. Hence, "Chicago Works Together" was born—a phrase still worn on pins by many city employees. During the Daley era, Chicago was known as the "city that works"—but not in the eyes of minorities. The Development Plan was not written in the Planning Department but under the leadership of DED and the subcabinet. Nonetheless, my staff had a great stake in it. We had helped shape it, and it shaped how we thought about our work. The plan was very well received on a local, national, and even international level.[2]

Public Participation and the Neighborhood Planning Process

While we were writing new policies, we also had to start to cope with demands for public involvement and access to services. What people really wanted was mini–city halls providing government service in their neighborhoods. The expense of decentralization made this approach unthinkable. Instead we provided low-cost new mechanisms whereby citizens and community groups could gain access to their government. These included community forums and usable, accessible information.

The Department of Information and Inquiry, the Latino and Women's Commissions, and our subcabinet came up with the idea of Community Forums: The mayor and all of his department heads visited a designated part of the city and answered prepared questions from community organizations and spontaneous questions from citizens. The Planning Department also recommended organizing a Resource Fair of city government services preceding the forums. The fair was like a trade show for citizens about their government. Each department developed a portable display to describe their program. Staff and brochures accompanied the displays. Bags were available (with "Chicago Works Together" logos and the mayor's name prominently displayed) so people could easily collect material.

I had assumed that the mayor's appearance at these forums would be carefully staged to give him maximum media coverage before a full house and whisk him away leaving all tough questions to his department heads. To my amazement, Harold Washington came early and stayed late. First he'd meet the community leaders at a reception prior to the public meeting, and often he would stay two or even three hours in the public meeting, patiently answering questions (or flipping them to department heads) even when half the audience had left. Department heads or top deputies were expected to be there, and often thirty or forty of us would attend.

The only section of the city where the mayor was met with palpable hostility was the white ethnic Southwest Side. He handled boos and jeers with humor and good grace and with the same respect for citizen's questions.

For each of these meetings the Planning Department regularly supplied demographic information as well as lists of infrastructure investments planned for that area. The MAPS project was one example of data collection efforts driven by our desire to serve neighborhoods and balance city investments between downtown and neighborhoods. Balanced investment strategies require accurate information on capital investments. The Planning Department compiled the first detailed, computer-mapped interdepartmental list of actual (not planned) capital investments.

The infrastructure investments data were part of a series of tools designed to help communities to plan for themselves. The most successful of such tools was a monthly list of buildings in Housing Court and their status. This list, called "Case Watch," makes it possible for community organizations to identify their worst slumlords and to go to court to protest against owner indifference. This was part of the Affirmative Neighborhood Information Program described in Kretzmann's chapter in this volume.

The mayor understood the value of such tools to community organizations and always created an opportunity at neighborhood forums for me to describe it. The compilation and use of data by the new administration was another demonstration of what "reform" meant.

Community Power:
The 1985 General Obligation Bond Issue

Our cultivation of community organizations and citizens provided a way to mobilize support for neighborhood investments, even during the "council wars" (discussed earlier in Gill's chapter). One good example is the 1985 General Obligation Bond Issue. At the Community Forums, we had heard a great demand for local improvements of streets, sewers, sidewalks, and alleys. The mayor proposed a $250 million General Obligation Bond Issue to satisfy these demands and catch up with the significant backlog of infrastructure improvements. The bond issue was bottled up by the city council, as was every initiative of the mayor's at that time. At some point a presentation of the contents of the bond issue was made to the development subcabinet, and it became apparent that there was no part of the city that would not benefit. In fact, there was a great deal of work scheduled for the Northwest and Southwest Sides because of the prevalence of "WPA" streets there. (These were streets built by the Works Progress Administration in the 1930s with neither curbs nor proper drainage.) It was also clear that low interest rates and debt refinancing could provide a bond issue at a very low cost to taxpayers. This struck me as such a salable package that the mayor might well make an appeal directly to the people. I suggested a simple brochure for wide distribution to show what people could get. It was also suggested that the mayor should get on a bus and go out to neighborhoods all over the city to show people the problems the General Obligation Bond Issue would solve. When we presented this strategy to the mayor he was delighted. With great relish he boarded the "Host Bus" with reporters and rode to potholes, broken sewers, and collapsed vaulted sidewalks. Many of these visits were in the wards of his aldermanic opponents, who in almost every case joined him as the mayor clucked over the need for repair. Meanwhile the city was papered with simple brochures explaining that, with rapid city council action, lots of work could be done at a low cost. Within a few weeks the council members (aldermen) bowed to public pressure and passed the bond issue.

Devising a Neighborhood Planning Approach

Early on we had some discussions about the formation of Neighborhood Planning Districts. However, my instincts told me that the neighborhood groups would look on these planning districts with a jaundiced eye. In many neighborhoods different groups competed for attention and constituencies. Few neighborhood groups were organized around ward boundaries, and in fact many saw themselves as alternatives to the aldermen as lobbyists and brokers for city services and investments. As an alternative, we adopted an approach that was responsive to opportunities identified by community groups and aldermen. The plans produced this way were guided by a very inclusive neighborhood planning community in which owners, renters, business people, local institutions, and the aldermen were represented. In each case these plans resulted in both public and private investments in areas that had seen little investment in the past decade.

Since the neighborhood planning staff never had more than eight people, we sought ways to stretch our resources through a series of partnerships. First we added a modest $100,000 to $200,000 annual planning grant program to the Community Development Block Grant program. This allowed five or six neighborhood groups a year to obtain grants to help them do their own planning for specific projects likely to lead to new investments. Also, we organized developers and real estate and architectural professional organizations to donate technical assistance to neighborhood organizations.

While none of these programs were very large, each was symbolically important to community groups. The Community Development Advisory Committee fought each year to maintain the Planning Grant Program in the CDBG budget (usually over the objections of the Budget Office, which saw the program as "soft"). Several community groups made useful alliances with downtown developers as a result of the partnership program, and there was widespread approval of the idea of linking downtown and neighborhood developers.

However, it wasn't until Harold's second term that we found the resources to do more comprehensive neighborhood planning. How this happened was another reflection of Mayor Washington's determination to be inclusive in his thinking about the city.

In 1987 a local political columnist wrote an article critical of the mayor because he had allowed a high-density development to be built in Lincoln Park (a North Side upscale neighborhood). He warned that Harold's supporters on the lakefront would not tolerate more density and absence of planning in their communities.

Scott Hodes, a North Side lawyer and political advisor to the mayor recommended to him that he create a mayoral task force on the subject of high-rise, high-density concerns. But Harold insisted that any such task force must have a broader agenda of planning concerns across the city.

What emerged was the Neighborhood Land Use Task Force, consisting of 60 members, chaired by Scott Hodes, but cochaired by a South Side black female neighborhood development director, Lauren Allen of The Woodlawn Organization (TWO). The agenda included high-rise/high-density issues, renovation of the 28-mile boulevard system; citywide commercial and industrial planning; and location of institutional care facilities. This grab bag of issues addressed the concerns of Lakefront yuppies; social service providers; a series of black, Hispanic, and working-class white neighborhoods along the boulevards; and the commercial and industrial community organizations throughout the city. The needs of a single neighborhood constituency were used as a vehicle to address a whole host of issues across the city. It set much of the planning agenda for the next several years.

The Task Force as a Policy Instrument

The mayoral task force proved to be a very common approach to policy-making in the Harold Washington administration. It suited our inclusive style and the necessity to coordinate departments in order to achieve change. The Department of Planning was put in charge of a number of these task forces because of our ability to handle policy development. Their success depended, in the end, on the will of the government to implement the policies. This will was strengthened or weakened by the level of mayoral interest, the power of the interest groups, and aldermanic interest.

The first and most successful task force that I chaired had all of the elements described above. It concerned the issue of the homeless. In 1984, the community groups, and public and private funders of shelters, were very frustrated by the absence of coherent city government responses to a pressing need. We asked everyone inside and outside of the government concerned with the issue to serve on the task force. It was evident from the outset that such groups as Travelers and Immigrants Aid, the Jewish Federation, and representatives of the State of Illinois were very surprised to be invited to the table as equal partners. We reconfirmed the equal partnership by giving leadership roles on subcommittees to both government and nongovernment participants. It was equally clear that departments such as Inspectional Services had little experience in participatory policymaking. The dynamic was very successful in balancing the conservative self-protective interests of the bureaucrats with the sense of urgency and realism of shelter providers and service workers. It also proved a good mechanism for communicating the resource limits and stretching limited resources by joint state and city funding of priority projects.

There was early and profound consensus on the need to fund small neighborhood-based shelters that would provide the best opportunity for the homeless to be reintegrated as permanent residents in a community. This perhaps self-evident policy was an important early decision and had such support that Chicago has successfully avoided creation of large "warehouses" for the homeless.[3]

Both zoning and building code regulations were required for shelters. This gave the task force the difficult task of deciding in which zoning districts shelters would be allowed. It also had to decide what code requirements were essential to safety that would not be so prohibitive in cost that it would have the effect of closing existing shelters. The zoning changes required aldermanic support. Negotiating an acceptable package for the city council without losing the support of the task force proved to be one of the most difficult tasks, particularly since the timing of negotiation (at some points on the floor of the council chambers on the day of passage) did not allow the full participation by the task force.

Two factors were essential to maintaining the consensus. One was the considerable trust that was built among members by insistence on full and open discussion and sharing of hard decisions. The other was the presence of politically savvy task force members from the not-for-profit side who could persuade other members that our compromises were not "sellouts." Our success in getting legislation passed during the "council wars" resulted in large part from the credibility and visibility given the issue both by the task force and the reality of the need.

During the early stages of this task force I called Mayor Washington at home one evening. (He had given his phone number to us all at a staff meeting and urged us to use it if we felt it necessary.) I was concerned because several members of the task force were going to be critical of our efforts in the next day's press. I wanted the mayor to be forewarned and not soured on our efforts. His reaction stunned me. "Hollander," he said, "of course we're going to get some criticism along the way. Don't worry about it. The important thing is that homelessness wasn't on the city's agenda before now and we've put it there."

Harold Washington and the Business Community

One of the reasons Harold Washington appointed me was to have a person in development who was known and liked by the business community. Rob Mier, commissioner of economic development, was an academic known for his interest in community-based economic development efforts and minority entrepreneurship. His appointment was somewhat scary to the business community, as was the election of Harold Washington. It is my theory that the election of Harold Washington helped to bring about a dramatic change in the organization and effectiveness of the business communities on city issues. They were forced to "grow up," which is to say that they had to find a new means of gaining access and influence rather than relying on an old set of personal networks.

When Harold Washington was first elected, business people would say to me "except for you we don't know anyone he knows." It was true. His closest advisors did not include anyone from the established business community. It was clear to me that the mayor was most uncomfortable in the presence of big business groups. He spoke very stiffly to them, and they seemed rather reluctant to ask questions that would give the mayor an opportunity for more relaxed dialogue. The "council wars" and the mayor's clear lack of enthusiasm for the World's Fair confirmed some of the business people's worst fears about the impact of his election. Harold Washington's unwillingness to "deal" with his city council foes and the consequent uncertainty and downright opposition on such matters as Navy Pier was keenly distressing to business people.

While many had complained privately about the purported payoffs that had gone on under Mayor Byrne (particularly telling of major pressure for campaign contributions), they were more distressed by the conflict. Certainty was clearly more valued than "reform." There was skepticism that "reform" really meant giving blacks the benefits that had been reserved for whites (e.g., jobs and contracts). There was a profound doubt as to whether there really was another way to do city business that was more open and fair.

But Washington's election brought with it both self-examination in the business community and new initiatives. One segment was heavily involved in the World's Fair effort. Don Perkins, the former CEO of Jewel Corporation, organized the Commercial Club into a Civic Committee, which published "Make No Little Plans," a far more sophisticated agenda of job-creating activities than a one-time World's Fair effort. Meanwhile, the Chicago Central Area Committee initiated a study of all the different business groups and their overlapping and conflicting roles.

While all of these efforts were going on outside of city government, the administration began to reach out to the business community. A series of lunches was organized (starting in 1984) to introduce the mayor to leaders in such sectors as finance, banking, trade, and transportation. In addition, a private resources council was organized to seek pro bono assistance on a whole list of city problems such as health insurance costs, and Bill Johnson, CEO of I.C. Industries, was asked to lead an effort to encourage local businesses in Chicago to increase their purchases from local firms. The level of trust grew on both sides to the point that the mayor asked the Civic Committee in 1986 to assist in long-term financial planning for the city. They responded by organizing a Financial Resources Advisory Committee.[4]

The business supporters of the World's Fair effort did not have the same success in winning the mayor's trust. The mayor's attitude toward the World's Fair was best demonstrated to me one day when some of the business leaders, including Tom Ayers of Commonwealth Edison, Frank Considine of American Can, and Bruce Graham of Skidmore, Owings & Merrill, were hustling him to a meeting at SOM designed to dazzle him with the latest concepts of the fair. Instead of allowing himself to be formally ushered into the conference room, the mayor spotted a young man waiting for an appointment in the outer office. "Hello," said Harold Washington, "I'm the mayor of Chicago. How are you?" The young man was completely taken by surprise, and Harold Washington had made his point about whom he considered his constituency.

The leaders of the World's Fair did not hear his message early or clearly enough. In all fairness, the mayor's message was not clear. He did not declare himself against the fair but instead urged his aids and appointees to concentrate on questions of cost and minority representation, and he gave full ear to the community groups against it. It was never clear to me whether the aim was a better fair or no fair.

I learned over time that Harold's stance on controversial issues was often intentionally ambivalent. He did not want to take a stand, but rather preferred to let the issue work itself out. For business leaders this contrasted with Mayor Daley's decisiveness even on controversial issues like the construction of the University of Illinois campus and McCormick Place. Of course, by the time Daley made those decisions he had gained a great deal of power and was being elected by large majorities.[5]

The demise of the World's Fair was a real shock to the traditional business community and a serious challenge to their leadership. The smartest of them, however, realized that more progress could be made on a substantive jobs agenda such as that proposed by the Civic Committee.

Harold Washington
and the Real Estate Development Community

The real estate development community went through a similar metamorphosis in response to the Washington administration. They were catalyzed into organized efforts by two events: the first was a surprise drive to adopt a commercial lease tax; the second, a community demand for exaction taxes on downtown development for neighborhood investment. An exaction tax is a dollar levy per square foot on new private developments (e.g., $5 a square foot). The tax was to be used for neighborhood improvements.

As indicated earlier, during the entire term of Harold Washington, the downtown area was experiencing an unprecedented development boom. In spite of concern that the "council wars" were driving investment out of the city, the pace of downtown real estate development never slackened. Since the city government was experiencing severe cutbacks in federal funding and rising expectations for neighborhood investment, it was inevitable that the downtown boom would be seen as a logical revenue source. The drive to tap this source did not come from the Washington administration.

Alderman Burke, a leader of the faction opposed to Washington, had first suggested a commercial lease tax, and when the Washington administration recommended it at the last moment over the Christmas holidays to plug the gap in the 1986 city budget, the development community was caught off guard. Frantic phone calls were made from ski resorts across the country. Richard Stein declared his signature on a North Loop Redevelopment Contract null and void because the city had taken a secret initiative that dramatically changed the rules of the game.

Several leaders in the development community, particularly Bob Belcaster of Tishman Speyer, representing a major portion of downtown office space, rolled up their sleeves to find alternative ways to fund the budget.

This was in contrast to such business organizations as the Chicago Association of Commerce and Industry and the Civic Federation, which regularly opposed new taxes and made unrealistic recommendations for budget cuts. The upshot was sufficient pressure to kill the lease tax and a compromise on other taxes. The debate also resulted in the formation of the Development Council. This group represents the largest commercial real estate developers in Chicago and meets regularly to discuss matters of public policy affecting their interests. It quickly became the group to consult on matters affecting downtown real estate, whether planning regulations or taxation.

The exaction issue was first raised by the Save Our Neighborhoods/Save Our City (SON/SOC) organization, representing the largely white ethnic Southwest and Northwest Side communities. The administration's main concern was to postpone this tricky political issue until after the elections. Its response was the creation of the Task Force on Linked Development. Community groups, developers, government leaders and some mediators (liberal business people, churchmen, foundation staff) were included. This task force failed (in contrast with the Task Force on the Homeless) because it lacked the ingredients for success. The appointments were unbalanced from the start. The developers were outnumbered and said so. The level of trust was low. SON/SOC came to the table with nonnegotiable positions. Others, like Robert Brehm (whose chapter in this volume provides an alternative view) felt downtown developers owed the neighborhoods something. Soon the term "exaction" was called "extraction" by the business community and "reparations" by some community representatives.

The Planning Department's first task was to try to develop a defensible rationale for taxing downtown development. Illinois law requires a "rational nexus" between exactions on development and the public impact of the development. In San Francisco and Boston, a rational nexus could easily be established between increased downtown development and housing prices. Each city has so little land that housing prices are driven up by central city commercial development growth.

In Chicago, we had to reach for a rationale that public infrastructure investments in support of downtown private development were adversely affecting neighborhoods. The report we produced was scoffed at by both developers and community groups. I had struggled for objectivity under great pressure to make it come out right for community groups. I did not believe that downtown development had a negative impact on neighborhood development. I also agreed with the developers that a tax on new development was a clumsy and discriminatory way to raise funds. I was much more sympathetic to alternative proposals to tax all large commercial space 5 cents a square foot.

The pressure from the community groups did result in some alternative proposals from the Development Council, including a voluntary fund-raising effort to be matched by an increase in the real estate transaction tax. SON/SOC, the initiator of the exaction proposal, was unwilling to compromise. They were being courted both by forces in the black community and by an aldermanic group that included white opposing aldermen and Hispanic Alderman Luis Gutierrez. If the Mayor had allowed them to be defeated it could have been damaging to him politically.

The final task force report was not a consensus document, and nothing resulted from it. As with the World's Fair, the mayor's position on the issue was never clear to me except when he indicated that he hoped the issue would "go away" until after the election for the second term. I realize, in retrospect, that I expected the mayor to exercise leadership on a tricky issue even though he did not yet have a majority in the city council and was courting a precious potential constituency in the white ethnic working-class wards.

The real estate development community realized that they could not take for granted political support from either the mayor or their more traditional supporters in the city council majority. They emerged from the debate with a strong, organized, well-connected political voice for large property developers.

Harold Washington and the Planning Agenda

Harold Washington was not a mayor with a physical vision for the city. He had no interest in urban design, nor was he "turned on" by big development projects. Nor, conversely, was he concerned about the adverse impact from rapid growth of the downtown area. The mayor was concerned about who would benefit from downtown development. In subsidized projects he insisted on strict affirmative action programs for contractors and the work force, and he promoted hiring from among the unemployed registered with the Mayor's Office of Employment and Training (MET). The mayor also understood, however, that there was a constituency that cared about planning and urban design and expected me to nurture it. He gave me both the credibility and a free hand to do so.

Early on the mayor took steps to signal my importance to him as the city's planner. Within the first three months of my tenure, he attended two very important events. The first was the annual meeting of the Metropolitan Housing and Planning Council where he told me "these people really love you, Liz." They did, and they also loved seeing me on the arm of the new mayor. At my request, Harold also came to deliver a speech to the

Midwest Meetings of the American Planning Association. It was the first time such a meeting had been addressed by a mayor of Chicago. Even more important, the mayor made it clear to the development community that he was not interested in a personal involvement in developments. He did not regularly see developers and their projects; and when he did, he made sure I knew about it and included me in such meetings. He never once told me how to view a project or asked me to change my recommendation to the Plan Commission.

Establishing the Urban Design Agenda

As I indicated at the outset of this chapter, I came to my task as Planning Director with strong ideas about urban design. These ideas were not the result of any formal planning training but rather a keen observation of the city from the perspective of the user and the viewer of the urban landscape. In the central city, this was combined with a concern that Chicago never have a dead downtown, like Detroit, where people would be afraid to go at night.

I was an admirer of Chicago architecture, both old and new, but felt that there was a self-centered quality to many buildings, especially new ones. Too little attention was paid to context or to the needs of the pedestrian user of the city. For example, the Associates Center Building on Michigan Avenue was a stark diamond-shaped building in striking contrast to the exquisite row of buildings to the south of it along Michigan Avenue, including the original Central Public Library, a handsome late-nineteenth-century building. It jarred me every time I drove into the Loop, and I swore to myself I would never approve anything like it as Commissioner of Planning.

Garages everywhere seemed to me a blight on the urban landscape, ugly necessities that were designed as if no one had to look at them. I was not concerned about a lot of density in the downtown area because Chicago had so much space and such a good transit system to handle it, but I was very concerned about the quality of the open spaces that gave people relief from those densities. That concern included the lakeshore, the river edge, and public plazas, arcades, and the like, which were experienced by the pedestrian.

In the neighborhoods, new commercial areas were designed like suburban shopping malls with parking lots in the front and poor pedestrian access. As an avid shopper who loved streets full of interesting, small shops, I considered this design antiurban.

Planning practice in Chicago had been to let developers take maximum advantage of a very generous zoning ordinance. The planned unit development (PUD) provisions of the zoning ordinance allowed very large buildings to be built by providing arcades, plazas, and upper-level setbacks. The PUD provisions were regularly used by developers not for the kind of flexible arrangement of space that was their intent in most jurisdictions but to maximize the amount of built space on valuable downtown land.

It was clear to me early on that the "council wars" would not allow us to make changes in the zoning ordinance to achieve urban design objectives. Instead, the Planning Department had to influence large projects by a combination of moral suasion and organizing the constituency for planning. I started by suggesting to developers that their projects should be reviewed by groups such as Metropolitan Planning Council and Friends of the River long before they were presented to the Plan Commission. Similarly, neighborhood projects were expected to be fully aired with community groups. We asked developers for contextual models and drawings and quizzed them on ground-level details.

By 1986 I organized all of the civic groups concerned with quality of design in the central area into the Central City Advisory Committee. Some twenty groups met with the Planning Department on a monthly basis, sharing the agenda. The mayor was not particularly concerned with or involved in this agenda except for big ticket items like the Chicago Theatre, the North Loop, and eventually the redesign of State Street and the library location. However, it was understood that the Planning Department was in touch with all aspects of the downtown constituency. I used this group as one of many sounding boards on matters of broader policy such as the budget.

In 1984 the Planning Department signaled its new interest in urban design standards by cosponsoring the first International Urban Design Conference in Chicago. The conference was used as a vehicle to involve the local architectural community and to communicate our approach to neighborhood planning, and the conference brochure contained pieces on the Development Plan and on the balanced growth policy.

A major downtown development project provided another important vehicle for establishing a new way of doing business with the Planning Department. It led to the establishment of two important principles: one was to seek input from civic groups; the second was not to expect financial assistance from the city.

The Chicago Dock and Equitable Trust owned a 50-acre parcel of land north of the Chicago River and directly east of the Tribune Tower. The completion of a new bridge across the Chicago River on Columbus Drive, east of Michigan Avenue, dramatically improved access to this land and made it ripe for development. In 1985 the Chicago Dock and Equitable Trust announced that they had hired Alex Cooper, a New York planner, to devise a plan for the entire 50 acres. The Trust wanted to bring the entire piece to the city as one planned development. Alex Cooper approached the Planning Department with his initial ideas but was very open to hearing the city's concerns about this key downtown land. Early on, he asked me to walk the site with him. His fundamental vision of the site was music to my ears. He wanted to extend the grid of the city onto the site rather than making it an isolated enclave. He saw the river edge as a potential major amenity for the site—to be used, not ignored. He knew about and respected the Lakefront Protection Ordinance and understood all land east of the outer drive should be designated for park use. We suggested the importance of the view corridors west of the Tribune Tower and Wrigley Building, and east through the site to Lake Michigan.

We suggested to the Trust that the Planning Department work closely with the Cooper firm to devise a set of urban design guidelines for the property that would be formally adopted by the Plan Commission. With that backdrop, it would then be possible to present the entire development as one PUD, consistent with the guidelines. This approach was used, along with involvement of the civic groups as the plan was developed.

Initially the Trust indicated to us that they would need tax-exempt financing for the $75 million worth of infrastructure needed to develop the site. We said we would help them, providing they met our requirements for affirmative action and local hiring in all aspects of the project. Eventually the group decided against tax-exempt financing but did agree to build the infrastructure systems to city standards and donate them to the city. They further agreed to subject themselves to a voluntary affirmative action plan and report on their progress annually to the Plan Commission.

Another project, the River North Urban Design Plan, was significant because it adhered to the same principles, and went beyond them in three ways: it was a truly public–private venture; it influenced development on a broad scale; and it established the role of planning principles as an important factor next to aldermanic preference.

One of the hottest areas for development was the River North area, that part of the city north of the Chicago River, west of Michigan avenue, north to Chicago Avenue, and bounded on the west by the North Branch of the river. Full of handsome old loft buildings, galleries and restaurants, upscale shops, and the like, it was attracting ever more investment in housing and offices. I was concerned that too rapid escalation of new investment would kill the very qualities that made the area attractive unless there was a set of urban design guidelines. The Central Area Committee shared my concern, and so their staff and mine, working closely with the River North Association, devised an urban design plan of award-winning quality. The first draft was completed in 1987.

Winning final approval by the Plan Commission took several years,

owing in large part to aldermanic opposition. Aldermen were used to calling the shots on major developments in their wards. Developers were
expected to share their proposals with the aldermen and get their reactions
to the zoning approvals. Planning Department and Plan Commission re-
views were a respected part of the process. What was new in the River
North plan was the extent of negotiation over design and planning
principles.

Even during the time that the plan was still in draft form, developers used
it as a guideline. The aldermen no longer had as free a hand as they were
used to in determining what development would be acceptable in their
wards. This was a dramatic change in the way of doing business in the
downtown area. Although several compromises were necessary (such as
calling it "guidelines" rather than a plan), the Plan Commission finally approved it.

Planning for a Balanced Economy:
Broadening the Planning Agenda

During the same time that the Planning Department was increasing its
influence over urban design in the downtown area, we were working on
significant neighborhood planning efforts that reflected my broadened vision of neighborhood development. One was a plan to project the 28-mile
boulevard system throughout the city's neighborhoods as a city amenity,
like the Lakefront and river edge, that had the possibility for generating
development. I believed that a plan to revitalize it would symbolize our interest in reviving all city neighborhoods and the Neighborhood Land Use
Task Force shared this vision. The plan was actually completed during the
Sawyer administration and, like the River North plan, was adopted by the
Plan Commission.

The other major planning effort that reflected my increased understanding of the economy of the city was the North Side Industrial Plan. I had
become convinced, as a result of the lobbying efforts of the industrial community groups, the DED and, to my surprise, the traditional Lincoln Park
community organization, that it was important to protect industry. This
was a changed point of view for me. Within the first year of my tenure, I had
approved the conversion of an empty factory building in the Clybourn area
at the west edge of Lincoln Park to residential units. I had been told by my
holdover staff that there was no industrial future in the area and the building would sit empty. I had bought the notion of the "postindustrial" city.
As I came to know the area in more detail, I recognized that it was possible
both to save industry and make room for new commercial and residential
development, but only with careful planning and innovative zoning.

When we first organized the Neighborhood Land Use Task Force, a call for citywide industrial and commercial plans had been made by the Chicago Association of Neighborhood Development Organizations (CANDO), the umbrella group of commercial and industrial community groups. We were also in the midst of devising innovative industrial protection legislation, called the Planned Manufacturing District Ordinance. This was a response to conflict over land use in areas such as the Clybourn corridor where industrial firms were being threatened by commercial and residential development around them, as described in more detail in Ducharme's chapter later in this volume.

To respond to CANDO's suggestion, and to support the Planned Manufacturing District (PMD) legislation, I thought it important to have up-to-date information on industrial land and its uses in the city so that we could target the areas most important to retain. I sought to forge an alliance for the industrial planning effort not only with the industrial area community organizations but also with the industrial real estate community. The two leading industrial real estate professional organizations, SOIR (Society of Industrial Realtors) and AIREB (Association of Industrial Real Estate Brokers), were asked to participate in the planning effort. This partnership proved a fruitful one, as members came to understand the purpose of PMD legislation and equated it to the covenants found in suburban industrial parks.

By the beginning of Mayor Washington's second term, I had articulated my increased understanding of the economy of the city in a speech called "Planning for a Balanced Economy." Everywhere I went, I espoused a new understanding of all aspects of the Chicago economy and warned against relying on the "postindustrial" cliché. I also painted the vision of the boulevard systems running through a series of diverse, revitalized communities. The mayor understood that I had broadened my vision, and he told me that he considered me to be one of his most articulate spokespersons for it.

Big Decisions in the Second Term

At the beginning of the second term, we were faced with the reality that articulating a vision was not enough. Frustration was widespread. Everywhere constituencies were seeking more action. Hispanics were disappointed in the hiring practices of city government. Blacks wanted jobs we had not had the ability to create. The cumulative impact of many neighborhood improvements was not recognized or considered sufficient. The Chicago Housing Authority was under siege by the U.S. Department of

Housing and Urban Development (HUD), and there was a cry to reform education.

At the same time, there was a series of blockbuster projects clamoring for our attention. I expected these projects to be handled differently by the mayor now that he had control of the city council and a clear electoral mandate. During the first term I had been frustrated by his indecision on both the World's Fair and exaction tax issues. In reflecting on his handling of large projects in the second term I must conclude that while Harold Washington had a passionate interest in reformulating the political ground rules, he had little interest in building monuments.

I was involved in two major controversial development issues during the second term: the installation of lights at the Chicago Cubs' Wrigley Field, and the location of the Central Public Library. The first issue, lights at Wrigley Field, involved deep community opposition and a belief on the part of community activists that they would, in fact, be able to choose lights or no lights. Harold brought to this issue a deep interest in sports and a sense of the importance of teams to the city's life and self-esteem. He often reflected on his depression as a young man when the Cardinal's football team left town. He clearly viewed the issue as a balance between citywide and neighborhood interests. However, he insisted upon a neighborhood dialogue to articulate every mitigating measure that could be taken to reduce the impact of bringing lights to Wrigley Field. In communicating the seriousness with which he took that dialogue, the community believed he had given them the right to determine their own destiny. I was asked to lead the planning effort because Rob Mier, who had been in charge, was known to be an avid sports fan and was not seen as neutral.

The neighborhood planning process on this issue was the most confrontational one in which I participated. Supporters of Harold Washington felt abandoned, and opponents took maximum advantage of the controversy to put him in a bad light. Nonetheless, we managed to get the community to list their needs. This process took more than a year. We counterbalanced their opposition with a survey of public opinion done by the Economic Development Commission that revealed the extent of support for the Cubs, even among those living near the ballpark. These two approaches proved to be important tools for positioning the mayor to support lights. He acted on behalf of the whole city but with respect for the affected neighborhood.

The resulting Lakeview Protection Plan, implemented under Mayor Sawyer, worked. Except for the impact of parking permits on local business, the negotiated measures were so successful that the neighborhood experiences less negative effect from night games than afternoon games.

The location of the Central Public Library proved to be an even knottier problem. It demonstrated the difficulties of accomplishing a major project when the mayor was unwilling to exercise strict control over either his own bureaucracy or his Library Board appointments. For sixty years the need for a new Central Public Library had been evident, and its site had been debated for fifteen years. In 1983 Mayor Byrne had acquired the Goldblatt's Department Store downtown, and as early as 1984 the Washington administration decided to pursue renovation of the building because it was a project that could be completed in the first term since architectural and engineering studies were complete. However, a Washington appointee to the Library Board, Canute Russell, favored a new building, and the Better Government Association, a civic group known for its watchdog, exposé operations as well as its Republican leanings, had been opposed to the project from the outset.

Russell, the Better Government Association, and the *Sun Times* undertook to discredit the Goldblatt's project, arguing it could never become a "world class library." Questions were raised about the accuracy of rehabilitation estimates and the credibility of engineering assessments of the building's load-bearing capacity. Commissioner of Public Works Paul Karas, a very independent young man who was new to the administration, undermined the administration's position by publicly expressing his doubts about both the load-bearing capability of the building and the wisdom of rehabilitation. The mayor had no effective mechanism in place to force consensus between his Library Board and his staff, nor did he exercise his own influence sufficiently to sustain the project. When Ernie Barefield, then chief of staff, indicated that the mayor was open to the alternative of new construction, the Planning Department exerted a lot of influence to select a South Loop site that Mayor Byrne had failed to redevelop. We sold the site on the basis that it would have the same upgrading effects as Goldblatt's, would be less expensive and faster to build on because it was a cleared site, and would not require relocation of first class retailing activities. Through Barefield's office, a consensus was achieved on the alternative South Loop site. I was then given responsibility for the project. I told Barefield that I could not do the job without a clear mandate from the mayor. I needed to be in charge and have a single mechanism for decision making that involved all parties. I organized the Library Policy Review Committee, which included all the key members of the Library Board, the library commissioner, and the essential members of the city administration (Public Works, Budget, Comptroller, Purchasing, Mayor's Office). This group, which met regularly and which I chaired, was recognized as the final authority on all matters concerning the library project. The Planning Department also organized an Ad Hoc Citizens Committee to advise us on the library project representing all of the constituencies concerned about the project.

Because of the history of the project, we recommended a design–build competition, an innovative approach that required teams of architects and builders to compete to build the project according to a set timetable and budget.

We prepared a detailed briefing book for the mayor that outlined the full costs of both the competition and the library construction (as well as some branch library projects to appease the city council members). The price tag was a whopping $175 million (as compared with $80 million for Goldblatt's). The competition reduced city control over choice of minority subcontractors and put the choice of the architects and contractor teams in the hands of a citizen jury. The mayor agreed to the package, and the city council passed legislation that put all of the decision-making power in the hands of the Library Policy Committee (which included no council members) and the jury. The mayor had final authority, but no one believed he would second-guess the jury. The jury, like all of the Washington-appointed boards and commissions, reflected the diversity of the city. It included a black historian, a Chinese businessman, a Hispanic artist, and a Hispanic developer, as well as an architect (from out of town), a local architectural historian, a black librarian (also from out of town), and a member of the Library Board. The chair was a businessman, Norman Ross, one of the few business people who was a long-term mayoral confidant.

One of the reasons we had chosen a design–build approach was that it gave an important opportunity for broad-based citizen involvement. In fact, the public display of the five competing schemes was widely viewed and discussed. Thirty thousand Chicagoans visited the exhibit, and eight thousand took the time to write their detailed opinion for the jury. Local newspapers gave the exhibit extensive coverage. A "Nova" program was prepared on the competition for public television.

In retrospect, it is clear that large projects were not seen by the mayor as something to be accomplished outside of the democratic process. Instead, an approach had to be found that provided sufficient consensus both within the bureaucracy and in the public realm to allow the project to proceed. This appeared as indecisive to many and was a great source of frustration to those of us in charge of the projects. It reflects the mayor's priorities, however, and his particular kind of leadership.

What's important about these stories from the second term is that they confirm my belief that development projects were not at the center of Harold Washington's concerns. Big projects were annoying necessities that did not fare well under the inclusive and democratic political style that were Harold's hallmarks.

The Real Legacy

Chicago, like most big cities, defines its success by visible, built symbols: the world's tallest building, Sears Tower; the Lakefront park legacy of the

Burnham Plan; or the nation's largest airport. Harold's leadership was similarly defined and found wanting by many. It was not the legacy he sought. The legacy that he sought was articulated for me by Bill Berry, a deeply respected black civic rights leader. At a fund-raising breakfast for the second campaign, Bill talked about all the press Harold was getting on the stadium issues and then told us, "That's not what is important. What's important is, how have we changed the lives of the ordinary citizen of the South and West Sides?" I remember thinking what an impossible standard that was.

The first step to changing the lives of the poor of the city was making their issues a part of the debate. As the mayor had said to me, putting homelessness on the agenda was the key. It was only in retrospect that the city began to understand how the nature of the agenda had changed. Groups representing every segment of the city—the Southwest and Northwest Sides, the West and South Sides, downtown, Hispanics, gays, the homeless, women, Asians—had all been built into the agenda-making process. The vehicles included appointments to boards and commissions, task forces, funding of delegate agencies, city staff appointments, and community forums. Decision-making processes for key items like the budget were permanently altered to give time for public input.

Community-based organizations were partners in every endeavor, whether combatting gangs or building housing. Major private development projects routinely provided amenities in exchange for building rights, even though the Zoning Ordinance had not been changed.

Harold was the cheerleader for the potpourri; he called this the patchwork quilt of race, income, and ethnic background that could be stitched into a beautiful city. He reveled in the democratic political process and fought for fair political representation. He had a singular capacity to inspire a vision of the city based not on its glittering downtown buildings but on its human potential.

Was Chicago ready for reform? A New York friend said to me, "Oh, you have that old-fashioned mayor who believes in all of that sixties stuff." Harold was promoting a vision of a grass-roots democracy in the midst of an era of worship of the private sector values of the bottom line, the big build, and making it without government help. Contrary to my friend's view, he was not old fashioned but ahead of his time. America, in the face of impending shortages of skilled workers, was rediscovering the human resource.

The recent election to the mayoralty of Richard M. Daley, Richard J. Daley's son, a politician dedicated to keeping the nitty gritty government services going, and silent on a larger vision, would seem to tell us that the city wasn't ready for the winds of change. On the other hand, the Chicago school reform effort is a dramatic experimentation in the power of grass-roots democracy to redirect resources. The business community, in partnership with parents and not-for-profit reform groups, overturned the city's best established bureaucracy in the name of educating children. That was an unimaginable strategy before Harold Washington's tenure. In 1983 the business community didn't know anyone Harold knew. In 1989 these same leaders were lobbying the state legislature with parents from Woodlawn and Pilsen. Harold's legacy is not on the skyline but in the halls of the legislature and hundreds of meeting halls across the city. His legacy is in the milieu in which he thrived.

NOTES

1.   In my last conversation with Harold Washington before he died, he said to me, "You're always objective, Hollander." I was deeply complimented.
2.   I was invited to a conference in Genoa, Italy, to present the plan to an international conference on cities in transition.
3.   As recently as the winter of 1989, Commonwealth Edison recommended converting closed hospitals to homeless shelters and there was an instant and total rejection of the idea by the task force (which still governs policy and implementation). Instead, the Department of Human Resources channeled Commonwealth Edison's interest into a business group on the issue to be staffed by the Chicago Association of Commerce and Industry and urged support for the rehab of single-room occupancy hotels, the first steps toward permanent housing.
4.   Even at this late date the mayor was still stiff with this group. He had been invited to lunch to discuss his needs with them. He arrived with an entourage and proceeded to read a half hour speech, badly. The business people had expected ten minutes of informal discussion. It almost soured the deal, but fortunately business people who had worked more closely with him prevailed.
5.   In the end, the clear political decision came not from Harold Washington but from the Speaker of the House, Mike Madigan. He organized a blue-ribbon committee chaired by Adlai Stevenson III that raised enough questions about the World's Fair to allow Madigan to recommend against state funding in June 1985. He said to me later he hoped the mayor was grateful to him for killing the fair.

Reforming the Role of Human Services in City Government

JUDITH WALKER

Some time in mid-May 1984, I got a call late at night from the mayor's chief of staff asking if I would take the post of commissioner of human services for six months. He indicated that they had to do something immediately. There was an upcoming Community Development Block Grant budget to be put in place, and the leadership was not there to make the needed cuts necessitated by Reagan's shrinking federal pot. I had talked to the mayor earlier that year when he asked to see me after a ground-breaking ceremony for a building of Provident Hospital, one of the few African-American-owned hospitals in the country, where I coordinated housing and community development activities. He said he was impressed with my résumé and asked why I had not submitted it. I told him, quite simply, that I hadn't because I was not interested in working for the city.

I had done policy work at the Department of Human Services, and served as deputy regional administrator for the U.S. Department of Housing and Urban Development (HUD). I had joined Washington's Housing Task Force in his congressional district and also participated on the World's Fair Committee organized to examine the proposed fair's impact on the primarily black communities of the South Side of Chicago. I worked briefly on one of the transition committee task forces, but I had no intention of returning to government service. My concern was to get more help in the community in which I was working.

However, Washington asked me to reconsider and when, after several more discussions, I was asked to become commissioner of human services I agreed to take the job for six months and help in the transition to a permanent commissioner.

While I felt that there were some needed new initiatives that could be launched, my primary goal was to reorganize the department, bring focus to it, find someone who really wanted the job, and get out in six months. I coupled this with a desire to improve the image of human services and to see its integration into the priorities of the city.

My second goal was to increase the advocacy for human services and enhance their importance in the mainstream of our thinking, planning, and funding. While the national politicians and the media were promoting the great recovery of America, in the cities things were getting worse. There were few voices raising objections to the sorry state of affairs. One exception was the progressive coalition behind the election of Harold Washington, and his administration was raising its voice.

Human Services as an Economic Partner

The classic definition of economic development includes the provision of goods and services. However, those services are seldom seen as social services. The belief that social services are something extraneous to the community is, in my view, detrimental to the rebuilding of communities and contributes to the negative view many people have of human services.

Prior to the Great Depression, social services were primarily the domain of reformers who set out either to protect individuals from the marketplace or to help those who were victims of it. Social intervention in the marketplace took several forms from the Depression through the Sixties. The Reagan revolution brought back a concept of unfettered economic growth that has wrecked havoc on cities. Therefore, one of the challenges to progressive administrations in the 1990s is to reintroduce the need for government interventions and promote the concept that social services can increase the productivity and therefore the viability of a society.

Social services employ people who earn wages that they can spend in the community. Agencies often provide services that allow more people to find work, supplying additional income for purchase of goods and services in their community. The clearest example is day care. While there is controversy around the country on how to provide day care, there is general consensus that it is needed in order to allow people to work. In America, the care of children while parents work has been viewed as external to the operations of the marketplace. In most other industrialized nations it is seen as essential.

Human services are not seen as integral to the basic functioning of a city, even though the human condition is a major factor that attracts or detracts from city life. Even education, the most basic of human services, is not held in esteem in the United States. Only within the past few years has the business community come to realize that poor urban education is having a direct impact on the ability to hire a qualified work force.

Redefining Human Services

In America, we make a distinction between "make-work" and "real work." The distinction seems arbitrary to me. I never understood why flipping hamburgers is real work and providing meals for homebound seniors is make-work unless it is done by a profit-making corporation. Day-care workers often make less money than parking lot attendants, without the possibility of receiving tips. Day care is often perceived as make-work, whereas parking lots are seen as a legitimate service.

This is especially evident in the poor neighborhoods. In many of the wealthier suburban communities, shopping malls, in addition to the stores, have recreational outlets like movies, bowling alleys, and skating rinks. There may also be health services and health clubs. Ironically, much of the infrastructure surrounding the development of shopping centers and suburban community expansion is subsidized by governments directly and through taxes. However, providing such assistance to low-income communities is seen as unprofitable or luxurious and not appropriate for government subsidy.

As I confronted the task of my first departmental budget presentation to Mayor Washington in the fall of 1984, I drew on my experience at Provident Hospital to support two priorities: maintaining existing city facilities as economic anchors to poor communities and increasing funding to community not-for-profits for local delivery of services. With a budget ravaged by federal cuts, such goals would require a redistribution of services, forging new partnerships and taking steps to build local capacity.

The Department of Human Services had roots in the War on Poverty of the 1960s and the Model Cities Program of the 1970s, and it was in charge of facilities in designated low-income communities around the city. But, over the years, the number of such facilities had dwindled significantly. The predisposition to have the city actually provide services and compete with local institutions was not contributing to the development of strong communities. Consistent funding cuts had left the department's staff demoralized and the agency inefficient.

My first challenge was the reduction of the department's budget. I had the recommendations from the previous commissioner and an audit performed by the city's Department of Personnel. Two things were immediately evident: the layoff recommendations disproportionately affected staff working in the field and were apparently compiled by job title rather than appropriate functions necessary to keep centers operational. So I revamped the staff reductions to have minimum impact on the field.

While one of Mayor Washington's major themes was a redistribution of resources to strengthen neighborhoods, the administration had not initially seen social service facilities as part of neighborhood development. In my first budget presentation to the mayor, I made the argument that facilities were critical to community stability and development. After that presentation in 1984, the department moved three facilities to more suitable quarters rather than close them. The amount of support a facility contributed to the community became a critical factor in location.

In a later controversial move made in a Hispanic community, we relocated a facility into a vacant building on a commercial strip. Part of the community objected because the corner involved had heavy drug and gang activity. Our position was that moving the city's facility to the vacant building removed the opportunity for drug sales from that site, which would have a positive impact on the situation.

Another commitment by Mayor Washington kept the construction of a city facility in the Capital Improvement Plan. When completed, the facility will represent the first time the city government has built a human service facility using local, nonfederal funds. This is more than a building; it is a statement that human services are a part of city government, not an adjunct to it. It is also an acknowledgment that they can play a role in the development and stability of communities.

Role of Not-for-Profits

My second priority was to increase funding to support the private sector of the social service community—neighborhood-based not-for-profit agencies, which I felt were the backbone of struggling neighborhoods, fighting economic exploitation while promoting community education and empowerment. During the Model Cities era, we learned that providing a new environment without the social supports did not necessarily turn a neighborhood around. Building cohesiveness, developing responsibility, sharing visions and hard work on the part of residents made the difference. At the heart of many of the successes were not-for-profits.

Investing in them makes sense because locally based community agencies are more likely to return their resources to the community and are often the last to leave. My view has consistently been that strong not-for-profits, whatever they do, help build the communities. Whatever the core services are, community-based agencies tend to become involved holistically in the surrounding area. Whether their primary function is day care or gang prevention, the nature of their services necessitates broader views and involvement. Thus, providing services at the local level through existing community-based organizations became one of the department's operating principles.

Redistribution of Services

Maintaining city-run programs while also increasing support to not-for-profits at a time of fiscal retrenchment was a tough equation. The Department of Human Services had developed over the years into an agency that both operated its own programs and funded other agencies to deliver programs, often in the same areas, without a clear reason for one or the other mode of operating.

Questions were raised about the department's fairness in making funding decisions: Were different monitoring and evaluation standards being used by the department for its own programs than for those operated by the private sector? What about the appropriateness and competence of city workers? Needless to say, the dilemma did not lead to strong planning, coordination, and advocacy for human services.

We made noncompetition with the private sector the goal. Collaboration and partnership became the operating philosophy. A general policy was adopted that the department would only run a specific program where there were no agencies capable of running that program. Also, in those instances, once a program was developed, it would be spun off as soon as possible. This gave a clear signal to the not-for-profit community that the city would not be its competitor. To be more specific, in 1984 there was $107 million coming into the Department of Human Services, including $48.5 million for direct departmental operations and $58.6 million for delegate agencies. After the policy shift went into effect, in 1986, of the total of $112 million, $47.1 million went to departmental operations and $65.4 million to delegate agencies. The increase of $7 million for delegate agencies supported 124 new agencies.

One example of how this was accomplished is in the approach to demonstration grants. The Department had run a program funded through the U.S. Department of Health and Human Services to reduce the incidence of child abuse. The basic premise was that good parenting and coping skills would reduce the incidence of child abuse and that those skills could be taught. Though the program met with some measure of success, once the demonstration ended, any attempt to replicate it or advocate for similar services was seen as a self-serving extension of departmental staff. But I believed there was another way to effectively use such demonstration grants. When an opportunity arose to establish a Headstart program for homeless children, the application was made jointly with the Salvation

Army, which already ran a shelter for women and children. The successful partnership that developed led to an advocacy program both for early childhood intervention and for help to the homeless, and it received national attention.

The department also ran a Battered Women Shelter, a Domestic Violence Court Support Program, and a Family Resource Center in the Robert Taylor Housing Development. All three were run with Department of Human Services staff. In these instances the department delivered services in a marginally acceptable fashion. There were many in the social services field who felt the department was ill prepared and without the expertise to perform the functions needed. By transferring the operational funding to not-for-profit agencies with track records in the field, we were able to improve services dramatically.

There was no question that the department had a number of talented staff; but it was trying to be all things to all people. Further, what it did best was to respond to crises, to provide immediate problem identification and response. The department was also good at identifying funds that could be applied for or that were available. It was not particularly good at the long-term, in-depth provision of services.

To some degree, staff resisted the changes, especially those who were working in special programs and felt this was a direct attack against them. However, as time went by many grew to accept the decision, some even choosing to work for the private agencies. As a result, several things began to happen: First, as new programmatic endeavors were undertaken, the agencies became a major participant in the planning and implementation. Second, there were a number of funding initiatives where joint applications were made, leading to exemplary programs. Third, a dramatic increase took place in funding community-based not-for-profits that were contributing to the economic base of their communities. Fourth, there was a dramatic improvement in the relationship between the city and the social service community.

Building Local Capacities

There was open competition for the contracts to provide services. Some of that competition was between the older, established social service agencies, many of which were predominantly white, and the newly emerging black and Hispanic agencies in the poorer communities. The experience of dealing with the city and its requirements was often more than the smaller agencies had bargained for. One of the major tasks facing our approach to redistribution of resources was the challenge of building local capacity to handle the funding and programming. There were agencies in the communities that had the basic expertise to perform the functions. However, it was not prudent for the city to fund programs and then just sit back.

I set out to organize the department to be an advocate for the agencies. My staff was directed to be ombudsmen and -women for those agencies, rather than a punitive monitor of them. Additionally, a major complaint of many of the agencies working with the city was that the system of voucher payments was too slow and cumbersome. In fact, many of the agencies continually worked at a deficit. While it was easy to claim mismanagement, the fact is that it is hard to manage without the resources to make payroll. We took several steps in response to these problems:

Technical Assistance   A special Technical Assistance unit was set up to assist agencies in the contract and vouchering process. The unit had direct working relations with the City Comptroller's Office, which actually made payments to delegates. This unit was responsible for working with agencies so that they understood up front the requirements of city funding. Manuals were revised and training sessions were held at the beginning of the contract year to ensure that agencies understood. Insurance requirements, for example, were built into the "Request for Proposal" package to avoid confusion.

Identification of Agencies at Risk   A system to identify agencies at risk was developed that focused support and monitoring on agencies having potentially serious problems in both the fiscal and programmatic area. Guidelines for programmatic monitoring were designed to identify "at risk" agencies based on reports and past monitoring visits. Consequently, some agencies were visited weekly whereas others were visited monthly, based on objective criteria.

Monitoring   Monitors were assigned to all agencies, and guidelines were developed that included a look at the fiscal issues that often led to audits problems. Monitoring in the Headstart and the day-care programs was very good, even routine. But the skills and experience in these areas had not been transferred to other operating divisions. One task was to transfer that skill and discipline, even though the function was not a directly allowable expense with funding sources. It was not an easy transformation. Even after training, many of the staff who were now assigned to monitoring did not see it as an important part of their function; rather, they saw it as administrative paperwork that got in the way of the real work.

Advance Payments   An advance payment program was initiated to assist agencies maintain cash flow. The city government normally operates on a reimbursement basis. In response to the concerns of the Headstart Directors Association, we initiated a pilot program that provided agencies which met established criteria an advance payment every month, for 95 percent of their contract, with the vouchers being used to reconcile payments over the year. We found that one of the best ways to help agencies was to ensure cash flow. It helped a number of agencies grow.

Training   The department instituted a number of training programs that were open to not-for-profit managers. A prime example is the Roosevelt University certificate course to provide training in management for not-for-profit staff. Also, we instituted an annual Emergency Service Conference aimed at improving and sharing the skills within the shelter community. Information on grant availability and training opportunities was regularly shared with the delegates.

The lesson in all this is that it takes work and innovation to improve the capacities of local agencies. In an era of dwindling resources a conscious decision has to be made to support this type of activity, and ways have to be developed to achieve this end.

Creating Internal Participatory Management

To make any of these changes work I needed to reorganize and revitalize the staff. I came to the position with a firm commitment to open up the decision-making process both within and outside of the department, consistent with the Harold Washington philosophy. I had accepted the position of commissioner only for six months. To be successful, I had to gain positive staff support and cooperation at all levels. There were more than a thousand staff at the agency, and only a handful of them were non-civil-service employees working at the pleasure of the commissioner, so changes had to be accomplished in a nonthreatening way.

I firmly believed that the only way to succeed was with a team consisting of people brought in new to the department along with those within the department who believed in a progressive, participatory approach to service delivery and advocacy. My decision to accept the job for only six months made staff recruitment difficult, and I was determined to make the department work with a minimum of upheaval. This position was not generally appreciated by some members of the new administration who were calling for an all-out purge and replacement of staff.

Establishing participatory management and shared decision making as an operating principle meant incorporating it into all actions. But this was a big challenge. I had approximately five weeks to balance the budget and implement a layoff. The staff of the Department of Human Services was primarily black, and many of them had worked for the previous administrations. They were elated to have the first black mayor, but at the same time they were the enemy. They were the patronage workers that Harold Washington talked about during the campaign. This resulted in an agency schizophrenia because the reform that was called for challenged their security and sense of worth.

But I went in with a positive attitude. The initial tone is always important, so I purposely established the initial review process to include all of the top management. A message of openness had to be sent to all staff. It required participation from all levels. There were division directors who indicated that for the first time they had been included in the decision-making process that affected their units.

I had worked with the department at one time, years ago, so I had some familiarity with the programs. The previous commissioner was not very popular, so I was successful the minute I walked in the door. I approached the department with what I call the "one-third philosophy," which I have about life. It asserts that in all things a third will be positive, a third will be negative, and a third will be in the middle. It is not original, but it works.

I found that one-third of the staff wanted change and were eager to work. I started out by asking for volunteers for task forces on programmatic issues. I just decided to send out a memo to all thousand or so staff, saying people who were interested in working on an issue should come to meetings on Saturday morning and after work. People came, and talent rose to the top. The end result was that the final leadership of the department was both from within and from without. It was not an upheaval of staff, and the method used was participatory in nature. Then, when I looked for people to bring in, I looked for people who had a set framework that was participatory and supportive of open management. The people we found fit this style, and we were able to get much of the staff excited about moving forward.

Morale and Image Improvement

Having signaled a participatory style, my next task was to do something about staff morale. Part of the morale problem related to the department's history of being the stepchild of city government, left to expand or shrink based on external forces. Part of the problem had to do with the low esteem many people have for the social service field. And part was based on how the department had been operated.

I maintained an open-door policy. I worked long hours alongside of staff and let it be known that I would meet with anyone who asked to meet with me. An appointment was necessary, and all appropriate administrative or personnel options had to have been explored.

Morale was helped by the fact that it was public knowledge that Harold Washington wanted me. The department began to be looked to for leadership and direction on city issues beyond those of the department itself. There were a number of task forces and work groups working on city policy and administration. Not only were individual commissioners part of the process, but the departments were represented in a number of avenues. I was a visible part of the management team for the city. I was part of the mayor's policy council, and when I was appointed chair of the community services subcabinet, it gave the entire department a morale boost.

Reorganization

I decided to have regular staff meetings, including sessions of all staff together. We set up a structure that required people to talk to each other. There was no question that there was overlapping of geography and focus. There is no way to isolate or compartmentalize human beings or their lives. No matter how you describe or delineate the categories, there will always be another way to look at the same issue and there is no simple right or wrong.

Is a family on the street with small children an emergency service case, a case management responsibility, or people requiring emergency food? To complicate the case, if they are victims of or part of a gang, do they belong as part of the Intervention Network programming? Current theory focuses on client-oriented organizational structures rather than service-oriented approaches. Our approach was probably somewhere in between. Interdivisional task forces and shared responsibilities became a way of operation. Those staff who were used to isolated action were not happy with this approach, and there were drawbacks in that in some cases there was no clear delineation of responsibility, a classic no-no in management theory.

However, the internal task forces became an established process by which programs were developed and problems solved, and this had a number of advantages. Staff bought into the problem solving. When we went through the agonizing process of improving the Home Energy Assistance Program, which had all but collapsed, staff became part of the solution rather than merely being defensive about a program that was not working.

As we moved to improve operations in the field, the concept of task forces and participation became more of the norm. This approach was used to improve black–Hispanic tensions in the agency and other problems related to program monitoring and management. A major antidrug program and a new youth initiative were also developed through this approach. By the time I left, the department had an internal structure in place that avoids program and staff autonomy and that requires people to talk.

Establishing a Mission

The development of a unified vision and mission for the department was necessary to pull the operations together and to promote collective action. It was a way to bring focus to the department and make sense of the reorganization. I decided that I would use the annual city budget process for that purpose.

The city allocation represented about 10 percent of the total budget, and the annual budget process had traditionally only related to that portion. The annual budget presentation to the mayor and later to the city council had not been seen as a point for discussion or disclosure. As part of his reform actions, Mayor Washington disclosed all federal and state funding during the annual budget process. Using this process to give focus to a department that was primarily federally funded, however, had not been done. To complicate matters, the Department of Human Services was funded by seven major grants with four different fiscal years, and there was no guarantee of funding from any of the sources.

Because of all this, staff of the various programs were to a great degree isolated, focusing on their programs and not seeing how they fit into a whole. The programmatic task forces I established not only developed leadership but also began to identify commonly shared goals. One of the first themes to develop was "To Protect the Child." This was followed by "To Help Victims"; "To Strengthen Families"; and "To Develop Youth," added a year later. These themes encompassed most of the programs of the department. A number of programs within the department were slightly restructured to fit the theme, and some new approaches were added.

We focused initially on To Protect the Child. There was no additional money, so we had to look outside the department for support. We enlisted the support of WBBM-TV to host a breakfast to initiate the program, and with the cooperation of a number of businesses, most noticeably Illinois Bell, we were able to put together a "safe child kit" for mass distribution, as well as improve the child abuse library and make it available beyond the day-care centers to all youth-serving agencies. A number of other initiatives fell into place, including a program to promote the use of fire detectors in the home and safety seats for automobiles. In each case, both internal and external partnerships began to develop. Thus, the clearer sense of mission dovetailed with the emphasis on participation, both through internal task forces and through the changed relationships with outside agencies.

Special Projects and Concerns

Increasing the department's neighborhood presence, improving not-for-profit funding, tackling the budget and staff reductions, and overseeing its reorganization would be enough work for most managers. But as my six-month commitment to Mayor Washington stretched into the length of his term in office, I found myself taking on other concerns. These included four areas of particular interest: the homeless, legislative initiatives, policymaking, and crime and youth.

Mayor's Task Force on the Homeless

The Mayor's Task Force on the Homeless was originally established in 1983 under the leadership of Elizabeth Hollander, commissioner of planning, in response to the rising incidence of homeless people in Chicago. Its November 1984 report raised a number of issues that needed continued attention, particularly by my department, including: community opposition to shelters; grant award procedures; the need for rehabilitation of existing shelters; creation of more shelter beds; and provision of resources, equipment, and technical assistance for shelter operators.

One of the major concerns of the task force was its continued existence and ability to influence the mayor. It had taken a year for the task force to develop some level of confidence in the city and its new leadership. The commissioner of planning felt that the workings of the task force had clearly crossed over into the implementation phase and that operations should be housed in a line department.

For many years the Department of Human Services had run an emergency service program that started out as a response to fires and evictions and had grown over the years to cover a number of other crisis situations. Almost all of the shelters and advocates from the homeless community had some contact with staff over the years and had developed a negative attitude. There was open hostility toward the department and its past relationship to the shelter community and toward the suggestion that I take the leadership of the Mayor's Task Force on the Homeless.

There were some very legitimate concerns about the possibility that there would be decreased importance and emphasis put on the activities of the task force once its work was placed within a line department. Also, the fact that I was only to be an interim commissioner made people unsure of my intentions. There also were some less legitimate concerns that I was insincere about improving the operations of the department and its relationship to the social service community.

After looking at our options, Commissioner Hollander and I decided not to force the issue and proceed gradually. I was concerned that the support from the Planning Department would abate once the leadership was shifted. I was assured that this would not happen. In October 1984 I hosted a luncheon of all shelter providers in anticipation of the upcoming winter season, to share with them our priorities and to begin the process of building relationships and trust.

This luncheon has, over the years, turned into an annual Emergency Services Conference held in the fall of each year to bring staff and shelter providers together for training, information sharing, and skill enhancements. This effort of reaching out to the providers was coupled with the response to those concerns we could handle. For a period of time, Commissioner Hollander and I cochaired the task force, and by March 1985, when the mayor announced that I had agreed to stay on, the transfer of its leadership seemed more of a natural evolution and was readily accepted.

Since 1985, the Mayor's Task Force on the Homeless has made significant improvements in the number of shelter beds. Also, a system of Warming Centers coordinated through the Inter-Faith Council was implemented during the winter months, and there has been an increase in funding to more than $3 million from the corporate budget in direct funding for shelters and another $1 million in emergency food resources. A number of innovative programs were added, including a Coordinated Clearing House and a toll-free hotline.

Equally important, Mayor Washington became an outspoken advocate for the homeless on the national level, and I worked on several major committees to improve conditions and produce more understanding of the issue of homelessness. Together, we developed an approach that focused on prevention and a common advocacy.

The Legislative Network

By late 1985, it became clear that the posture of the department was to encourage participatory decision making and implementation of programs. The Mayor's Task Force on the Homeless had been operating and expanding. Also, several legislative efforts on the state level had been implemented to increase funding for day care and for welfare grants. It was clear that there were a number of advocacy efforts under way and that often one group did not know what the other group was doing and why.

We decided to establish a legislative network by having monthly brown-bag luncheons, inviting all of the intergovernmental staff from major social service agencies, as well as some of the advocate groups that work regularly in the social service community. The purpose of the meetings was to exchange information on a regular basis. This type of informal advisory structure made the advocacy community part of the department's operation without creating cumbersome structures. It provided for an extension of the open government policy established by Mayor Washington.

The luncheons also were instrumental in the development of policies for the Work, Welfare, and Families coalition, whose platform became the focus for the advocacy for welfare reform actions finally undertaken by the State of Illinois in the late 1980s. It became the springboard for ideas to improve the social service delivery system in Chicago.

But in trying to bring this new agenda into the legislative arena with our new partners, we encountered another problem. New federal restrictions on not-for-profit lobbying had put a stranglehold on community agencies and coalitions. Proponents of the restrictions always point to the day-care lobby or the Headstart lobby as an example of people being self-serving, using tax dollars to influence the spending of tax dollars. I look at it differently.

It is grossly unfair to pit poor people against the defense lobby and say that their organizations cannot use tax monies to influence government in their favor. Defense contractors can lobby government officials and claim a legitimate business expense. Yet, poor people are expected to pay for such activities out of their already limited incomes. The expectation that they can, from a deficit position, raise money to advocate for their survival is grossly unfair.

It became clear that there was a need to put money into advocacy and community education. Our legislative network allowed groups to do some things they could not do under current resources. Thus, it became clear that in order for human services to survive, advocacy had to be a continuing part of our work.

Setting Policy

The progressive agenda called for government intervention and responsibility in many areas such as health, day care, and welfare. Although not articulated in this precise fashion, the election of Harold Washington signaled a reentrance of government into dealing with some of the basic human issues. The main constituency that elected him had major expectations that he could make changes in their lives in terms of health, housing, education, and employment.

The policy framework for the department was partly set by the administration in terms of openness, fairness, participatory style, and focus on neighborhoods. It was further refined by a belief in self-determination I shared with Harold Washington. But, to a greater extent, programmatic policy was established by the funding sources that provided the resources to operate the department. Of the approximately $115 million dollars that constituted the department's operating budget, I had flexibility on less than 15 percent.

In reality, my agenda and programmatic thrust was more often than not formulated by the media. A youth is shot by gang members—do something immediately! A homeless man freezes—do something immediately! Calls for action and resource development were stimulated by the nightly news. While most of us understood the complexities of the problems facing the cities and the poor, and regularly sought funding to deal with them, we seldom could get attention or additional resources unless there was a news bite. It is extremely difficult for government to plan comprehensively and systematically for the development of human services. There are two fundamental reasons for this:

First, the money is controlled by a philosophy of "let's cut back and reduce the waste," as opposed to resolving problems. The answer to most problems is costly, and we seem to believe that we can put it off until tomorrow. Whether this philosophy is merely a selfish response or whether there is some other explanation, there is a disinclination to spend money on prevention and long-term investment. Both are essential in the human services field.

Secondly, we have developed a system of societal response that is trendy. It calls for a quick fix, but most social problems have grown over many years and take years to resolve. In contrast to the 1970s, when comprehensive planning was in vogue and management by objectives was seen as the way to manage, people want the simplistic solution. Just say no! Too often, unfortunately, human service policy is driven by media attention. The challenge for cities is to be in a position to take advantage of press interest—or to stimulate that interest. The Chicago Intervention Network grew out of just such a situation.

Chicago Intervention Network

In November 1984, Benji Wilson, a prominent black high school basketball star, was killed in a senseless act of youth violence. Through the spotlight of media attention came a hue and cry from the community for the city to "do something about the issue." The problems of youth gangs and delinquent behavior have existed in Chicago for generations. Trying to draw attention to these problems in a comprehensive orderly fashion had proved futile.

Benji Wilson's murder captured the full attention of the media as well as the warring factions of the city council, where the opposition was intent on embarrassing and hamstringing the administration. Members of the opposition were calling for increasing the police force, ridiculing the position taken by the administration, which sought to hold the line on police costs. Mayor Washington responded by establishing the Mayor's Task Force on Youth Crime Prevention to develop a programmatic response to the issue. There was immediate agreement to set aside resources in the corporate budget. However, there was no agreement on what approach should be taken, how the money should be spent, or which city department would manage it.

The task force was established to represent the full spectrum of the city, including all relevant governmental agencies, the private sector, and representatives of the communities most affected. It was decided that the task force would be staffed primarily by the Department of Human Services and the Mayor's Office.

Since the problem is different in each neighborhood around the city, hearings were held in each of the 24 police districts. More than 2000 people participated, sharing successful programs in their areas and offering to volunteer. The consensus was that the response to the problem was not to be found in police action alone. To a great extent the problem was how to get the community to accept responsibility and buy into the solution.

The task force presented specific proposals, and there was great pressure on the administration to move quickly or be doomed to criticisms of footdragging and indecisiveness. There was also pressure from the city council for quick action; many of those calling for action were members of the opposition pressing to fund programs in agencies not under the mayor's control, such as the state's attorney, the city colleges, and the Chicago Board of Education.

Even while holding to the concepts of citizen participation, the task force had developed a comprehensive program that responded to the majority of the concerns of the neighborhoods by March 1985. It included street intervention workers, victim assistance, alternative youth programming through locally based youth-serving agencies, and the development of neighborhood watch activities. To continue citizen and governmental involvement, the Chicago Intervention Network (CIN) Coordinating Committee and nine neighborhood advisory councils were established.

Though the CIN Coordinating Committee focused much of the program on prevention, there were others who urged intervention and mediation with the so-called hard-core gang members. In the Black community, gangs had been institutionalized to such an extent that turf-related violence was not the major problem. There, the violence was often related to drug activity and weapons trafficking. But in the Hispanic community, the gangs were newly formed and there was turf-related violence, again in most instances related to drug trafficking. There was often tension within the advisory structure as to what was the best approach. In the end, the preventive focus won out.

During the early days of the program there was continued criticism from the press and city council opposition because the $4 million program had not in six months solved all of the city's gang and youth problems. To a significant degree it was the steadfast involvement and support of the advisory structure that enabled the continuation of the program. As the CIN program matured, there were a number of improvements made as a direct result of advisory committee deliberations, including deployment of staff, incorporation of additional high-risk communities, implementation of a safe school zone and an anti-graffiti component, and restructuring of the mobile units.

Many community-based agencies that received CIN funding also became involved in the coordination effort consistent with a commitment to the participatory decision making. CIN has awakened communities to take back their neighborhoods from the gangs and stands to have a lasting effect on the way this type of problem is addressed in the future. Implementing a broad array of crime prevention strategies through local agencies with the expertise to do them strengthens communities. The city does not have to do it all by itself.

Lessons Learned

The Harold Washington years had a dramatic effect on government and Chicago. The man was bigger than life and embodied a spirit and vision for the city. His leadership set the tone on issues basic to human dignity, as well as fairness, openness, and good government. Perhaps the first lesson learned is that good government goes beyond the efficient and effective management of city services. It includes setting the parameters and purpose of those services and the manner in which they are delivered.

We learned that development of partnerships committed to change can make a difference. And that a key element to success is the willingness to listen, take chances, and try things that were suggested. We were able to accomplish the Warming Center program and the toll-free hotline in the homeless arena because someone in a meeting suggested the approach as a solution. Rather than saying why we couldn't do it, we said let's try.

From the CIN experience, we learned that one could have a process within city government that included broad-based decision making and participation and that it could be done quickly and efficiently. We were in a position to take advantage of press attention to an issue and implement programs consistent with the fundamental views of the administration. We were able to do both of these in large part because we had the citizen outreach mechanisms in place and a commitment that we get something done.

Another important lesson is that change can be made without dramatic upheaval, especially when you are dealing with large organizations or bureaucracies. Change can be accomplished by melding old with new, identifying from within those that have a predisposition to the change— and there will undoubtedly be some there. Also, forcing contact with outside actors by establishing partnerships creates a teamwork approach to solving problems and delivering services. Outside agencies gain respect for the organization and the direction it is going, a dynamic that will force and enforce change. The staff will see the movement. People naturally tend to go with a winner, and to fight the change is seen by most people as destructive.

Perhaps the hardest lesson learned was that it is extremely difficult to change public opinion on social issues regardless of the facts. Human service issues, more so that any other area, are clouded with emotion. It is very difficult to change that emotion. When you can make change, it takes time and it is costly. For example, everybody wants immediate action and quick response to do something about the homeless, as long it is "not in my back yard." There was great resistance to services when they were located in a community. After the advocates, religious community, and staff worked in a neighborhood for months, and sometimes years, they were able to gain acceptance and even support.

Resistance was also felt against sufficient allocation of resources for human services. Everybody wants somebody to do something about social problems, but nobody wants to pay for it. We were unable to increase funding much, except at crisis points. So we had to be prepared to take advantage of those points when they arose.

One of the things I set out to do was to get back the funding to not-for-profit agencies. We were very successful, and we learned, or relearned, that the not-for-profits usually made a contribution to the community bigger than just the service paid for. It was possible to set up mechanisms that were responsive and responsible. We were able to protect the public's investment while being innovative and flexible. These community-based agencies were the backbone of the communities and by redistributing services back out to the communities, we saw some increased stability of the economic base for the community.

Finally, I started out, as a child, clearly understanding the impact of race and racial prejudice. I grew up knowing about racism. I believed that education and doing "right" would overcome it. After all, there were examples of individual African-Americans who made it. I then began my career in the days of the Great Society, which essentially dealt with race and class. It aimed to tear down the institution of discrimination and compensate for the inequalities of poverty. The individual could then make it.

In the 1970s, I believed that there was some rational economic approach to solving the problems of the city. I believed that concentrated incentives could create stabilization and growth where there had been disinvestment and that, with the appropriate support and training, all communities and citizens had a chance to make their communities whole. Essentially, I believed that race was not the issue; the real issue was a lack of resources and opportunity.

I have come back to the belief that fundamental to the fabric of life in America is racism and classism. Both shape the public and private policies that guide this nation. The reason we have poor people is because we live in a capitalistic society, which by definition places higher value on those who have capital than on those who don't. What we learned in the 1970s was that we could not, in a comprehensive, holistic fashion, respond to the needs of *all* the citizens without challenging the basic economic structure of the country.

In the 1980s, America began readjusting its economy downward. Providing for the health and welfare of its citizens cut into the profitability of its industries. There was a resistance to government intervention direct or indirect. The policies of deregulation and reduced social programs implemented during the Reagan years have had profound impact on the human fabric of our nation and the problems facing progressive city administrations. Industries were downsized and salaries reduced. More low-income jobs were produced. At the same time astronomical wages were being paid corporate executives and mind-boggling profits made in leveraged buyouts. We have a minimum wage that does not provide for basic survival.

We enter the 1990s with a growing schism between the haves and the have-nots. An outright attack on affirmative action resulted in the acceptance of racism and indifference to the impact of racism on the people. We see the impact in increased racial tension in cities and an abandonment of those programs and services that could make a difference. We have not been able to shift public attention and support to the less fortunate. We have, in fact, become more strident in our negative attitudes toward them.

The final lesson that we have not yet learned is that we, as a nation, must take better care of the poor since they are an integral part of the economic base and ultimate stability of this country. And that elimination of racism is essential to economic stability and national security. The Harold Washington years began to deal with these issues and showed that you could have a fiscally responsible government that was fair and cared.

The Commission on Latino Affairs: A Case Study of Community Empowerment

MARÍA DE LOS ANGELES TORRES

On October 5, 1983, fifteen Latino community leaders who had actively campaigned for Harold Washington held a press conference in the press room of the second floor of city hall to announce that they were forming a Commission on Latino Affairs. The night before, as we had sat in Juan Velázquez's office in Pilsen, a representative of the Mayor's Office had threatened that we would "fall out of bed with the mayor" if we went to the press. Yet we knew that the mayor's support in the Latino community—which some credited with his April victory—was quickly eroding as months had passed and many campaign promises remained unfulfilled. For us, it was the integrity of the independent movement in our communities that was at stake. Despite a phone call from the mayor at midnight asking us to delay our plans, we decided to proceed. Days later, Mayor Harold Washington signed an executive order creating a Mayor's Commission on Latino Affairs.

This chapter will explore the background of the independent political movement in the Latino community; analyze the emergence of the black/Latino electoral alliance that led to the 1983 election of Harold Washington; and, through the experiences of the Commission on Latino Affairs, discuss key events that allowed the Latino community to have an impact on the city's reform agenda. In conclusion, it will reflect on the lessons learned and on the political future of Latinos in Chicago in the aftermath of Harold Washington's death.

Background

To most observers, Chicago is a black and white city, especially when it comes to its politics. Race has been the medium through which larger issues of municipal reform, economic development, and democracy are played out. Yet, between black and white, other communities have emerged that are bidding for a space within the city's political arena. One such community is the Latino community.

According to the U.S. Census Bureau, 8.1 percent of the U.S. population—some 19.4 million people—are of Latin American origin.[1] Census estimates project that by the year 2010 the Latino community will number more than 30 million, making it the largest minority in the United States. In 1986, a Chicago-based research and advocacy group, the Latino Institute, estimated that Latinos constituted 19.1 percent of the city's population and that by the year 2010 Latinos would be a third of Chicago's population.[2] Today, the community is one of the most diverse in the world: Mexicans make up about 57 percent; Puerto Ricans, 25 percent; Cubans, 2 percent; Central and South Americans, 7 percent; and the fastest growing sector, children of multinational marriages, 8 percent.

Beyond national differences, deep economic, political, and social cleavages accentuate the diversity among Latinos. Distinct immigrant generations add to the complicated texture of the community. And geographic disparity fuels the turf-minded political divisions so characteristic of Chicago politics.

Despite these differences, the communities do share a common language, some culture, and—perhaps most importantly—discrimination and political marginalization. These commonalities have contributed to the emergence of "the Latino," an ethnic/political category that has facilitated the joining of these disparate communities into a bloc that has come together at certain political junctures.[3] These two seemingly contradictory realities—diversity and attraction—have been the backdrop that highlights the political development of Latinos in Chicago.

The national press heralded the 1980s as the decade of the Latino. Burgeoning population numbers, minority rights legislation, and increasing nationwide registration numbers had established Latinos as an important political force in the country. An unprecedented number of Latinos had been elected to office, and three major cities had Latino mayors. Yet, Latinos in Chicago were far removed from the local seats of political power. While electoral mobilization characterized Latino politics outside of Chicago, the lack of meaningful possibilities for community political empowerment in the electoral arena had caused young Latino political activists in Chicago to adopt other strategies. They were more concerned with building community organizations and with U.S.–Latin American relations.

In the Mexican community, the most active and progressive organization was CASA, HGT (Central de Acción Social Autónoma, por la Hermandad General de Trabajadores). Founded in 1968, this national organization's original purpose was to unify the struggles of Mexicans in the United States and in Mexico. One of its aims was to protect the rights of undocumented workers. Years after the national organization had disappeared, Chicago's chapter was still active, concentrating on providing services to the community, working with student organizations, and advocating immigration reform. Individuals like Rudy Lozano, Art Vázquez, Linda Coronado, Jesús García, and Juan Soliz were all active in CASA. Other activists like Juan Velázquez had been community and labor organizers since the 1960s. Later, they were to become the leadership of the progressive electoral movement in the Mexican community. In Puerto Rican neighborhoods, community activists and Puerto Rican independence supporters had built a strong base through the West Town Coalition of Concerned Citizens. This advocacy group had succeeded in bringing together community organizers and progressives into one organization. The Reverend Jorge Morales, its first president, became one of Harold Washington's principal supporters in this community, along with Peter Earle, María Cerda, and José ("Cha-Cha") Jiménez. The Cuban-Americans, like myself, who were involved in the Harold Washington campaign, had come from the movement to better relations with Cuba and the Democratic party. Colombians, Central Americans, and Chileans like Rodrigo del Canto and Neri and Lucía Barrientos, who were active in the campaign had concentrated their efforts on building support for the antimilitary movements in their countries. Electoral politics was not the principal form of struggle for Latinos in Chicago.

Prior to 1983, no Latinos had been elected as members of the city council (aldermen). Only 2 percent of city employees were Latino, only two Latino-owned firms had been awarded municipal contracts, barely a handful of Latinos had been appointed to serve on major boards and commissions, and there was no specific office established to advocate for the needs of Latinos.

In four years following Harold Washington's mayoral victory, these trends were reversed. By 1987, four Latinos sat in the city council chambers, more than 5 percent of city employees were Latino,[4] 8 percent of city contract dollars were going to Latino-owned firms, 20 percent of those serving on major boards and commissions were Latino, and there was a Mayor's Commission on Latino Affairs.[5]

The conceptual framework for understanding the transition from community progressive politics to an electoral urban reform movement includes three major components: minority political empowerment (the goal), coalitions (the method), and urban municipal reform (the agenda). These three interrelated phenomena arise from a group's desire to live and participate in a society free of inequalities and to have a responsive government. In the 1950s and 1960s, blacks and Latinos in the United States organized and mobilized to demand social, political, and economic equality. As a result of this pressure, political space was created in the 1970s and 1980s that allowed for increased minority representation. The intensification of the struggle to create structures that facilitate equal political representation of minority groups and mobilize minority communities to take advantage of openings in that political space is known as the movement for minority political empowerment.

In the case of Chicago, the movement for minority political empowerment involved a unique political coalition of various minority communities and progressive whites committed to a fairer city. The coalition manifested itself in several forms: between blacks, Latinos, and progressive whites; and among Latinos.

The political demand from minority communities in Chicago went beyond a call for equal representation to include a reform agenda for municipal government. Recalling the classic municipal reform agenda, Chicago's reform agenda of the 1980s called for professional and efficient government, yet it incorporated two new features as strategic objectives: fairness in the distribution of municipal services, and opportunities and democratization of decision making in city hall. This made Chicago's reform agenda distinctive. It also made the leaders that called for this agenda and the coalition progressive, for they challenged not only the outcomes and methods of politics but also the underlying assumptions about the economic and political system. While they became part of the political system during Harold Washington's administration, they did not come from the political machine but rather from community organizations that had vehemently fought against the machine and from progressive movements in each community, thus bringing a broader vision of politics and change.

Genesis of the Latino/Black Political Coalition

Despite Latinos' long-term presence in Chicago, the city's political machine had practically ignored this community. During Mayor Richard J. Daley's administration, a loose network of Latino families known as "Amigos for Daley" would periodically appear before elections. Daley made a few Latino appointments to the Board of Education and one to the Regional Transit Authority (RTA), and he retained a Latino liaison in his office. A number of Latinos were slated for citywide posts, like Cook County Board Commissioner Irene Hernández, but they were not part of the powerful political machinery nor were they slated for aldermanic seats.

It was not until the Jane Byrne administration that Latino leaders called for independent political activity in coalition with the black community. This occurred at two levels: one through community struggles, the other in the electoral arena. Latino and black interests came together on a range of issues: affirmative action in city employment and contract, defense of communities against developers, education, and some foreign policy issues.[6] This coalition was further solidified by President Ronald Reagan's assault on poor communities. Since the federal government allowed states to decide where to make budgetary cuts, national opposition was minimized. It made local organizing the only strategy left for poor communities to pursue. In Chicago, this contributed to the progressive movement's emphasis on gaining local political control at a time when the national government was taken over by the political right.

In the electoral arena, blacks and Latinos coalesced in 1981 to challenge the state's redistricting. But it was Jane Byrne's blatant gerrymandering of Latino and black neighborhoods in redrawing the city council districts in 1981 that consolidated these efforts. Black and Latino activists came together to sue the city and seek redress through the courts for new ward boundaries and special elections, which were finally held in 1986.

This joint effort led to a series of initiatives. One was the formation of a citywide alliance called the Black/Latino Alliance for Progressive Politics.[7] The other was the launching of two Latino independent candidacies for state representative in the 1982 elections, one on the North Side, the other in the Near West Side.

In 1982, North Side activists called for a community political assembly that endorsed an independent candidate, José Salgado. Unfortunately, Salgado did not survive the machine's challenge to his nominating petitions. Nevertheless, these efforts did not go unnoticed at City Hall. Jane Byrne named Joseph (José) Martínez to the 31st ward aldermanic seat. And to appease regular Democrat State Senator Edward Nedza, who had supported another candidate, Joseph Berrios, she slated him for the state representative slot that the community had wanted to fill with a politically independent representative. Byrne's actions forced Puerto Rican activists into a more complicated political struggle in which the issue became not only one of no Latino representation but rather one in which machine Latinos had to be distinguished from independent Latinos.

Events on the West Side unfolded a little differently. There, community activists had a more cohesive base organization, CASA. This organization endorsed one of its members, Juan Soliz, an immigration lawyer who had made his name by defending the rights of undocumented workers, to run for state representative of the 20th district. The machine regulars on the West Side endorsed Marco Domico, an Italian precinct captain in 25th ward Alderman Vito Marzullo's regular Democratic organization. Therefore, the electoral fight that ensued was more clearly defined along ethnic lines. The regulars had Soliz disqualified in the primary, but he ran as an independent in the general election of November 1982, garnering 33 percent of the vote. Soliz had been endorsed by the Black/Latino Alliance for Progressive Politics as well as Harold Washington, the new black South Side congressman from the 1st congressional district. These political milestones in the Latino community laid the foundation for the 1983 aldermanic and mayoral races. Whereas from 1963 to 1982 only thirteen Latinos had entered aldermanic races, in 1983 eleven Latinos made it on the ballot.[8]

Latinos and the 1983 Mayoral Race

In late 1982, after four years of joint community and political struggles, blacks and Latinos entered a mayoral challenge that was to change race and power relations in Chicago as well as fundamentally redefine the acceptable and expected political discourse. Unquestionably, the main force behind the movement to take power at city hall was the black community, which had reached a consensus on a single candidate, Congressman Harold Washington. The congressman only accepted on the condition that a massive voter registration drive be launched. While this drive fell short of its goal, Harold Washington announced his candidacy for the Democratic party's mayoral nomination in mid-November.

In the Latino community, it was activists from the Mexican and Puerto Rican community along with progressive Cuban-Americans who first called a series of meetings to line up support for Washington. In the Mexican community, Rudy Lozano's aldermanic campaign in the 22nd ward and Juan Velázquez's in the 25th provided the precinct structure for Harold Washington's campaign. In West Town and Humboldt Park, community activists were coordinated by the Reverend Jorge Morales. In Logan Square, José ("Cha-Cha") Jiménez, an unsuccessful earlier aldermanic candidate, coordinated the district for Washington.

Most of us had at one point or another been invited to participate in breakfast meetings in the homes of black activists. In early November, friends of mine from the Third World Foundation organized a breakfast meeting. Congressman Harold Washington spoke to a group of about twenty and laid out his ideas about his mayoral bid. I remember asking him how he planned to bring in Latinos. He responded that Latinos were going to play a key role in his campaign and that he had recently met with Rudy Lozano to see how this could best be done. Lozano had come to the campaign through the labor movement, others like the Reverend Morales, the black/Latino political alliance, and myself through Latin American solidarity work and university colleagues.

Early on, we decided that we needed a high-level Latino in the campaign structure. Despite repeated requests for a person to be named as head of Latino Operations, critical months passed and it was not until twenty days before the primary that Renault Robinson named Linda Coronado to head Latino Operations. She had been the director of Mujeres Latinas, the only social advocacy agency for women in the Latino community.

Most of the established Latino community organizations were reluctant to openly support Harold Washington. The business sector was squarely behind the incumbent, and the young professionals in the Latino community were backing Richard M. Daley, the former mayor's son. Nevertheless, a group of Latino activists began meeting and volunteering at the campaign headquarters. We made sure that we had people in the precinct operations and the issues committee.

The issues that had brought these Latinos to the Harold Washington campaign included his support for bilingual education, his fight against federal cutbacks of social programs, his opposition to the Simpson–Mazolli Immigration Bill, his advocacy for peace in Central America, his vote against Radio Martí, and his successful floor fight against Reagan's attempt to dilute the Voting Rights Act. Through this last action, Harold Washington had consolidated his relations with key national Latino leaders, who encouraged local Latinos to support him. The Latino network worked with the issues committee to further define Washington's position in regards to neighborhood improvements and local control of government.

According to a Midwest Voter Registration and Education Project's exit poll, more than 66,000 Latinos, or 68.6 percent of those registered, turned out to vote in the Democratic primary.[9] Of those interviewed: 12.7 percent said they voted for Harold Washington, 34.5 percent for Richard M. Daley, and 51.4 percent for Jane Byrne. In the primary race, support for Washington was stronger from the Mexican community than from other communities, partly as a result of the stronger precinct organization of the aldermanic candidates that endorsed Washington. Rudy Lozano came within 17 votes of forcing Frank Stemberk into a runoff, and Juan Velázquez received 42 percent of the vote in Marzullo's infamous 25th ward. Both independent candidates received a majority of black votes in their wards. Harold Washington won more than 79 percent of the vote in the black community, and with a small percentage of liberal Lakefront votes, became the Democratic party's nominee for mayor.[10]

Between February and April 1983, there was a political realignment in the Latino community. The progressives who had organized Washington's primary campaign successfully brought into their camp most of the young professionals and party regulars who had supported Daley. The Latino leadership aligned with Byrne transferred its support to Bernard Epton, the Republican party's nominee.

Washington's campaign committee facilitated the entrance of Latinos. Latinos were added to the Campaign Steering Committee. The Issues Committee, the Special Events Committee and the Press Committee hired Latino staff. Latino operations was made part of precinct coordination. In precinct operations, two Latinos were hired to interface with the operations in the neighborhood. However, requests to hire a Latino to a high-level position in the campaign were never honored.

In a shift from the primary, most of the Latino media endorsed Harold Washington. The only exception was APLI (Asociación de Periodistas y Locutores), an association at that time controlled by right-wing Cuban reporters. Along with the Cuban-American Chamber of Commerce and various operatives of the machine, this group organized Epton's campaign in the Latino community. An inflammatory leaflet stating that "Baboons are going to take over City Hall" and that "Harold Washington was a child molester" was traced back to a member of the Board of the Cuban-American Chamber of Commerce, who was later ostracized for this activity.[11]

No formal "Latino Committee" was ever established within the Washington campaign. Latinos working within the campaign formed an informal caucus that met two times a week. The network among Latinos was too new, and those on the steering committee did not want to formalize a structure in such fluid circumstances.

Nonetheless, there was a consensus reached on a "Latino Platform." This included: a call for affirmative action in contracts, hiring, and appointments; a request that one of the five proposed deputy mayors be Latino; and a call for neighborhood-oriented economic development and the establishment of a Commission on Latino Affairs.

This last idea had emerged from our need to build a structure that could continue to bring us together as well as to stand up for the needs of the Latino community. In March, Maurice Ferre, former mayor of Miami, had come to Chicago to campaign for Harold Washington. We had gathered a group of Latinos from the various communities to brief him on the campaign and tell him about their community. At one point, he asked each person to identify their nationality. Almost every major Latin American and Caribbean country was present. Someone made a point that we needed to continue this exchange among ourselves even after the campaign. In part, the idea of the commission grew from this need. In early April, a Latino Unity Dinner was held, and Harold Washington endorsed the Latino Platform and promised to establish a Commission on Latino Affairs.

Latino voters responded to the Washington appeals by casting an overwhelming number of votes for him on election day. According to the Midwest Voter Registration and Education Project, 62.2 percent of those registered voted. This election, Puerto Ricans (82.3 percent) favored Harold Washington in a higher proportion than Mexicans did (62.7 percent). Surprisingly, 48.2 percent of Cuban-Americans interviewed also said that they voted for Washington. In total, 75.3 percent of Latinos reported voting for Harold Washington.[12] This translated into approximately 45,000 votes. Harold Washington won the election by 51,000 votes. According to Abdul Alkalimat and Doug Gills, "the dramatic turnabout in the Latino vote [was] the key aspect of the general election voter mobilization, which provided Washington's campaign with its margin of victory."[13]

While Latinos gave Washington the margin of victory, his campaign had profound political impact on the Latino community. First, his campaign legitimized the progressive sector of the various Latino communities. Since progressives were the first to join the political coalition, they in turn were credited with the victory, thus providing them with a political legitimacy they had not enjoyed in the past. Secondly, this new political leadership was one that was rooted in progressive community struggles, and therefore the issues that they put forth were ones that would fundamentally change the relationship between city hall and the community. Thirdly, the campaign had provided both a structure and a purpose by which the various sectors of the Latino community came to know and work with each other. For the first time, Latino progressives had built a solid and profound relationship with each other that showed that unity could have dramatic political successes. All this combined to change the political expectations of Latinos as well as the political discourse in the community.

Governance and Politics: Latinos and Harold Washington's First Term

From the Neighborhood to City Hall

A grass-roots movement elected Harold Washington, but his administration was dominated by a more bureaucratic and elitist style. The different styles of the new bureaucrats and the expectations of the Latino organizers of the Washington campaign came into conflict. Very few Latinos were named to the "blue-ribbon task forces" or to the Transition Team. None of the committees were headed by Latinos. The administration contracted a "talent" agency to screen résumés generated by the campaign, and none of the Latinos who submitted theirs were found eligible for jobs at city hall.

The larger political context at city hall was defined by the attempts of the organized opposition in the city council to block the mayor's program. This faction included 28 white aldermen and the first Latino to be elected to the city council, Miguel Santiago, who was loyal to the machine.[14] Within the bureaucracy, the mayor found very few loyal supporters among the 41,000 city employees.

In the Latino community, the political coalition that had emerged during the campaign fractured as a result of the competition for high-level positions by members of the leadership. These three situations—the elitism of the new bureaucrats, the difficult political conditions, and the disunity among Latinos—helped create tension between Latinos and Mayor Washington. In the first three months of the administration, the mayor made no major Latino appointments. By this time, much of the support that had been garnered in the community was lost.

In the summer of 1983, Rudy Lozano, the mayor's closest advisor in the Latino community, was shot and killed in the kitchen of his home.[15] Weeks before his killing, he had testified before the National Labor Relations Board that several tortilla factories on the West Side were bringing indentured slaves from Mexico. Lozano had come within 17 votes of a runoff election for alderman of his ward. After the election, he had been central to Latino effort to develop a community network that could both defend the mayor's programs and pressure the mayor into fulfilling his promises.

Rudy's death helped galvanize the leaders of the Latino community. After Rudy's death, Juan Velázquez and the Reverend Morales took the lead in continuing Rudy's efforts. We alternated between meeting at San Lucas' church in West Town and Velázquez's office on 18th Street. Jesús García, Art Vázquez, Carmen Velásquez, Miguel del Valle, Juan Montenegro, Ada López, Peter Earle, Carmelo Rodriguez, Daniel Ramos, José ("Cha-Cha") Jiménez, and I continued to organize and to meet with the mayor. (In the interim, Art Vázquez and Peter Earle became deputies in the Departments of Economic Development and Neighborhoods, respectively, and left the group. Mario Aranda and Linda Coronado took their places. We did not want to have people on the board who were also employed by the city.) Although Mayor Washington had promised to form a Commission on Latino Affairs, Bill Ware, the chief of staff, had advised against it, arguing that it could become a "runaway commission."

From July to September 1983, we negotiated with the mayor and his staff about the structure, function, and members of the commission.[16] At every meeting, his staff promised that we were days from the announcement of the commission. Yet weeks would pass and nothing happened. Concerned about the disunity in the Latino community and the fading legitimacy of the independent movement, we made plans to announce the formation of a commission focusing on the interests and needs of Latinos ourselves. We invited the mayor to attend a press conference and despite his continued promise that the commission would be formed in the near future, we announced it to the press. A week later, the mayor signed an executive order creating "The Mayor's Advisory Commission on Latino Affairs" for a period of two years. The board was composed of the original members and an extra person, Homer Alvarado, added by the Mayor's Office.

The board members formed a search committee, asked me to serve as acting director, and after a month recommended that I become executive director. The board then elected Miguel del Valle, then executive director of the Association House, to serve as chairperson.[17] Del Valle served two years and was replaced by Linda Coronado.

In early November, I arrived at city hall. We had no office, budget, or staff. Every department and commission had a liaison in the Mayor's Office. Bill Ware assigned us to Charles Hunter, who tried to shelve the Commission on Latino Affairs within the Commission on Human Relations. In fact, he offered us a desk with a phone within the Office of Human Relations. We did not accept the office or the definition of the Latino Commission as a "desk" within the Commission on Human Relations. Instead we demanded that the Latino Commission be treated as a separate Office of the city administration and that we be guaranteed monthly meetings with the mayor.

In a few days, the Mayor's Office had found a temporary office for us on the sixth floor of city hall and had budgeted two positions to hire an administrative assistant, Esther Nieves, and me. We established an ongoing dialogue with the mayor. We held monthly meetings in which all the commissioners would be present.

The second major battle fought was with the city council and Ed Burke, alderman of the 14th ward and chairman of the council's powerful Finance Committee. Just weeks after the mayor created the Commission on Latino Affairs, Alderman Burke proposed the creation of a different Latino Commission. His commission would have been established by ordinance, with the city council controlling all the board appointments. His proposal mandated that the commission's functions include a series of busywork duties instead of the research, policy, and advocacy functions that the mayor had already granted. The budget proposed for Burke's commission was higher than that offered by the Mayor's Office. The existing Commission on Latino Affairs asked for a higher budget and lobbied against Ed Burke's proposed ordinance, which in reality would have taken powers away from the commission, not the mayor. Finally, the city council backed down on their proposed ordinance and the higher budget was approved.

Once in place, we started to organize the board and develop a work plan. The mayor had asked Juan Velázquez to organize a breakfast meeting with the publishers of the Latino press. While we wanted to stay away from "public relations" events, we complied since we wanted to establish a better relation with the mayor.

Two days before the breakfast meeting was scheduled, we met with the mayor. We asked him about his promise to name a Latino deputy mayor. He assured us that this would happen but said that he had no one in mind. That afternoon, a member of the commission was called by the press to get his reaction to the mayor's pick for a Latino liaison in his office, Ben Reyes. Outraged at the mayor, half of the commissioners boycotted the breakfast meeting.

Besides feeling that they had been lied to by the mayor, the commissioners felt betrayed because they had lobbied the mayor to secure a high-ranking Latino liaison who had been part of the reform political movement. Ben Reyes had not worked on the campaign and had moved from the city during the general election. The Mayor's Office replied that they had yet to name the "deputy mayor" and that Reyes's duties only included overseeing the infrastructure departments. Reyes had been told differently. While the liaison's duties were administrative, Reyes acted like a roving Latino ambassador in the Mayor's Office, often counteracting community demands which surfaced through the commission but which the administration did not like. Mayor Harold Washington encouraged the formation of parallel structures: a Commission on Latino Affairs and a top Latino advisor; a Planning Department and an Economic Development Department; a chief of staff and a deputy chief of staff. These structures provided a forum for internal debate, but they were also a great source of destructive tension inside government.

Reyes attempted to dismantle the Latino Commission but was countered with the same independent spirit as the mayor and his administrators had experienced. In part, he saw the commission as a threat to his access to the mayor. And in part, he wanted to prove to the administration that he could manage conflict in the Latino commuity. He first tried a divide-and-conquer strategy of pitting Puerto Rican against Mexican-American commissioners. When this failed, he tried to organize the staff of the commission against the board.

From its inception, the commission was more of a community project than a city hall agency. When we could not get results for our requests from departments, our mayoral liaison, or the mayor himself, we would take our case to the press. Strategically, the members of the commission chose not to be the "insider" advisors to the mayor but, rather, the inside advocates of the community. I supported this strategy, and every move I made had the approval of the commissioners. This strategy also required going outside of city hall to mobilize the community.

"Democracy in Action": The Dialogues, Task Forces, and Monitoring Committees

Despite these internal battles, the Commission on Latino Affairs ensconced itself on the seventh floor of city hall. The commission set three goals for its first year: (1) to establish a citywide network of Latinos from various communities and nationalities; (2) to develop a process of policy formulation that included the community; and (3) to create a mechanism in city hall to voice the concerns of the community.[18]

The first goal was accomplished by naming representatives to the commission's board from every Latino neighborhood in the city as well as from every major nationality. This representation was also reflected in the composition of the staff. The second goal was met by holding a series of "Community Dialogues" on the following issues: economic development and jobs, housing, health, public safety, human services, and education. The third goal was accomplished in part by creating the commission itself and by organizing a network of Latino senior employees. We were also able to ensure a voice within city policy development by participating in two subcabinets, Human Services and Development, the latter being an important forum through which to have an impact upon major decisions.

The Community Dialogues were community-based public hearings and were intended to bring to the table members of the Latino community who could define the concerns in the various Latino neighborhoods and recommend policies to the mayor. In order to help unify the seven Latino neighborhoods of the city, we chose to hold these dialogues on the basis of issues rather than neighborhoods. We held the dialogue on economic development in Little Village, on health in South Chicago, on hiring in Uptown, on housing in West Town, on public safety in Logan Square, on human services in Pilsen, and on education at the University of Illinois at Chicago. People from all the neighborhoods attended each one. At each dialogue, the participants broke down into smaller groups to define the problems and prepare a list of recommendations, which were then presented to a general session. We then asked for volunteers to serve on a task force that worked with our staff shaping the policy recommendations into a document. At the end of this process, which took about two years for all six documents to be completed, more than 1500 Latinos had been consulted about the major problems facing their communities and had helped shape governmental solutions.

Once the policy recommendations were completed, we asked task force members to continue in the monitoring committees, which we made sure had at least ten members each. We sent the reports to the Mayor's Office and the appropriate departments with a request for a written response to each recommendation. With their response in hand, the monitoring committee would initiate a series of meetings with the commissioner to work out timetables on those recommendations accepted and to lobby for those not accepted. These committees became the focus of the work of the Latino Commission in the third year, when for the first time community representatives had an opportunity to meet with department heads and representatives from the Mayor's Office on a periodic basis.

At the end of the third year, each committee called another community meeting to meet with department heads and get a full report as to what they had done with each of the recommendations. In these accountability sessions, the chair of the monitoring committee would ask the department heads to account for the progress they had made on each of the recommendations that had been presented to them.

In November 1986, each committee evaluated the progress the administration had made on each of these recommendations and found that the city government had been slow in initiating specific projects. Each committee gave priorities to three recommendations that had not been accomplished.[19] This became the agenda which the commission suggested to the mayor as part of his 1987 election platform.

Yet despite the lack of progress on specific programs, most committee members felt that Mayor Washington had taken an important step forward in opening up city hall to the community by allowing the commission to be established and to struggle for community issues and positions. The committees concluded their reports by citing that, with the exception of hiring, there had been progress at the policy level and in contracts awarded to the community.

At the end of the four years, Marta Ayala, the person in charge of community outreach for the commission, calculated that almost 4000 people had in one way or another participated in the commission's discussions. We entitled our 1986 report, "Democracy in Action."[20] We unveiled the report at the commission's annual celebration at the Preston Bradley Cultural Center in October. The mayor was thrilled to hear us praise him.

The Proposed 1992 World's Fair

Besides the issues that surfaced through the Community dialogues, the commission took on other issues—especially when community representatives asked us to get involved in some pressing concern. One was the proposed 1992 World's Fair that was being planned for a site near Pilsen, the largest Mexican neighborhood.[21] The Commission on Latino Affairs had held a hearing in Pilsen in September 1984. That community would have been directly affected by the proposed World's Fair plan. Almost everyone who testified at the hearing opposed the fair and particularly the use of public monies in that venture. Our commissioners also visited New Orleans to see the impact of that city's fair on the Latino community. And a delegation went to Los Angeles to study the effects of the 1984 Olympics on that city's minority communities.

By the winter of 1984, the mayor had not publicly decided one way or another. The Planning Department was cautiously promoting the fair. The Department of Economic Development was quietly opposing the fair. The World's Fair Authority, supporters in the Mayor's Office of Intergovernmental Affairs, and Ben Reyes lobbied commissioners to support the fair. When the vote was taken, there was one abstention, Mario Aranda, who sat on the World's Fair Authority Board, and one vote in favor of the fair, Daniel Ramos, a Puerto Rican businessman who said that he had been offered contracts; the rest voted to recommend that the mayor oppose the World's Fair. Through this action, the commission again demonstrated its independence from the Mayor's Office.

Affirmative Action

The equitable hiring of Latinos at city hall and their appointment to policy positions and boards and commissions quickly became a primary concern for us. The commission was more successful with appointments than with hiring: 10 percent of all mayoral appointments were Latinos, and 20 percent of appointments to major boards and commissions were Latinos. Hiring, both entry and high-level hiring, was another story. Some key department heads did appoint Latino senior staff, but many important departments did not. Only one major department was headed by a Latino, the Mayor's Office of Employment and Training.

At the beginning of 1984, the Latino Commission board members met with all department heads concerning their hiring of Latinos and gave the mayor a set of recommendations on how to increase the pool of eligible Latinos and increase hiring and retention of Latinos.

Several of the recommendations were implemented. For example, at the beginning of 1985, the commission successfully lobbied the Mayor's Office to sign an executive order that prohibited city departments from collaborating with federal immigration officials and from making any reference to immigrant status on any city applications—including employment forms.[22] The measure automatically increased the pool of Latino applicants, and the mayor became a hero in immigrant communities throughout the city.

Because the administration failed to move on other recommendations, and hiring of Latinos was very low, we decided to crank up the pressure. In the spring of 1984, we issued a report card grading each department on its hiring record. From then on, every six months the commission would issue a report card on departmental hiring records and on the mayor's overall record on hiring of Latinos. Some departments responded constructively, but others did not.

The city's hiring of Latinos was lower than the mayor had promised and much slower than the hiring of blacks. The commission was feeling tremendous pressure from the community for results. This was an issue that was splitting the black/Latino coalition apart.

On December 31, 1985, after intense lobbying efforts on the part of the commission, the mayor established an Affirmative Action Council to oversee a hiring plan with goals and timetables.[23] He also extended the life of the commission for another two years.

But the Affirmative Action Council did not help the situation. In fact, it may have aggravated it. Sam Patch, the chairperson of the council, did not even hire a Latino to its staff. So the body that was supposed to oversee the implementation of the affirmative action plan did not even have affirmative action hiring practices. Hiring of Latinos, especially in high-level positions, considerably decreased in the middle of the first term. As already noted, going into 1987 a Latino headed only one major department, the Mayor's Office of Employment and Training. The Graphics Department and the Commission on Latino Affairs were also headed by Latinos. Out of 110 deputy commissioners, only seven were Latino, and the Mayor's Office staff had three Latino aids.[24]

Moving Beyond City Hall

While the commission's primary focus was municipal government, we understood that we needed to move beyond that arena. State and federal policies and legislation deeply affected the availability of monies for important programs and many times limited what the city could actually do. We developed a state legislative agenda, which among many issues included opposition to an elected school board. This gave us an opportunity to lobby in Springfield and begin to understand other aspects of government. On this particular issue, we had a group of seven students who helped develop a fact sheet, researched the impact of the elected school board system in New York and other cities, and spent a day in Springfield talking to state legislators. Most of the students had never met an elected official. The proposal for an elected school board was defeated in 1986.

After a federal court ordered special aldermanic elections in 1986, four

Latino districts were created. Three new Latino aldermen were added to the city council's body, which already included Miguel Santiago. The members of the commission began meeting with them to develop a city council agenda as well. In 1987, by working closely with Alderman Jesús García, we successfully placed on the city's general election ballot a referendum question on the deployment of the state's National Guard to Central America. This question was placed on the primary ballot in the 1988 April presidential primaries, and an overwhelming 70 percent of the voters said they did not want the governor to deploy the National Guard in Central America.[25] This issue allowed us to hold hearings on a foreign policy matter that directly affected the Latino community. I participated in a fact-finding trip to Central America and reported back to the community in a special hearing held in West Town and in a state hearing held by the General Assembly. We wanted to move the political agenda of the Latino community beyond city hall to include state and federal perspectives.

The Interrupted Second Term: Unresolved Creative Tensions and Changing Strategies

The commission's role in the 1987 reelection campaign was to build consensus around a Latino platform and create pressure on Mayor Washington to support it.

The platform[26] consisted of the following planks:

1. *Political empowerment.* This plank supported formation of a citywide task force to monitor the 1990 census count so that there could be a more equitable basis by which to assess the needs of the Latino community and, just as important, to have the building blocks to redraw the city, state, and congressional districts to maximize Latino voting strength. It also called for a commitment from the mayor to lobby Springfield for the redrawing of congressional boundaries to build a Latino congressional district in 1991.

2. *Jobs and neighborhoods.* This plank called for enforcement of the city's Affirmative Action Plan, and development of Affirmative Action Plans for all the other governmental agencies where the mayor appointed the boards, negotiations of the "First Source" agreements into contracts of companies doing business with the city,

expanded business opportunities, and special programs to develop business exchanges with Latin America. There was also a special request to initiate neighborhood planning boards that could help the city determine how to target neighborhood monies.

3. *Human rights and youth.* This plank supported establishment of a city program to document cases of discrimination resulting from the new federal Immigration and Control Act. In terms of youth, Latino leaders wanted the mayor to be actively involved in educational issues such as dropout prevention, alleviating overcrowding in Latino schools, and naming a citywide committee that could plan a festival celebrating the "Meeting of the Three Worlds: The 500 Years of the Americas" as a way to allow young Latinos to learn about their history and culture.

But while building consensus among Latino leaders was accomplished, getting the mayor to publicly support the platform planks was another story. One plank that created quiet a stir was the one calling for the mayor to support the drawing of a Latino congressional district. Jackie Grimshaw, the mayor's deputy campaign manager, did not want the mayor to make this commitment. We had asked Mayor Washington to announce his commitment at a Latino rally for him, and he had agreed. Grimshaw removed the agreement from the mayor's speech, but at the last moment Harold Washington was alerted and he announced it at the Unity Rally in April 1987.

In 1983, Harold Washington's margin of victory was the Latino vote. And, although the administration was slow in responding to the Latino community, at least key advisors shared in the need to maintain Latinos as part of the coalition that was under seige. In 1987, Harold Washington won by a slightly larger margin, 80,000 votes. Thus, the Latino vote was not viewed as critical. Also, in the first city council vote following his reelection, the mayor succeeded in gaining 40 votes for the reorganization of the council. Again, the importance of the Latino aldermen's vote was diminished. Thus, despite the Latino voters clear support for the mayor, the community did not have as much leverage entering the second term, in which the mayor was much more in control.

A new confidence characterized the incumbent administration. Projects that had been held up by the city council opposition could now be implemented. The mayor now had in place experienced administrators. Ernie Barefield, the chief of staff, organized more than a dozen committees to help develop the strategies to implement the "Mayor's Action Agenda"; initially, with the exception of one committee that had a Latino representative, no Latinos were asked to serve on these crucial committees. When a protest was lodged, several Latinos were named to four committees, but they were never called to meetings. The core group, that is, the chairs of each of the committees, continued to meet. There were no Latino chairs.

The hiring situation was no better. In June, Mayor Washington made eight cabinet-level appointments. Although he had résumés of numereous qualified Latino candidates, not one of his appointments was Latino. At the same time, Ben Reyes was stripped of his administrative duties. While the mayor kept his campaign promise of establishing a program to document cases of employment discrimination, the director of the program was not Latino.

As in 1983, the support that the mayor had garnered during the campaign began to dwindle. A result of these events was that in June, 100 representatives of community organizations met with the Commission on Latino Affairs to ask for a status report. The community representatives decided to build a citywide coalition to pressure the mayor for more jobs and contracts and asked the commission to provide them with information and assistance. From this meeting emerged the Citywide Affirmative Action Coalition, which continued to pressure Harold Washington's successor, Acting Mayor Eugene Sawyer.

In August 1987, more than four hundred West Town residents came to the meeting demanding that the mayor be more responsive to the high infant mortality rates in poor communities of the city. Dr. Jorge Prieto, a long-time health advocate in Chicago's inner city and president of the city's Board of Health, publicly criticized the lack of action of the city's Department of Health.

Knowing that a second term would be an altogether different ball game, we decided to continue transferring the advocacy role to community organizations. Therefore, plans were made to start dismantling the community committees and changing the role of the commission from one of frontline advocate to one of providing information and resources to the community.

We began by reorganizing the Latino senior staff network as well as a new network of Latino appointees and a community coalition that could receive information from the commission and at the same time help set its agenda. Another strategy was to work through the Latino appointees, who many times had authority but no staff to document distribution patterns for them. For instance, the commission started working with the Latinos on the Cultural Affairs Board giving them information on how the city was distributing cultural monies. They, as board members, could ask the hard questions. In the past we had only kept contact with them but not developed joint strategies on particular projects.

The same was done with the Latino aldermen. From the legislative branch they could pressure the executive branch. But this strategy was now possible because we had succeeded in getting Latinos in key positions and the community had succeeded in getting political representation.

Conclusions

A month before Harold Washington died, Gary Rivlin, perhaps the best political reporter covering the Washington administration, published a *Chicago Reader* story entitled "Is the Black/Brown Coalition Coming Apart."[27] Latino leaders were very critical of the administration. What had been a coalition of two powerless groups trying to get into city hall had not translated into an administrative coalition. The Latino community was not in control of the fifth floor of city hall. While Latinos certainly fared much better under the Washington administration than under other administrations, the community was also the most rapidly growing community in the city. Grass-roots blacks also complained that city hall administrators, especially Jackie Grimshaw and Ernest Barefield, excluded them from the decision-making process. But for Latinos, the situation played out as a split between blacks and browns.

Despite these tensions, it is interesting to note that when Harold Washington died, the four Latino aldermen in the city council coalesced and cast their votes for Alderman Tim Evans, Washington's floor leader and heir apparent to the Washington mantle. For their steadfastness in the days following Washington's death, two of the aldermen, Jesús García and Luis Gutierrez (who would later join the Daley camp and declare the death of the black/Latino coalition), were lionized as folk heroes in the black community.

Alderman Tim Evans lost the city council vote to select an acting mayor until special elections would be held to choose a permanent successor to Harold Washington. Alderman Eugene Sawyer won the city council vote with the backing of a coalition of machine white aldermen and several black aldermen. Even though Sawyer was beholden to the white aldermen, he was compelled to maintain many of Harold Washington's programs. In August 1988, Acting Mayor Sawyer signed a city ordinance creating a permanent Chicago Commission on Latino Affairs.

During Harold Washington's tenure, the commission successfully brought a Latino voice to city hall were none had existed before. Enough pressure was brought to bear to ensure at least one Latino on every major board and commission. In comparison to past administrations, there was more Latino representation in the higher echelons of important departments.

Provisions and programs were put in place to defend the rights of immigrants. An affirmative action plan was launched, albeit not successfully implemented. And the commission had succeeded in broadening the participation of the Latino community in policy development, thereby democratizing decision making to some extent. The effect was to empower the community with experience and information.

Nevertheless, all this was accomplished through a "creative tension" that had a political cost. Although the commission was supposed to be an inside advisor to the mayor, its advocacy role made many top administrators uncomfortable. Many of these administrators were not committed to bringing Latinos into the administration or to ensuring an equitable distribution of services and opportunities to all minority communities. Our open confrontation with the mayor over the issue of hiring became a Latino vs. black issue instead of an issue of implementing a progressive municipal agenda.

At the community level, the commission also had some negative effects. One was the institutionalization of much of the Latino community's leadership. The commission was after all a city agency. While this provided it with legitimacy, it also robbed the community, and many community-based struggles, of an independent leadership.

But the community gained as well. Understanding the inner workings of city government is important knowledge for communities to have. There was capacity building and a collective experience that sharpened the community's demands. The commission did provide a forum to bring together Latinos from different nationalities. Networks of people working on the same issue were brought together to determine a common agenda. Neighborhood rivalries in some instances did give way to citywide networks. The youth network, for instance, not only overcame national and neighborhood boundaries but built a solid network with black youths.

In part, the Commission on Latino Affairs worked because it grew from a community struggle for a voice in government. We gave this movement a structure to maximize unity and find a common agenda. We stayed away from becoming a public relations arm of the Mayor's Office. We did not become a direct service provider.

The commission also worked because, despite Harold Washington's complaints that "Latinos were too pushy or moving too fast,"[28] he gave an equal chance to those who fought for equality.

Whether or not this would have continued into a second term, or whether he would have found the pressure from the Latino community too bothersome to effectively respond to the demands, is impossible to guess. What is certain is that for the Latino community, a new political standard emerged calling for an independent political style that defended the rights of the community.

In order to govern Chicago, whoever is mayor will have to continue to bring the Latinos into city government. Politically, representation will continue to increase, and population pressures will push Latinos into the ranks of public employees. In the long run, Latino leaders who are successful in coalescing alliances beyond their particular neighborhoods will be able to have a citywide impact.

In the meantime, the political split in the black community severely hurt the rest of the reform movement. The "new machine" has successfully co-opted some of the leadership of the "Washington movement." We do not know how long it will take to effectively bring together the old progressive forces and the new ones that will be forged in the struggle against a government threatening to turn the city over to the developers. And a larger question remains unanswered: whether or not city government can really satisfy the needs of poor communities.

Yet it can be said that the Harold Washington administration provided a forum through which community-based movements did impact city government. And, during that time, Latinos did gain a foothold in the city's local political and administrative apparatus.

NOTES

1. U.S. Department of Commerce, Bureau of the Census, *The Hispanic Population in the United States: March 1986 and 1987 (Advance Report)*, (Washington, D.C.: U.S. Government Printing Office, August 1987).

2. John Attinasi and R. Flores, "Latino Perspectives for 1990: New Numbers, New Leverage," Latino Institute Report, Chicago, 1987.

3. Felix Padilla, *Latino Ethnic Consciousness: The Case of Mexican Americans and Puerto Ricans in Chicago* (Notre Dame: University of Notre Dame Press, 1985).

4. M. Torres, "Democracy in Action," Annual Report of the Mayor's Commission on Latino Affairs (MACLA), Chicago, November 1986.

5. MACLA, Roster of Latino Appointees, Chicago, updated 1987.

6. M. Torres, "Latinos Evaluate Harold Washington at Midterm" (paper presented at the Latin American Studies Association Meeting, Albuquerque, New Mexico, April 1985).

7. Roberto Rey, "Latino Politics in Chicago" (Master of Arts thesis, University of Illinois at Chicago, 1984). For an analysis of the 1980s in Chicago, see Teresa Córdova, "Latino Politics or Politics by Latinos: Harold Washington and the Rise of Latino Electoral Politics," in D. Montegano, ed., *Essays in Contemporary Chicano Politics* (Albuquerque: University of New Mexico Press, forthcoming).

8.   John Attinasi, Rufin Osorio, and Raymundo Flores, "Al Filo: The Empowerment of Chicago's Latino Electorate," Latino Institute Report, Chicago, 1986.
9.   Midwest Voter Registration and Education Project, Mayoral Primary Exit Poll, Chicago, February 1983.
10.   Board of Elections Results, Mayoral Elections, Chicago, 1983.
11.   This news story was covered by TV Channel 7, Chicago ABC, several days before the election.
12.   Midwest Voter Registration and Education Project, Mayoral Elections Exit Poll, Chicago, April 1983.
13.   Abdul Alkalimat and Doug Gills, "Chicago: Black Power vs. Racism—Harold Washington Becomes Mayor," in Rod Bush, ed., *The New Black Vote* (Chicago: Synthesis Publications, 1984).
14.   Gary Rivlin, "How Did This Guy Get to Be An Alderman? Hacienda Politics: The Story of Miguel Santiago and the Machine That Made Him," *Chicago Reader*, 15, no. 3 (May 16, 1986).
15.   Gary Rivlin, "Who Killed Rudy Lozano?" *Chicago Reader* 14, no. 30 (April 26, 1985).
16.   Proposal for a City of Chicago Commission on Latino Affairs, 1983.
17.   In 1986, Miguel del Valle became the first Latino elected to the state Senate.
18.   MACLA, Annual Report, Chicago, 1984.
19.   MACLA's Monitoring Committee Reports, Chicago, 1986.
20.   Torres, "Democracy in Action."
21.   MACLA, "Proposed 1992 World's Fair," Chicago, 1984.
22.   Mayor Washington signed an executive order instructing all city departments not to collaborate with any U.S. Immigration and Naturalization Service (INS) investigations not mandated by federal law.
23.   On December 31, 1985, Mayor Washington signed Executive Order 85–5, creating an Affirmative Action Council.
24.   MACLA, Update on Hiring, Chicago, October 1986.
25.   *Boletin* (MACLA's Quarterly Newsletter), Summer 1987.
26.   Ibid., Spring 1987.
27.   Gary Rivlin, "The Blacks and the Browns: Is the Coalition Coming Apart?" *Chicago Reader* 17, no. 7 (November 6, 1987).
28.   Alton Miller, *Harold Washington: The Mayor, The Man* (Chicago: Bonus Books, 1989).

Throwing Rocks on the Inside: Keeping a Progressive Administration Progressive

Timothy Wright

In 1984, before I was working for the Harold Washington administration, but having been a campaign activist I wrote a letter to the mayor expressing concern about how the administration was operating. I told him that outsiders could clearly see the disunity and disagreements among staff in the Mayor's Office and that this made him look bad. People like me, who had contributed to the political movement that elected him, had no access to his office to discuss the important issues. The decisions that were being made seemed nonprogressive and out of step with the movement that had brought him into power. The staff was constantly fighting with each other instead of dealing with issues such as the regressive city utility tax or an ordinance against doing business with South Africa. I began to fear that the Washington administration, by operating the machinery of government in its inherited form, might be just like other minority-controlled administrations, which have, over time, lost touch with the people.

It wasn't until two years later, in 1986, that I received a call from the mayor's secretary asking me to come in and see Washington the next day. After the traditional hour and a half wait, the mayor began by asking me about the letter. He wanted to know how I had come to the conclusions and what I would do about the situation. I made clear there was no doubt about my support of the administration but that there were some real problems. I said it was essential for people to have better access to him—not just to talk but to ensure that information got through to him. Harold appeared to be very upset about my letter and asked me to write a follow-up as to how I would approach those problems. I did this, and a few months later we met again; I wound up accepting a position as assistant to the chief of staff.

I had once told Matt Piers, who had joked about me throwing rocks at the administration and yet enticed me to join the Washington team, that if I did join the administration I'd always keep a few rocks in my pocket to throw them from inside if necessary. The first day I came to work for the administration, Piers said, "I see you got rid of those rocks in your pocket." So I told him, "I'm here to help Harold Washington, not the bureaucracy. And I still keep one rock."

In this chapter I will describe some of the difficulties the Washington administration had in pursuing a progressive agenda. It focuses on both the *external* obstacles, reflected in the "council wars" and attempts to strip traditional city powers, privileges, and governance and lodge them in the county and/or the state, and the *internal* ones, related to the heterogeneous nature of Washington's coalition. My main conclusion is that the fight to keep a progressive administration in power and progressive is constant—and never won.

On the Outside

I had first met Harold Washington in November 1982 when I was involved in a fund-raiser for him in Los Angeles. It involved a number of politicians and activists—people like Willie Brown, the first black Speaker of the House in the California State Assembly, Tom Bradley, the mayor of Los Angeles, Assemblywoman Maxine Waters, and quite a few others. I had heard of Washington's advocacy in a number of different areas, such as the Civil Rights Amendment and the debates around designating Dr. Martin Luther King's birthday a national holiday, and I had become interested in him.

That was the first time I had met Harold, and seeing him next to Mayor Bradley really brought out some differences. Tom Bradley was a good friend of my family—my mother had grown up across the street from him and had been in his wedding—but he never moved me politically. I had never become particularly involved in politics with him because I saw him not as a black leader but as a leader who was black. He was never really a major presence in the black community, but we voted for him because he was black and it was the first time we had that opportunity. By contrast, Harold Washington was expressing a politics of empowerment not only for blacks but for everyone who had been left out of the system.

Thinking about Bradley and Washington also pointed up some contradictions in my own life. I was planning to go to work for a major law firm, and I wasn't really putting my talents to work for change and progress. Yet, I was clearly a beneficiary of the struggles of a lot of people who had fought for the social, political, and economic rights of blacks. Thinking about these things really made me want to work with Harold, to address this next stage of black political struggle, or at least to help him get elected.

Most black leaders lose sight of the issues on which they were elected once they are in office, and they become as political as anybody else. That was true of Bradley, Coleman Young in Detroit, and Marion Berry in Washington, D.C. Berry, for example, had worked with the Student Nonviolent Coordinating Committee (SNCC), a radical student group. But once he assumed power, he became a very traditional politician. Harold seemed different. Movement politics got him elected, and he seemed to stay thoroughly conscious of that. In that sense, he differed from Tom Bradley, and in my mind Bradley represents the old and Harold the new. With Washington running for mayor of Chicago, surely the most important step that would move blacks forward as a race, the most important progressive political fight to enfranchise blacks, was going to take place there. Washington had the most significant political and social agenda for the people since Dr. Martin Luther King, Jr. What happened in Chicago would affect the whole country, the whole world. So I thought that was the place one had to be and that one had to become involved.

Even though I had not been heavily involved in traditional politics before, I had helped organize people on issues such as Angola and South Africa. Traditional politics, whether with Democrats or Republicans, seemed irrelevant to me: as a black, I couldn't leave my community and enter a white neighborhood without getting stopped. As I grew up in this situation, it was clear to me that it didn't matter who was president—the same thing still occurred. But I felt a sense of kinship and self-empowerment with struggles such as the civil war in Angola, and the fight against oppression wherever it was taking place. So, while in college, I participated on the board of a national organization protesting U.S. involvement in Angola.

In the early 1980s I was in law school after having quit my previous job as a senior cost engineer for a construction company. Around the time Harold decided to run in the primary, I started coming to Chicago for job interviews with law firms; I would only do interviews in Chicago. Every time I came I would add a few days to my stay, spending anywhere from four or five days to two weeks, and then head back to Los Angeles. During that time, I did what I could to help, whether it was going door to door in Chicago or raising money by taking buttons back to Los Angeles.

After the primary I had to stop coming to Chicago so often because I had to complete my law studies and take the bar exam. But one week after I took the bar, I moved to Chicago. I didn't have a job secured, and I really didn't know very many people, although I had gotten to know some during the primary campaign. My main contact was Alderman Bobby Rush, who was a friend of one of my professors who had been in SNCC and had also worked with the Black Panthers and the Crusaders. The first organization I joined politically in Chicago was Bobby's. There was always a certain paranoia about new people, and when people would ask questions about me, Bobby, who knew me, would be my ticket to legitimacy. So, when I moved to Chicago, I moved to the second ward—Bobby Rush's ward.

My first job in Chicago was to be a clerk for a conservative judge with the District Court. He was one of the few black judges on the bench, but he had tried to keep Dr. Martin Luther King out of Chicago! After a few weeks of trying to be there, I left and joined a not-for-profit law firm called Business and Professional People for the Public Interest (BPI). The group provided mostly legal services around public interest issues, such as energy issues affecting poor people, poor conditions in the Chicago Housing Authority, or some other similar problem.

As the first black attorney with BPI, I became involved in a number of different things—from suing U.S. Steel for reneging on their promise to build a rail mill to drafting legislation aimed at restructuring the utility tax system. I also worked with State Representatives Carol Mosely Brown and Woody Bowman and State Senator Dick Newhouse to draft legislation prohibiting state investment in South Africa. I did this because as a lawyer I knew how to do it, and also because I wanted to stay involved with progressive issues as a way of supporting the Washington administration. While drafting and lobbying city legislation, I got to know Aldermen Ed Burke and Ed Vrdolyak, the leaders of the "Vrdolyak 29" faction in the city council who opposed Mayor Washington. You had to have made that contact if you wanted to pass legislation in the city council. They didn't necessarily identify me with the mayor (other than being black) because I was focusing on specific issues rather than partisan lobbying. I believe the first unanimous legislation that was passed in the city council in 1983 was a piece I had drafted and for which I lobbied.

Through BPI, I became involved in several issues that helped Harold Washington in his struggle to gain control of city hall. These related to Washington's ethics statement; the ward remapping case; and the Park District Board.

The Struggle for Control of City Hall

When Washington was elected in 1983, his ability to govern was seriously hindered by the fact that he could count on only a minority of aldermen and -women. At the first session of the city council, his opponents had very effectively pushed through a reorganization that put all committees under their control. The split ("council wars") between the

"Vrdolyak 29" and the "Washington 21" dominated the city's politics until the special elections in 1985 gave the mayor control.

One major issue early on with which his opponents tried to harrass the mayor revolved around his ethics statement. They brought suit to have the mayor removed from office for failure to file his ethics statement on time—which had indeed been a mistake on the part of his staff. Working for BPI, I was one of the attorneys supporting the Washington administration on this. One of my colleagues, Doug Cassel, and I worked on the case, and we went through numerous law books to look for legal precedents to support Harold's case. Very late on the night before the hearing on the case, we called Jim Montgomery, the corporation counsel, and told him we had put together a legal theory that would support the administration. We took it over to him that night—his staff was still in the office—and at the hearing the next day they used it. It proved to be the prevailing theory. It felt good to play such a role in the outcome of the case, and sometime afterward the mayor and Montgomery thanked Cassel and me. That was the second time I was face to face with Harold Washington.

The next time we had a real opportunity to meet again was in connection with the ward remapping case in 1985. Based on a lawsuit, the boundaries of the wards had to be redrawn. During the special elections that were required because of this, I and others helped get several groups of lawyers together to work for Washington's candidates on election day. Ultimately, the special elections gave Washington control over the city council. When I met with Harold that time, during the victory and thank-you reception for the lawyers, he seemed to remember me, but he didn't really let on. He tended not to trust people he didn't know well.

The next major struggle started in the fall of 1985 and involved the Park District Board. Harold was trying to place his nominees on the various boards and commissions, and the city council held the appointees hostage, refusing to confirm any of the nominations. The Park District, controlled by Superintendent Ed Kelly, represented a particular problem in that its large patronage army would continuously be used to undermine the Washington administration. First, through various contacts and relationships we had, we were able to quietly convince one of the Kelly Park Board members to go along with supporting Mayor Washington. As a result of growing public pressure, Ed Vrdolyak and his "29" relented and allowed one more Washington appointee to the Park Board, believing that this appointment would not affect the balance of power on the board; after all, they would still have the majority of votes on the board and Superintendent Kelly would still have his seat.

Once we had architect Walter Netsch on the board, however, we knew that Washington would have the balance of power, because of the other board member who had already agreed that the mayor should have the right to appoint his own people. Through an exhaustive search of arcane law we discovered that with a majority of the Park Board we could modify its charter. For political reasons we couldn't fire Kelly, but we could take away all his powers and put them into a new office called the executive vice-president, to which the board could then appoint a Washington supporter. We knew there would be some court challenges by the "Vrdolyak 29," so we did thorough legal research and came up with an airtight case. Then we launched the strategy: We got Walter Netsch on the board and made him its president. Next, we changed the Park Board charter and created the new office of executive vice-president, and the new Washington majority appointed Jesse Madison, a Washington ally and his former commissioner of consumer services, to that office. Kelly didn't attend the meetings because he thought they were illegal and the actions taken null and void. Kelly and his allies complained, but when the court refused to entertain his complaint, the superintendent resigned.

It was through cases like this, and most decisively through the remapping of the ward boundaries and the ensuing election of four new aldermen sympathetic to Washington, that he was able to gain control over city hall from the "Vrdolyak 29." When I came to work for the Mayor's Office in 1986, though, there turned out to be just as many difficulties on the inside as there had been on the outside.

Life on the Inside

Within the first few days of coming to the Mayor's Office as assistant chief of staff, I found myself sitting in the Chicago office, running the operations because everyone else was down in Springfield. The Illinois state legislature was trying to take control of O'Hare Airport from the city in part for what we did to Superintendent Kelly at the Park District. The Republicans and ethnic Democrats had come together to create an Airport Authority that could control O'Hare from the suburbs, in exchange for their giving up Ed Kelly's job at the Park District. I quickly began calling various people for support and was working with the legislature, drafting arguments against the regional Airport Authority and Kelly, to be used in debate. I put together briefing papers on Kelly's history. Since I had worked on it, I knew a lot about his seemingly questionable deals on Soldier Field and some other real estate deals. We faxed this information to be used as ammunition on the floor of the legislature. Washington spent the day trying to reach people on the phone. In the end, we prevailed by one vote.

Soon after Harold Washington and I spent that Saturday in the chief of staff's office responding to this crisis, he asked me to move over to the Mayor's Office of Intergovernmental Affairs because they really needed help in the legislative area. I began working with the head of that office, Jackie Grimshaw, on legislation and pulling the office together, structuring, supervising, and doing some preplanning. After Jackie left to direct the 1987 reelection campaign, the mayor appointed me acting director of the office. I addressed such issues as the White Sox ballpark, the ethics ordinance, and securing the voting block for the mayor, among others. After dealing with intergovernmental affairs for some time, the mayor and I began to develop a real relationship. Initially, he would ask me how I saw a certain issue, and sometimes he would respond, "You know, that's stupid." I would feel embarrassed, so I began to change the way I approached him with my solutions. I would give him several ways to look at a problem and suggested a solution for each perspective. He appreciated that approach. This way, I was able to make the mayor feel very comfortable about legislative issues. For instance, I worked on the ethics ordinance a great deal. When it was time for the reelection, I told the mayor that if he changed the ethics ordinance in certain ways he would surely pick up the votes. The mayor agreed, although he wasn't sure it would work. I told him the votes were lined up and he would get 47 votes. Harold didn't believe me, but the votes came through and he was pleased.

As we were becoming more successful the mayor began to trust me more, but others were jealous of that relationship. This led to several conflicts with other senior staff. For instance, once I wasn't invited to a legislative reception owing to these conflicts. When the mayor found out about it, he insisted that I attend. He knew about the feuding within the administration, but I think he liked it that way because he thought that in this way every issue would be well thrashed out.

When the year I had promised was up and I decided to leave, there were about twenty people who went to the mayor and suggested I remain in office. Some of them offered to resign if I left. When I told the mayor I was leaving, he asked me to make him an offer. I said if he made me his lawyer, I would consider staying another year. Now that was a problem, because as he said, "I have a corporation counsel," but he said he would think about it. After a few days he named me special counsel. He wanted me to handle the city council, which had been in Intergovernmental Affairs' jurisdiction. This left the Office of Intergovernmental Affairs with only the state and federal government relations, again a source of dissension.

The mayor and I grew even closer when my father died. I flew back home to Los Angeles for the funeral on March 7, 1987, which was right after the primaries. I spent some time with my family, and the mayor called to console my mother. When I rushed back from Los Angeles to deal with the election, the mayor shared with me the feelings he had when his father died.

The relationship and trust between the mayor and me continued to grow. He began giving me more responsibilities, and he wanted my viewpoint on a number of important issues.

All the while, I felt that one of my responsibilities was to keep the administration progressive. However, several of the people who surrounded the mayor didn't turn out to be as progressive as he was. As a result, the bureaucracy was not fully capable of achieving the mayor's vision. Operating the same bureaucracy that had been shaped and operated by the "machine" would not produce the progressive results the mayor had envisioned even if all those who operated it were truly progressive—let alone when they were not. What it did was to create contradictions for the progressives in government. Matt Piers was one of those persons who were deeply caught up in the contradictions of working for the city government. He was in the corporation counsel's office and often defended policemen accused of harassment and beating people in the streets. He felt that this was his job, and that it didn't matter what kind of person you were or what your moral and political beliefs were: once you were in a job, you had to perform the tasks of that job—and that meant defending the city authorities. We all had to face that same contradiction in one form or another. I attempted, through advocacy, debate, and policymaking to ensure we were progressive and democratic on as many issues as possible, and I thought a few other people in city government were trying to do the same thing, including Mayor Washington. But at times, when policies came to be implemented, they got completely confused and ended up looking completely different from the way they started out. Even though the mayor sought to implement progressive policies, at times he was unable to because of his senior and junior staff.

Not all staff shared the mayor's progressive philosophy; some senior staff did not truly understand the undercurrents, issues, and people that brought Washington to power. Nor did they understand his responsibility to the various elements of his constituency or their responsibility in transforming the bureaucracy into a progressive, inclusive, democratic institution that served the best interests of all Chicagoans. While it was difficult enough for Mayor Washington to gain control of an intransigent bureaucracy full of the political patronage workers of the "machine," many of the people who were brought in with the mayor weren't especially progressive. Only some had truly participated in the politics of the movement that elected him. The others tended to be skilled people from various areas, and they were bureaucratic in their approach. As a result, the mayor was being isolated from the progressive concerns of his constituency; the Praetorian Guards had set up shop.

There were many constituencies—nationalists, liberals, progressives, rich, poor, whites, Hispanics, and blacks—that wanted access to the mayor, but many never got it and their issues were not addressed. At times, the mayor would hear from a constituency group and make a commitment, but there would be no follow-up. Usually, he wouldn't be aware of this until the issue arose again.

One of the ways we tried to address this problem was to have frequent meetings and bring information to the mayor, but many people opposed this. The chief of staff made it his job to control access, and issues had to be brought to him before going to the mayor. Bill Ware, the first chief of staff, was nicknamed "Bottleneck Bill" because he never sent much on to the mayor. Those of us who had links to the community and to constituency groups tried to get as much information to the mayor as possible, and Harold Washington began to reach out and appoint representatives from various constituencies to advisory groups to be better informed.

There were many fights on the inside, but my friends on the outside thought we weren't fighting enough. They felt Washington's administration was no different from Byrne's or Daley's or Bilandic's. From the outside looking in the administration was not acting very progressively and not enough was being done. Yet from the outside it was hard to see the difficulty that confronted those of us on the inside. From the inside you could see that some senior staffers were not operating effectively. For example, they had not submitted the mayor's ethics statement on time. The other problem was one of leadership. People had trouble perceiving objectives, working together to achieve them, and then moving on. They needed someone to provide leadership and create a sense of a team effort.

Another example of these problems is that even during my time in city government it was difficult to get a proposed anti-apartheid ordinance past various individuals. It never got to the mayor. If the mayor wanted something done, very seldom did that happen. Only after heightened pressure from constituency group on these issues did we finally get results. But you could never get things past various senior staffers because they didn't understand the importance of certain progressive issues. This wasn't so much a matter of different ideologies. Many senior staffers didn't represent a large constituency, the poor, or the people that had elected Washington. They were power oriented and represented the same old way with new faces.

Some of this may be inevitable. Even when there is a new mayor, the operations of government are still carried on the same way. There are certain boundaries and formalities one has to obey. But certainly some things can be modified to produce needed reform and change, to make government more responsive to the people while still running the city like a business. In operating the bureaucracy, it is too easy to get involved in the day-to-day issues of government and lose sight of the progressive reform to which one is committed. For instance, we were involved in the deal for the new White

Sox Stadium and got a great sense of accomplishment from it. But what difference did it really make in the end? We should look at what kinds of changes are needed to make institutions like city government more responsive to the people it affects. That's what some of us struggled for, while others thought power for the sake of power was important. Even they had a point, though, because if you can hold on to power you will gain time, and time brings the ability to change things.

In the middle of 1987 Mier urged me to consider the position of commissioner of economic development. When I finally had an interview, I became the number one candidate for the position. My education and employment history were the strongest argument for hiring me. My experience was well rounded and met the job requirements. But Ernie Barefield and Brenda Gaines, the chiefs of staff, didn't want me to be commissioner. I felt they had considered me only to be able to say there was a local black candidate. After I had been ranked number one, Ernie Barefield opened the process again to search for other candidates. Again I was voted number one. Barefield told me that since I was so close to Harold, it would be harmful for both me and the mayor if I moved out of the Mayor's Office. I think he was sincere in saying this, but I felt he was wrong. I believed I could maintain my relationship with Harold and still help the administration as commissioner of economic development.

Harold and I talked the Saturday before his death. We talked about economic development and what we needed to focus on. I felt that we needed to define economic development as empowering people, and that we should focus especially on problems of blacks and Hispanics. We talked over a lot of ideas that I have continued to work on in the department. He said that he would announce at a press conference the next week that I would be named commissioner of economic development and that it would go into effect after the new budget was passed. We met on the Monday, Tuesday, and just briefly on the Wednesday morning of that week on various matters. After the Wednesday morning encounter, I went upstairs for a few minutes to deal with some city council issues. When I came back downstairs, the paramedics were wheeling Harold out of his office. He died that day.

The Future

The mayor's approach on some of the things we talked about the Saturday before his death really led me to believe he had a grand strategy, a big game plan. He knew he had to confront others one-on-one to gain political power. Without that struggle, he wouldn't have gotten respect, been able to gain control of the government, and he wanted the position of authority. He could never back down politically or make deals with Ed Vrdolyak. He did not want to be seen as having any political weakness.

He saw economic development in this larger context and did a lot more thinking about economic development in the city than I ever knew. He saw that for the right kind of development to occur it was necessary to create strength and political relationships. He viewed the issue of job creation as important, because there were real needs and demands. But the real issue wasn't jobs: it was economic empowerment in areas and for people that were previously ignored.

Harold Washington saw the major battle as a struggle for regional political power. Historically, black mayors who have risen to power in major urban areas have come at a time when the central city was losing white population to the suburbs and so was becoming less powerful relative to the suburbs. As a result, the cities have fewer resources and cutbacks have to be made, and hence power tends to diminish. Atlanta is a perfect example, and there are many other such examples across the country. The real locus of power thus becomes the region. Harold had begun to see this clearly. He felt that the next stage for Chicago would be an effort by the state and county government to shift powers from the city to the county and the state. His political opponents such as Richard M. Daley and Ed Vrdolyak were shifting to county government, with Daley as Cook County state's attorney and Vrdolyak running for county office as well. Several of the white ethnic aldermen were also beginning to run for county offices, or were switching to the Republican party, rather than staying in the city in a Democratic party soon to be controlled by black politicians and electorates. Simultaneously, the state legislature kept trying to shift control of the airports and public transportation away from the city. Ultimately, because of the city's needs for state funding, the city might lose control over most city institutions, such as the Park District. There already is a School Finance Control Board, the Metropolitan Sanitary District, the Regional Transportation Authority, and noncity agencies that control the new White Sox stadium and the McCormick Place exposition center.

Mayor Washington tried to address this by putting together a racially balanced, agreed-upon slate for the countywide offices, and that is why he endorsed certain people who in the past opposed him. The mayor felt that by endorsing a mixed slate of candidates he could join hands with white ethnic Democrats, greatly reduce the political antagonism between blacks and whites, and wield a strong regional hand. But unfortunately he never was able to fully pursue this agenda. Clearly, though, he knew the struggle for control was a continuous one, and that is why he always said he was going to be mayor for twenty years. It probably would have taken that long.

The Affirmative Information Policy: Opening Up a Closed City

JOHN KRETZMANN

The election of Harold Washington shook Chicago's governmental and political structures to their very foundations. Long-accepted policies and practices, not the least of which was government's habitual secrecy, were suddenly open to scrutiny and debate. In fact, one of the first major challenges facing the new Washington administration in 1983 involved prying open the doors and windows of a government in the back room for half a century, whose business had been conducted in private, and in which public participation in policy formation was considered anathema. The populist orientation of Washington's movement-style campaign virtually guaranteed that this closed and secretive system would be exposed and challenged.

In fact, Washington's populist campaign themes, backed by strong neighborhood-based demands for increased citizen participation, set the context for creating policies that signaled not simply an *open* government but an *invitational* one. This account will touch on a number of these participation strategies but will concentrate on one particularly innovative thrust which came to be called Affirmative Neighborhood Information. This approach was conceived basically as a systematic response to the shortcomings of Freedom of Information Acts when viewed from the perspective of the empowerment agenda articulated by community organizations in consort with a populist-oriented city administration.

My own involvement in the development of a set of inventive information-related policies for the Washington administration grew out of a neighborhood-oriented information project at Northwestern University's Center for Urban Affairs and Policy Research.[1] From that base, an action research team had collaborated with a number of community organizations in Chicago to experiment with ways of collecting and using neighborhood-specific data. Some of our work had introduced microcomputers into the organizations and had experimented with new ways of making data easily digestible. Involvement in the Washington campaign and transition team presented us with an opportunity to involve city government as information partners with neighborhood organizations.

The City and Information:
A Legacy of Closely Held Secrets

Reforming public information policy in the Chicago city government meant substantially reversing the practice of at least five decades of carefully constructed and jealously guarded secrecy. We conducted a series of background interviews with public officials, reporters, and civic leaders active during the Richard J. Daley, Michael Bilandic, and Jane Byrne mayoralties, which documented the tight control of information.[2] Our respondents emphasized time and again the extraordinary amount of time and effort they invested in trying to discover what government was doing. Without a Freedom of Information Act, repeatedly introduced by city council independents but killed by machine legislative leaders, "I was always running into court to sue for disclosure of one thing or another," recalled one former independent alderman.[3]

Often, city bureaucracies simply didn't collect relevant data. One former alderman, an independent, reported, "The fact was that they didn't keep a lot of the information we wanted. For instance, they didn't keep statistics on city agencies by ward. . . . About the end of Daley, beginning of Bilandic, they finally started including performance data in the budget that allowed you to see how much it was costing the city to perform a certain service and you could compare it to other cities."[4]

Furthermore, the members of the transition teams for both Mayor Byrne and Mayor Harold Washington, charged with the task of profiling the operations of city departments and agencies, reported finding "huge gaps" in the data collected by the city. Said one transition team head, "The city was this giant closed file cabinet. When we pried it open, we found out how little was in there. For the Washington transition report, we had to assemble a team of 150 people to put together information that any normal city would already have had."[5]

Interviewees also reported that Chicago's bureaucrats were adept at delay. One researcher for a civic group recalled, "Lots of times I was told they just couldn't find what I wanted, or that it would take five people weeks to copy it."[6] Another independent alderman reported that

under Mayor Byrne the delays got worse. She instituted a formal regulation whereby any request for information had to go through the

Corporation Counsel. This would take weeks; there was this huge bottleneck. Sometimes I'd send a series of letters, and I'd finally get a nice letter back saying, yes, these were public records and they'd give them to me. But if I'd come back and ask them for an update, more recent records of the same kind, they'd make me go back to the Corporation Counsel and get still another legal opinion as to whether these records should be released. There was certainly, on one level, an official policy to obstruct.[7]

All of the evidence indicated, then, that Chicago's bureaucracies were quite steadfastly committed to the protection of information and were adept at a variety of strategies aimed at excluding the public. But embedded as they were in the center of a machine style of government, these "natural" bureaucratic tendencies were reinforced by a "politics of secrecy" as well. In fact, most observers located the reasons for secrecy more centrally in the practices and values of machine politics than in those of bureaucracies.

Both insiders and outsiders emphasized that key decisions in government were nearly always the prerogative of a very few people at the top of the machine hierarchy and that they were based most often on criteria that were politically determined—the rewarding of friends and the punishment of foes. It appeared to active observers of the party that, within its highest echelons, the characteristics of information exchange were essentially three in number: the "ownership" of information was assumed to be a private matter; its exchange was interpersonal; and the predominant mode of exchange was oral and informal.

These decidedly nonbureaucratic assumptions and practices, explained one former machine alderman, were "based on the clear understanding that information is a form of power." Obviously, being "in the know" resulted in tangible benefits, benefits that were both hoarded and parceled out with greater frequency the higher the rung one occupied. Being on the bottom, or worse, on the outside, meant that one knew very little about the operation of government or about the opportunities for gain such knowledge opened up.[8] The case of the city council is perhaps even more telling. According to one former machine alderman:

There was *no* access to information, especially for us. Even records that the public got were not made available to the aldermen. . . . We'd be in the city council and they would tell us the title of an ordinance that we were voting on but they wouldn't let us see it. Tom Keane [former Finance Committee chair and confidant of Mayor Daley] would be sitting there with the ordinance on his desk and he wouldn't let us see it. Sometimes he'd hold up the ordinance and say, "There, you just saw it."[9]

City council members who were active in the Daley years provided at least a partial listing of the most common techniques used by the mayor and his legislative leaders to thwart the flow of information in the council:

- Titles of ordinances were vague and contained little information about the contents of the bills.
- Ordinances were often introduced and called up for a vote on the same day.
- City council leaders resisted the introduction of an ordinance numbering system.
- Leaders frequently slipped something controversial through the council by making it part of an "omnibus" package.

Given these consistent practices in pursuit of the protection of information, it is ironic that the avenues for obtaining information occasionally appeared to be more accessible to the antimachine independents in the council. "They didn't care about making noise and making enemies," explained a machine stalwart. "They could raise hell, go public, go to the media, and maybe they'd get something."[10] One independent reported constructing an elaborate set of procedures for keeping his own records of council legislation and votes. Similarly, reporters and representatives from civic and community groups occasionally found that unfavorable publicity or legal action were successful strategies for obtaining information about legislation.

This commitment to a closed flow of information persisted during the Bilandic and Byrne administrations. Our interviews produced little evidence that much, if anything, changed during this period. Perhaps the clearest summary of the state of the city's information, both its collection and its dissemination, at the conclusion of the Byrne administration is contained in the Executive Summary of the first volume of the Washington administration transition report, *Blueprint of Chicago Government*. The report stresses throughout the extreme difficulties encountered by the authors in their pursuit of information. The "Findings" section begins:

We have, in the process of this detailed investigation, discovered certain general conditions which are nearly universal in all of these municipal agencies.

One of the most obvious and pervasive facts about Chicago city government that has repeatedly been evident in our research is that basic information needed to understand how the City works, to assess how well services are provided and to determine who is responsible for various city programs is incredibly difficult to obtain. Simple questions like what an agency actually does, the total amount of money an agency spends, and the names of people who run the agency are difficult to answer. Getting even this simple descriptive information requires consulting several different sources, many of which are hard to decipher.[11]

Modernizing Information Systems in the City

Against this backdrop of both bureaucratic and politically determined secrecy, however, the numbers of professionally trained administrators in Chicago government grew steadily during the Daley, Bilandic, and Byrne years. One longtime city computer expert recalled, "I remember it was about 1970 that I started to get piles of job applications from people calling themselves 'systems analysts.' That was the time when I think it really dawned on the powers that be that we couldn't really keep track of the money and the personnel without drastically upgrading our information capacities."[12]

But in Chicago, of course, these developments did not signal a final shift from the old-style political mode of information management to the new-style administrative, or "reform," mode. Rather they appeared to lead to the existence, for at least a decade, of a peculiar two-track system of information collection and use. On the one hand, a number of agencies and departments, staffed increasingly with technically trained administrators and information experts, collected and stored "systems" data concerning their programs and operations. These data, increasingly computerized, were reported as required to the externally located bureaucracies, often federal, that controlled and to some extent monitored program funds. In addition, data were utilized internally for routine bureaucratic functions like building inspections. At the same time, however, the older "political" mode of handling information persisted. That is, privately held, personally and informally communicated information continued to determine, in many instances, what "really" happened in a department or agency. Hiring and firing, budgeting and programming decisions continued to be based almost entirely on the personal, political calculus of the machine politicians—not on the administratively defined needs of the particular department.

In Chicago, this two-track system for handling information existed in precarious balance for considerably more than a decade. While it held sway, it seemed to foster an extremely circumscribed, narrowly utilitarian view of the politics of information. That is, systematically collected information was most often thought of as helpful neither to the departments themselves, except for routine purposes, nor to clients or constituents, nor to policymakers. Information collection constituted rather a set of hurdles to be overcome mainly insofar as external agencies demanded that they be overcome. Since virtually no important decisions were connected with what was known or collected systematically, the data often did not need to be timely, accurate, or relevant to decision making.

Not surprisingly, and also not unique to Chicago, one of the outcomes of this two-track approach to information was the gradual and almost surreptitious development of an interdepartmental network of people whose jobs involved the collection and analysis of data, and whose inclinations were, as one department head put it, to "really *care* about information." One important magnet that drew these people together around it was in fact the city's Data Center, only half-jokingly described by a city computer veteran as "a haven for technical refugees from the Pacific Northwest."[13]

Increasingly numerous, however, these information professionals appeared to be politically isolated, considered marginal and unimportant by the city's patronage work force. What possible incentive existed for department workers who owed their positions to their ward-based political activity to respond to distant supervisors operating within a totally foreign and irrelevant administrative framework? Insofar as the cooperation of workers is necessary for the collection of accurate and timely data in a particular department, these barriers were quite significant.

The isolation of the information professionals also limited the uses to which data, once collected, were to be put. Politically connected department heads were often both products and beneficiaries of the old political style of decision making—or they were at least compelled to adapt to it. Many were themselves familiar only with the oral, informal style and lived by Daley's dictum that "good politics is good government" and vice versa. Decisions were thus based on the calculus of the political quid pro quo, requiring deep familiarity with a set of "signals" and information almost totally divorced from systematically collected data within a given department. The constant care and feeding of the network of political obligations known as the machine superseded all other criteria for decision making. There was no place in this network for the information professionals, and little outlet for their work internal to the departments. As a consequence, information collected and reported by these isolated professionals was quite often not even seen by department heads, who understandably regarded it as irrelevant. Clearly these arrangements affected both the quantity and the quality of the data collected.

Openness and Participation:
Two Key Themes in the
Washington Campaign

This, then, was the state of the "politics of information" in Chicago as the city approached the mayoral campaign of 1983. But from the outset of Washington's populist-oriented campaign the promise of "open government" was a central theme. This commitment was expressed in an early and oft-repeated pledge to issue an executive order on freedom of information (FOI) on the first day of a Washington administration.

This emphasis upon FOI as the cornerstone of reform in Chicago government was wholly understandable. Illinois had been the last state to enact such an ordinance—it finally did so in 1983—and Chicago virtually the last major city without one. The symbolic importance of such a step would mark a significant break from past practices and would in fact provide clear evidence of the reform intentions promised by the new administration. Furthermore, powerful constituencies extending beyond independent politicians were lined up behind the FOI thrust. These included the press, as well as many important civic organizations. Washington and his advisors were intimately familiar with the legislative history of FOI acts and were clearly committed to bringing the city in line with the rest of the country.

In addition, early in the Washington campaign, another seemingly unrelated theme emerged, one which would open the possibility that the government's approach to information policy might be extended significantly beyond the standard FOI conception. This second theme held out the promise that citizen participation would become the hallmark of this particular, populist version of reform and that local, neighborhood-based activity would be nurtured and validated.

The emphasis on neighborhood initiatives and citizen participation in the Washington campaign reflected accurately the perspectives of many of the key figures involved in the often disorganized, chronically underfunded, yet highly energetic Washington effort. Many of the field organizers and members of the policy formation team brought years of antimachine activity to their campaign work. A group of about a dozen staff and volunteers argued consistently for the kinds of decentralist empowerment-oriented policies that reflected their extensive experience in a variety of community organizing settings.

In fact, the voting blocks targeted by campaign strategists were made up almost entirely of groups that could be expected to resonate positively to the participation theme. First and foremost, of course, came the necessity to knit together the disparate elements of the black community into a uniform, activated base of support. Clearly the participation theme was one key response to the almost universal feeling among blacks that they had remained peripheral for too long.

In addition, the long-time community organization leadership in both Latino and white areas of the city responded quickly and positively to the emphasis on open governmental processes and local neighborhood initiatives. Until the Washington campaign, most of these groups shared an aversion to electoral political involvement. This aversion was based on both experience and strategic principle. The shared experience involved years of interaction and often conflict with the closed nature of the patronage-based local ward organizations. The strategic presumptions, particularly for the activist multi-issue groups, stressed the need to bring independently organized pressure to bear continually upon all elected officials.

But the participation themes stressed by the Washington effort proved promising enough to break this pattern of electoral aloofness. Here was a candidacy that did indeed look more like a populist movement than a modern campaign, one which featured an unimpeachably "progressive" candidate thrust into contention by an unprecedented mobilization of the most excluded residents of the city. Further, the platform expressed in *The Washington Papers* reflected not only the *content* of a program favorable to local participation and empowerment but also a *process* that had involved community leadership centrally in its production.

If it were in fact possible that significant city resources would be redirected from big downtown projects to the neighborhoods; and if a new administration were to commit itself to open government in place of the closed machine style; and if the developing proposals for active neighborhood participation in planning and development were to be implemented—then the context for local activity would be significantly changed. Slowly and steadily during the Washington campaign, the virulent and reality-based skepticism of many community groups began to lift.

Even as community groups continued, with considerable success, to push the Washington platform toward placing even stronger emphasis on the participation theme, the constituencies backing FOI were also gaining in both numbers and impact. "Secrecy" in the Jane Byrne administration became a central issue in the primary campaign, and candidate Richard M. Daley featured a commitment to FOI as prominently as did Washington. And when, after his primary victory, Washington's transition team began the attempt to collect data about Chicago's governmental operations, the obstacles they encountered only served to reinforce this pledge among key policy development insiders.

Still, the link between the commitments to open government and to community participation had not been articulated. As community-based actors talked about FOI they revealed that, in their views, a traditionally construed FOI Act, however broadly drawn, would help neighborhood groups very little. Three basic limits of FOI presented themselves. First, FOI is basically a statement of the willingness to react and respond, not to initiate. Community-based organizations (CBOs) would be the initiators. And few community-based groups possessed the resources, in time or staff, to aggressively pursue data that were physically distant and of unproved relevance to local agendas. Civic organizations and coalitions located in the downtown area, with adequate staff and a developed research agenda, could be expected to join the press and some public officials in taking advantage of the FOI opportunities—but not neighborhood-based organizations.

The second limitation of FOI with respect to CBOs concerned the form of the data that would be made available. FOI implied no obligation to make information intelligible, let alone systematically useful for community constituents. When it was obtained, it came in the form collected and used by the department involved, not by anyone on the outside; often, it required considerable expertise to "decode" and make intelligible.

And finally, FOI presented community groups with an opportunity that was ironically at odds with the overall policy directions of a populist administration, one aimed at developing consistent neighborhood policy in consort with active community organizations. FOI policies respond most readily to tightly drawn requests aimed at a single item or set of items. For CBOs, the targeting of such discrete and specific information needs would be most often embedded in a process of issue identification and action that could be characterized as serial, disconnected, and frequently ad hoc. Further, targeted lists of information obtained from the government were more likely to be appropriate to a protest agenda than to a development agenda. (For example, ownership of slum buildings had been one commonly sought piece of information.)

Thus, from the point of view of CBOs, there was an irony in the Washington campaign's commitment to FOI. These organizations were being handed a tool whose utility was best suited to an adversarial relationship with the public sector, but this tool was being offered by an administration with a strong commitment to ending that kind of relationship and to building CBOs' capacities to act for themselves in partnership with the city administration.

New city officials from the Mayor's Press Office, the Data Center, the Department of Neighborhoods, and the Budget Department joined transition team members in the conviction that an "affirmative" approach to information on the part of the new administration could overcome these objections and was both feasible and sensible. The city government collected and stored data covering a broad range of subject areas. Some of it, no doubt, was potentially useful to constituencies beyond the bureaucracies that collected it. Should it not be possible to design a system for sorting out what was useful, for making it understandable to "nonexperts," and for making it available on an "affirmative" basis (that is, proactively) to neighborhood groups?

The route from conceptualization of the project to its initiation, however, was to prove circuitous indeed. All of the relevant actors, both in the neighborhoods and in city government, needed to be convinced that affirmative information was an innovation worth pursuing, that in fact it extended their capacities for accomplishing already existing objectives. Inside city hall this effort centered on defining the Affirmative Neighborhood Information proposal in relationship to the existing commitment to FOI. With CBO leadership, discussions took place mainly within the context of the transition team's efforts to define an overall approach to neighborhood policy for the new administration. This latter set of discussions had virtually nothing to do with "information needs," focusing instead on the definition of neighborhood needs, particularly for resources, authority, and vehicles for participation in decision making.

CBOs in the Transition Process: Neighborhood Needs Begin to Include Information

During the transition process, which spanned the new mayor's first months in office, two particular task forces drew widespread interest and participation on the part of neighborhood groups: one focused on policy recommendations in the housing area, and the other more generally on neighborhood-oriented initiatives. The importance of these efforts transcended the particular policy recommendations set forth (although a sizable proportion of those were at least partially implemented by the administration in its first year). Rather, these task forces, and the forums and hearings that they convened, marked for Chicago's CBOs their first officially sanctioned opportunity to discuss needs and priorities across neighborhood boundaries, to discover both common issues and significant differences, and to share together some reasonable (yet often skeptically held) expectations that a cooperative stance vis-à-vis city hall was possible.

Though they were themselves, obviously, important exercises in open communication, none of the discussions within the transition process focused directly on the information needs of communities. Yet valuable lessons were learned that reconfirmed the importance of increasing neighborhood access to and sophistication about city-held data. One illustration of the way in which information needs entered these discussions concerns that segment of the Neighborhood Task Force that was to examine the possibilities for a formalized neighborhood planning process. During these discussions, some of which I convened, the wide variance in neighborhood-based capacities and interests was made very clear. Sophisticated neighborhood organizations with existing development capacities saw little need for an expanded city role—in fact, such a role was seen as potentially competitive, a drain on resources already cornered by the group. On the other hand, small, struggling CBOs tended to welcome any and all forms of city initiative in their neighborhoods, more or less on the theory that "anything is better than nothing." The conclusion drawn from these divergent viewpoints was in one way no conclusion at all—yet, in another, a very important recognition of community diversity. The transition report argued that no single formal system of neighborhood planning could possibly satisfy everyone. But in addition to that decision to back away from the universal installation of some form of Neighborhood Planning Board came a closer examination of exactly what kinds of resources the city *could* provide—resources that would aid both the established and the struggling groups. In that context, information came to be regarded as a more universal, nonthreatening commodity that the city held and could distribute.

Thus CBOs began to raise their expectations concerning the information programs of the city. They began, in fact, to constitute themselves as an expanded marketplace for public information. Hundreds of community representatives, for example, attended public hearings on the city's fiscal year 1984 budget, and hundreds more a day-long forum with administration officials on the Year X Community Development Block Grant budget. The status of informed consumer of information clearly appealed to CBOs across the city as the most logical and universal position to take vis-à-vis the new administration, for it left open the full range of local options for defining neighborhood-based activity and response.

Though this general stance by CBOs fell short of the vision of full support and partnership hoped for by some in the new administration, it nonetheless represented a highly significant shift in the historic relations between the neighborhoods and city hall. Expectations were being heightened on each side, at least some of which began to center on the expansion of shared information as the base on which to build further partnership arrangements.

Meanwhile, inside the new city administration, officials were focusing quite clearly on information issues, particularly the issuance of

Washington's oft-promised FOI executive order. But, not surprisingly, complications appeared, delaying the order's appearance for some three months.

How would the executive order be worded? What kinds of information would it cover, and what kinds would it exclude? Where would responsibility for its implementation be lodged, and how would it be structured? The answers to these questions did not appear as a rational construct, full-blown at the inauguration, but rather emerged gradually through a process of proposal, reaction, response, and personnel shifts. The ad hoc nature of this process was consonant with the overall mode of operation within the Washington administration during its first year. And it was understandable, given the constant shifting and redefinition of the political ground rules in Chicago's politics.

In fact, during the administration's first year and a half, five different persons served as the city's FOI officer, and each brought a different set of perspectives and skills to the task. What they had in common was a shared understanding of FOI as *politically* central to the Washington definition of reform. Each had been an active participant in the campaign and had absorbed the political importance of the promise to "open up city government." If the new administration could not deliver on that promise with some dispatch, a major chance for maintaining credibility would be lost. Further, quick delivery on this commitment seemed politically feasible, in a way which other initiatives did not, since the problematic legislative approval process could be bypassed, and authority could be lodged in an already budgeted position within the Mayor's Office.

The first person appointed to the newly created position was an anti-machine former state legislator, James Houlihan, a lawyer with some experience in FOI legislation. Houlihan was ensconced in the Mayor's Office of Intergovernmental Affairs—a division of the Mayor's Office whose major function normally was to facilitate the city's legislative agendas with other bodies of government, particularly at the state level. His placement there reflected both an acknowledgment of the political nature of FOI and the fact that, as he put it, "There was no place else to put me."[14]

Under Houlihan's guidance, the executive order was drafted, circulated among administration officials for comments and reactions, redrafted, and proclaimed—a process that was completed within three months of the new regime's tenure. The content of the order, according to FOI experts, reflected a quite liberal interpretation of both the kinds of information now available and the means provided to gain public access to it.

Houlihan and his staff were immediately responsive to the conception of Affirmative Neighborhood Information. Both the reasons for their enthusiasm and their contributions to the process of initiation are important to note. From the first meetings with these officials, it became clear that they regarded Affirmative Neighborhood Information as a logical extension of FOI and, further, as an approach that could help provide solutions to problems already evident in the implementation of that policy.

These problems were numerous. Virtually no city department was structured to facilitate public access to information. Further, most had no central, systematized method for collecting, storing, and assessing the information it used. Many top- and middle-level officials who were holdovers from previous administrations were at least wary of the new policy and tended to define publicly available information, in one staffer's words, as "whatever they've always given out when somebody bugged them enough." And newly appointed department heads most often had little idea of what kinds of information their departments regularly collected, in what form it existed, or how reliable it was.

As Houlihan began circulating the first draft of the executive order for departmental comment and reaction, he began to discern two major areas of concern. The first was legal in nature and was almost immediately regarded by FOI advocates as "mostly a smoke screen."[15] The second and more serious concerned the lack of resources to implement the policy. In the short term, department heads would be required to reshuffle duties so that the position of information officer could be established and a listing of data held by the department be produced. In the longer term, department heads were fearful of the additional workload imposed by frequent and unpredictable FOI requests from the public.

These resource-oriented concerns led Houlihan to seek outside technical assistance from a variety of sources. Computer manufacturing representatives were involved in an assessment of the hardware system needs of the city's departments. The state's archivists were called in to help departments decide when stored information could be discarded. Department heads were urged to include projected FOI resources in budgetary planning.

In this context of scarce resources, Houlihan and other city officials began immediately to regard "Affirmative Freedom of Information"—as it was initially labeled—as an efficiency measure. Fearing that a wave of information requests would follow the issuance of the order, they viewed the affirmative approach as a mechanism for routinizing public access to the most frequently requested items, thereby facilitating departmental compliance with the order. In addition, the political experiences that Houlihan and others brought with them to their positions led them to understand immediately both the public relations potential of affirmative FOI and the potential benefits to that part of the Harold Washington constituency consisting of community organizations. Thus, Affirmative FOI found a "home" in the bureaucracy and legitimacy within the new administration. In the meantime, support for affirmative information was solidifying within city hall: consultations with community organization leaders were defining the *content* of the data that it would be most useful to receive. Not surprisingly, virtually all of the leaders of major CBOs and of coalitions of organizations named housing data as the most useful general area—more useful, for example, than data concerning crime, health, economic development, or education, reflecting accurately the state of community organizing and development practice in Chicago.

Community groups next gathered to specify priority information items in the housing area. Which items would be most useful to them? Setting priorities was necessary both because of the city's limited resources and because of limits in the CBOs' capacities to absorb and use information— what one organizer referred to as "the dusty stacks of paper syndrome" in CBO offices.[16] To facilitate the process of choosing priorities, the city and the Northwestern group compiled an accurate and detailed "catalog" of all housing-related items of information collected and stored in computers in city departments.

Discussions aimed at producing the Housing Data Catalog taught participants valuable lessons about city-held information. It became clear, for example, that it was one thing to collect and record data for internal department use—corners could be cut, shorthand could be used, and building inspectors, for instance, would understand and adjust. But it was quite another thing for information to be collected with "the public" in mind—stricter standards of accuracy, clearer recording practices, or at least a process of informing the public about the "in-house" nature of data were now clearly demanded. Thus the tone of conversations with departmental data experts was often set by a series of apologetic explanations concerning the shortcomings of internally oriented information. As one expert put it, "This stuff was never meant to see the light of day."

Put somewhat differently, the conviction grew throughout these meetings with department officials that the city organized and understood housing information in a framework very different from that used by CBOs. The city officials' primary way of categorizing information—based on which department developed, maintained, and used that information— could not have been further removed from the neighborhood leaders' consciousness. From the community vantage point it made little or no difference which department or agency was responsible for a given set of data.

For this reason, the Housing Data Catalog reflected a thorough recategorization of city-held information into a format corresponding much more closely to neighborhood perceptions. These categories included Housing Status Inventory, Building Code Enforcement, Housing Assistance, and Land Acquisition/Disposition. Each of these broad categories contained diverse sets of data within it, but each set of data pointed to a distinguishable kind of use or activity on the part of CBOs.

Interestingly enough, this catalog soon began to revise the understanding of housing-related data for both the city administrators and the community-based organizations. For the city people who produced and dealt with parts of the information on a daily basis, the catalog both placed their own narrow slice of information within a broader interdepartmental context and led them toward understanding the very different perspective on "their" information which prevailed among community groups. For leaders from these groups, the catalog both expanded and concretized their understanding of exactly what the city *did* know and hold. The process of transforming city information into a resource—a "commodity" to be assessed, valued, and bargained for—had begun. And for CBOs, this commodification process began with the destruction of two opposing myths about city data that had grown naturally out of their historic adversary relationship with city hall: one myth held that "the city knows everything, if only they'd let us get at it," and the other that "the city knows nothing that is useful to neighborhoods, so we must produce the information which we need ourselves." The Housing Data Catalog, in contrast, began to establish a realistically complex marketplace for city data, one that defined the ground rules anew for community groups. The catalog told community groups that the city did indeed hold a variety of kinds of information (but *not* everything), information whose use-value varied in part depending on the groups' own definition of priorities, as well as on the data itself—its subject matter, accuracy, and timeliness.[17]

Further discussions of the catalog with groups outside of city hall began to clarify not only the groups' information priorities but also their evolving perceptions about and relationship to the new administration. They began to limit their expectations of what data government might provide, and they accepted the fact that this particular project might be stalled by any number of barriers—for example, technical, fiscal, legal, or political factors. That is, computer programming or compatibility issues could stall the project; the resources available in the city, modest though they were projected to be, could prove inadequate within the context of a tight budget; decisions by the corporation counsel could severely limit or prohibit the availability of information the communities wanted; and politically motivated opposition to the project could derail administration support.

The representatives of local community groups were cognizant of the modest nature of the initial step being proposed. They stressed the importance of "access to everything the city's got," as one leader put it. But much more quickly and eagerly than downtown groups, the CBOs plunged into the discussion of exactly which data items they would like to receive on a regularized basis. The prospect of "getting the city to do some of the work we have to do anyway" was immediately evident. And the specific, localized nature of the information available appealed directly to those groups' agendas, fostering a quick and clear recognition that they formed the core constituency for the affirmative information initiative.

After extended discussion aimed at defining criteria for choosing their data priorities, these groups targeted *information that fit their agendas, was timely and frequently updated, and which only the city could provide.*

The only category to fit each of the three criteria was "Building Code Enforcement." Narrowing the priority choice to this single major category represented a consensus among diverse members of the users' panel concerning both the nature of the groups to be served, at least at the outset of the project, and the programmatic utility of the information. Everyone agreed that the initial thrust of the project should be aimed toward providing resources that allowed groups to do better what many of them were already doing—in effect, stretching existing agendas. It should be noted, too, that the agreement on the major category did not end the process of raising cautions among members of the users' panel. One technical assistance provider, for instance, warned that asking for "too little" could easily lead the city to expend all of its time and resources "diddling with the insignificant" and ignoring broader questions of availability and access.

Shortly after the construction of sample housing reports based upon community groups' priorities was completed, the proposal was forwarded to an interdepartmental group within the administration, along with what proved to be a wildly optimistic eight-week work plan for completing the necessary technical steps and initiating the program.

In fact, troubled political and bureaucratic waters would delay implementation of Affirmative Neighborhood Information for nearly a year and a half. The delays were caused by three kinds of problems, each of which was in some way characteristic of the dilemmas faced by the new administration. The first area of difficulty involved the mostly predictable array of bureaucratically defined reservations about the program—concerns about resources and personnel, about organization and responsibility for implementation, about legal questions, about losing control of the information and its uses, and about revealing shortcomings in the operations of the departments themselves. The second set of problems involved the shifting status of FOI responsibility, with four different information officers serving during the first nine months of the Washington administration (a fifth was appointed eight months later). The last set of hurdles resulted from the political pressures on the new administration induced by the paralyzed Chicago context. The mayor's foes, who held the power to block legislation in the city council, were alert to the political ramifications of virtually every policy initiative. So, for example, when the Department of Neighborhoods emerged as a major communications conduit between city hall and the communities—sponsoring popular Neighborhood Forums, coordinating outreach, and providing support for initiatives like Affirmative Neighborhood Information—the city council gutted the department's budget and forced the resignation of its head.

In fact, Washington's opposition was redefining the rules of the political game. And the new political context created by this continuing opposition redefined the tone of the administration's policy discussion in the direction of defensiveness. More and more key administration officials were convinced that a rapid consolidation of power by the new regime was out of the question and that the prospect of four years of maneuvering and confrontation between polarized blocs seemed ever more likely. The effect of this defensive tone on policy initiatives was palpable. One department head quoted above now talked about "reform" as a "process that has to be gradual, quiet, almost invisible." He was also the first person I heard using a military metaphor that would become a commonplace over the next year "We've got to fly low," he explained, "under their [the political opposition's] radar."

Even within this difficult political context, however, it was bureaucratic inertia that proved most difficult to overcome. Gaining support for the new information initiative from ten different city departments, each with new leadership, all facing severe budget constraints and a volatile political milieu, proved a daunting task. Many of the bureaucratically defined objections to affirmative information concerned a well-defined and deeply held orientation to knowledge and information generally, and are likely to be applicable to situations beyond Chicago. At one point in our long series of discussions, we combined some of the objections we were hearing from the administrators into a summary package:

We (the agency/department/bureaucracy)

1) know what information we need for our purposes;
2) understand how and why such information can be adequate for these purposes, but not accurate;
3) know how to interpret the information we gather;
4) know what uses are appropriate to this information, and what uses are not;
5) know how to determine who is and who is not an appropriate recipient of this information; and
6) know how to instruct appropriate recipients in the proper uses of this information.

You, on the other hand (community organizations)

a) cannot possibly understand the reasons we gather the information we do;

b) will accuse us of gathering inaccurate information rather than information which is adequate for our purposes (but not for yours);

c) cannot know how to interpret the information we provide;

d) cannot possibly distinguish between appropriate and inappropriate, responsible and irresponsible uses of this information. Furthermore,

e) you (community organizations) may very well want to use our own information to criticize our operations; and

f) you might even decide to sue us for providing "inaccurate" information.

Taken in the aggregate, these two sets of propositions summarize the most extreme positions taken by city bureaucrats.

Most often, the officials advancing these more protective arguments were either holdover employees, hired by previous administrations, or middle-level "line" bureaucrats with immediate responsibility for department functions that might in fact be expected to draw criticism from community groups (e.g., the Housing Court division of the Law Department). Other officials, including a number of department heads, continued to express support for the initiative.

In the final analysis, however, the impetus for breaking the bureaucratic log jam could be provided only by the decision to schedule a press conference at which Mayor Washington would actually announce the program. This press conference indeed resulted from the continuing pressure and mounting frustration emanating from the community groups, who were growing impatient at the delays. The groups made both the Mayor's Office and the press office aware of their dissatisfaction, and the response was remarkably rapid. By the time the press conference occurred, nearly two years had elapsed since the idea of affirmative information had been conceived. Perhaps there was a trace of irony in the mayor's voice as he intoned, "Ladies and gentlemen, for those of you who have asked me continually what I mean by 'reform,' let me simply point out, *this program* is what reform is all about."

Reflections on the Affirmative Information Experiment

What is to be learned from this policy initiation effort? Final verdicts concerning the viability and usefulness of this newborn, as well as its capacity to thrive and grow, must await further experience and analysis. On the other hand, both the conceptual and practical efforts that defined the inception of this modest model project may well carry implications ranging far beyond the boundaries of Chicago.

Perhaps most importantly, it is clear that the development of information technologies is now far enough advanced that serious and potentially fruitful attention can be given to the construction of decentralist, or democratized, information strategies. The sheer quantities of data currently collected and stored in centralized computer facilities, particularly those facilities operated by public sector organizations, present policymakers with a challenging "fork in the road" set of choices: systems design may continue to respond almost exclusively to the technically and bureaucratically determined needs for larger, faster and more efficient data operation—without regard to the likely political consequences; or policymakers may choose to take advantage of the technology's increasing malleability to rethink the purposes and directions of information policy.

In pursuit of this latter goal, at least three interrelated political challenges we faced in Chicago may be relevant for other cities as well.

First, it was necessary to build a set of advocates for decentralized information in the neighborhoods. CBOs, along with allied city-wide civic organizations, were found to be both interested in and capable of defining their own organizational agendas and their corresponding information needs. They required some measure of technical assistance in order to expand their knowledge of exactly what kinds of information the city held, but once that assistance had been provided they quickly became enthusiastic advocates for the decentralist thrust.

The basic preconditions for developing constituencies interested in decentralizing information are ubiquitous. Large governmental bodies everywhere collect and store information about smaller geographic units. These locality-based data, covering a wide range of substantive areas, have potential utility not only for the centrally defined and operated programs they already serve but for locality-based groupings of citizens as well. It seems probable that for the variety of types of local groups, like Chicago's CBOs, the capacity systematically to collect and store their own data is beyond imagining. But the process of receiving data collected centrally does not drain scarce organizational resources and raises the potential for planned, systematic activity based on locally defined agendas. Furthermore, as the number of local groups with access to microcomputers continues to grow, capacities for storing and using information should develop apace. Electronic transmission and even exchange of data between central and local organizations may soon be possible to contemplate.

Secondly, in Chicago it was necessary to build the *political* commitment to a decentralized information thrust. Most public sector bodies are legally constrained by some version of a FOI Act. But the Chicago experiment makes clear the conceptual and practical gaps separating FOI's requirement of passive receptivity to outside requests and "affirmative information's" commitment to active distribution.

The crucial first step for political leaders may not depend on any particular ideological predilections but may be fundamentally conceptual in nature: information must be viewed as a *resource with wide distributive potential*. In a time of stagnant or shrinking public budgets, government leaders everywhere, and particularly in cities, face the political fallout resulting from program cutbacks. Viewed as a negotiable resource, even a commodity, information constitutes one potentially valuable "public good" with significant potential for expansion. Needless to say, the political credit for this expansion may provide leaders with more than adequate motivation to innovate.

Finally, as the Chicago case makes clear, it is necessary to build some level of bureaucratic support if the democratization process is to go forward. Indeed, we discovered even strong doses of community-based and top-level political support for the initiative could not guarantee efficient and enthusiastic cooperation from the city hall bureaucracies. Probably many of the problems placed in the path of decentralized information policy by Chicago's bureaucracies will crop up in other cities as well. Questions concerning accuracy and liability, ownership and control, resources and efficiency are germane to planning, law, and other affected departments in virtually any municipal government.

Yet the role of the bureaucracies in the Chicago case was probably skewed by a number of rarer circumstances. First, of course, Chicago's bureaucratic structures are larger than those of any U.S. city except New York and therefore more unwieldy than most. In addition, Chicago's unusually stormy and contentious period of political and governmental transition provided a somewhat unusual context for policy reform—a context whose effects on the bureaucracies' capacity to respond can only be judged as mixed. On the one hand, it is certainly true that most of Mayor Washington's top-level bureaucratic appointees were quick to grasp the potential political benefits of Affirmative Neighborhood Information and to understand the initiative as an integral part not only of a broader commitment to open government but of a more general populist policy agenda. Further, the traumatic transition period represented a context in which policy changes were *expected*, even within the normally routinized bureaucracies. On the other hand, the new mayor's appointees were themselves relatively few in number and almost universally new to the departments they served. They were faced initially not only with the predictable administrative challenges—familiarizing themselves with ongoing structures and functions, with personnel, and with workable levers of control—but also with a series of dilemmas defined by Chicago's uniquely polarized political context.

Although a detailed account of the fate and utility of Affirmative Neighborhood Information is beyond the scope of this chapter, a few notes may be helpful. The program was in fact institutionalized within the city's Planning Department. After a couple of months of experimentation, department staff routinized the monthly reports to community groups so that they demanded a minimal amount of time and attention.

The number of community groups receiving the reports quickly grew to more than 175. From an extensive survey of user groups conducted some months after the program was initiated, two findings stand out. First the amount of good will toward the administration that was generated by this simple outreach program was striking. From many different kinds of neighborhood groups, from virtually all sections of town, came comments much like that of a staff director from the Southwest Side: "We've never before gotten anything that's both free *and* useful from the city. It makes us feel like a real partnership is possible."

A second survey finding worth noting concerns the wide variety of uses that CBOs found for the reports. Most, predictably enough, used the reports to identify problem housing and to track buildings through the court system. Many groups, though, invented new uses for the reports—for instance, locating rehabilitation and community investment opportunities, or helping to prevent housing abandonment. The reports proved to be adaptable to a fairly broad range of community-based agendas in the housing area.

The usefulness of the reports led CBOs to begin asking for an expansion of the program and for the inclusion of more kinds of information. One set of groups, for example, pursued data concerning the city's capital budget, whereas others worked at extracting useful information about everything from city-owned vacant land to listings of city contracts. Where these ongoing projects and discussions will lead in the post-Washington era is difficult to predict.

It is clear that opening up city government in Chicago, given the situation inherited by the Washington administration in 1983, is a task that is still far from completed. But in this modest experiment called Affirmative Neighborhood Information, and in the ongoing projects to which it led, we have at least begun to meet the challenge to create in our cities a more democratized politics of public information. One might hope that more cities will soon accept that challenge as well.

NOTES

1. Other members of the group were Andrew Gordon, John McKnight, Robert Le Bailley, and Eric Nyblad.
2. Many of these interviews were conducted by Susan Reed.
3. Interview, Alderman Martin Oberman, July 1984.

4. Interview, Professor Dick Simpson, former alderman, July 1984.
5. Ibid.
6. Interview, Better Government Association, July 1984.
7. Interview, Alderman Oberman.
8. Interviews, former aldermen, August 1984.
9. Ibid.
10. Ibid.
11. *Blueprint of Chicago Government: A Study for Mayor Harold Washington by the Agency Review Unit of the Transition Team*, May 1983, Executive Summary, p. 2.
12. Interview, city employee, September 1984.
13. Ibid.
14. Interview, FOI official, August 1983.
15. Ibid.
16. Interview, community organizer, 1984.
17. Catalog available from the Center for Urban Affairs and Policy Research, Northwestern University.

Planned Manufacturing Districts: How a Community Initiative Became City Policy

DONNA DUCHARME

It's August 1988 in Chicago, and it's sweltering in the gym at Christopher House. Well over two hundred people have gathered for a public hearing on the proposed Clybourn Corridor Planned Manufacturing District. Every person I don't recognize makes me nervous, so I'm nervous as hell.

The proponents are hopeful that Chicago's first Planned Manufacturing District (PMD) will emerge from this community hearing ready for passage—first by the Chicago Plan Commission and then by the city council. The opponents are hoping for a minor miracle. The press is here—TV cameras and all. A front-page article this morning in the *Chicago Tribune* lambasted the PMD as ill conceived, politically motivated, and lacking manufacturing support.

Those of us in the middle of the issue know that the support base is strong, diverse, and well organized. It crosses most of the political barriers that plague Chicago. But we've been through a lot; we know where the pitfalls are and that anything can happen.

Harold Washington has been dead for nine months. Eugene Sawyer is now the acting mayor. Alderman Marty Oberman, a Washington ally, whose support signaled the start of the PMD development process, left office more than a year ago. The candidate he endorsed as his successor lost the election. Edwin Eisendrath, often an opponent of Harold Washington, is now the alderman of the 43rd ward. Rob Mier has been replaced by Timothy Wright as commissioner of the Department of Economic Development (DED) and Bob Giloth, who nurtured the PMD within the city bureaucracy as deputy commissioner of DED's Research and Development (R&D) Division, has moved to Baltimore. Now, Greg Longhini, in the Department of Planning, is the point person. The PMD hasn't died. It has survived a lot of change and has actually improved along the way.

It was five years ago that the first proposal to convert a manufacturing building in this area to residential lofts was approved. Within just a few months, three or four additional zoning changes were requested for other

industrial properties in the Clybourn Corridor. Surrounding manufacturers raised concerns about their future if additional zoning changes and
conversion proposals were approved. A clear city policy and an area-wide
solution were needed. Case-by-case consideration of zoning changes was
discouraging continued manufacturing investment, causing lengthy land
use battles, and doing nothing to discourage speculation and rapid increases in the cost of land.

The PMD concept was originally created to address the displacement
concerns of these Clybourn Corridor industries. It was designed to ensure
that certain manufacturing-zoned areas like the Clybourn Corridor would
continue to be used for industrial purposes despite upscale residential and
commercial development pressures. It was also designed as a flexible zoning tool. Each PMD will specify what types of land use changes, if any, will
be allowed, where, and under what circumstances. These rules assure manufacturers in the district that new development will be compatible with
their operations. Like the Clybourn Corridor PMD, additional districts
will be constructed to address the unique land use questions facing that
area.

This hearing has been a long time coming. Commissioners Elizabeth
Hollander (Planning) and Timothy Wright (DED) preside over it together. I
know that this, in and of itself, is a major success. No deputy commissioners running this one—it's too important. The PMD is not yet the
law, but it is city policy. Their presence is also an important signal. Both
departments own the PMD now. This display of unity and cooperation was
years in the making.

Alderman Eisendrath speaks first. I've already read his testimony, so I
know we'll be off to a good start. He summarizes the four-year effort to
preserve the manufacturing land in the face of development trends that
threaten to replace the existing industrial base with upscale residential, office, and retail uses: "Over the past year, I've felt like a marshal in the Old
West presiding over a range war. Some people want to farm; others want to
run cattle over the land. We've gotten past that speculation, but now it's a
question of balance." Eisendrath goes on to explain why the PMD is important and why it has his strong support.

His testimony is followed by workers, union officials, manufacturers,
community organizations, residents, and real estate developers and
brokers. The vast majority speak in favor of the PMD.

"Preserving the industries here (in the Clybourn Corridor) is one thing
that workers and companies can agree on," says a Black union vice
president.

A Hispanic area resident and worker says:

> I used to have a $75 apartment in the . . . area and I walked 1½ blocks
> to my job. . . . That $75 apartment is now $1700 and the job where I

had a good union wage is now a condominium. . . . The choice is this: working at a good manufacturing job or working at a service industry job to get McDonald's wages. I'm for protecting manufacturing and protecting jobs.

Another area resident makes the arguments of the wealthier white opponents, "I cannot be an enthusiastic supporter [of the PMD]. It's environmentally questionable . . . and there are no tax studies to demonstrate that residential development wouldn't outweigh the tax revenues from heavy manufacturing."

His arguments are countered by a wealthy white supporter: "Our city cannot survive as just a service economy, as just a consumer economy. We don't see industry at odds with residential Lincoln Park. Most opposed [to the PMD] are those who say, "When I get out of the city, I want to make my bucks so I can build elsewhere."

Our guys are doing great! A commercial developer testifies on our behalf. He was "converted" earlier in the summer and has helped us enormously with the other developers and retail businesses. The president of the largest and heaviest industry in the Clybourn Corridor, a steel mill, explains: "Our workers average $40,000. . . . We're a heavy, hot industry, but we've been a good neighbor. We'd like to be here for another 100 years, but we need certainty. We need stability to plan."

Another industry owner states his opposition to the PMD. "Someday when we want to leave, all this [the PMD] will do is keep our property values low." A third owner counters, "I'm a firm believer [in the PMD]. I disagree with . . . my neighbor. I think [he's] looking at the holy buck." A fourth owner sums it up this way: "I didn't move into Clybourn thinking it would become condo row. When I moved there, people thought I was crazy. Now, I'm considered visionary. To people who don't want to live near factories, I say, 'Don't move there.' We were there first and it's zoned for that [manufacturing]."

I'm really proud of these guys. They were all afraid to speak in public two years ago. When my turn to testify comes, I aim straight for the reporter who's front-page story that morning enraged and energized us. I'm sick of the biased way that the *Chicago Tribune* has covered this issue. It has the power to shape public opinion, and I wish it would be more accurate, if it can't be supportive. So methodically, fact by fact and point by point, I refute his article. Everyone knows who I'm talking about, and he's in the audience squirming. There have been a lot of things during the long process that have made me angry, but none have made me angrier than his article.

I miss the next testimonies because the reporter and I are embroiled in a heated exchange in the back: I'm talking about the responsibility of the press to be accurate and to represent issues truthfully, and he's telling me that I'm naive—"It's controversy that sells papers, not harmony." One of my staff comes to tell me to cool it. I look up. All eyes are on us. We part company.

Then comes the testimony we'd hoped for. An opponent whose outrageous statements make us look all the more responsible. She introduces herself as a "resident," neglecting to mention that she's also a real estate broker: "The manufacturing district here started 100 years ago. Things change. . . . We can't legislate what works for people. . . . If Finkl (Steel) needs to be protected, draw a line around *him* and make him a zoo—show our children how steel is made." Even the opponents tell her to sit down.

The former alderman, Oberman, who has stayed closely involved, finishes off the hearing: "We are breaking new ground here. . . . Old zoning tools did not seem to be working. We here in Chicago are setting a pattern for the whole country. Look on it as a pilot program. . . . We've worked on it over four years. Now it is time to put it into effect."

Two months, two more hearings, and a few days later, the Clybourn Corridor PMD was passed into law, unanimously and without fanfare in an omnibus bill, by the city council. This was the first time that I really felt like celebrating.

The Context

Establishing the Local Employment and Development Council

The concept of industrial displacement began as an attempt to make sense of our observations in the field, grew into a community issue, and then into an accepted cornerstone of Mayor Washington's economic development policy. This process was exhilarating and exhausting, inspiring and frustrating. Mostly it was a roller coaster ride and a lot of hard work. It wasn't planned—it evolved. It was only sort of what I'd had in mind when, fresh out of MIT's Master's program in city planning, I started the Local Economic and Employment Development (LEED) Council as a unit of the New City YMCA in 1982. It was the last year of Mayor Jane Byrne's administration.

Before graduate school, I helped run youth advocacy and employment programs for the local YMCA. Frustrated by the social service approach that helped people but never addressed the more fundamental problems in the community, I left to study community and economic development at MIT. The New City YMCA was built during this time, replacing an old YMCA and expanding its constituencies and services. Community development was to be a key component of the new "Y."

The director of the New City YMCA asked me to put together my ideas about what types of community economic development activity could be done from a YMCA base. Ultimately, I wrote my Master's thesis as an answer to his question and was hired to implement it. I knew the area, understood economic development strategy, and had figured out how to get started. I had no idea what would evolve.

I started by convening a nine-month planning process that brought together large and small manufacturers and community groups to look at the economic development needs of the community and what could be done to address them. It was a diverse group, including public housing residents from Cabrini–Green, managers from Montgomery Ward and Procter & Gamble, settlement house staff, and owners of small companies. This group operated on the basis of unanimous consensus throughout the planning process.

This diverse group of planners was convened in order to get people working together who had never even talked to each other before. Most community economic development organizations either were started from the business community *for* the business community or were started from a low-income residential base *for* that base. I was trying to create a hybrid by bringing the businesses and low-income residents together from the start. The interests of the low-income residents and the manufacturers, while not necessarily the same, could (I hoped) complement each other. A potential employment link existed between the residents and the manufacturers. And by working together they might be able to counter the mounting displacement pressures that threatened both communities.

The LEED Council's goals, determined by this planning group, were consistent with this underlying strategy: retain businesses and jobs; provide employment opportunities for residents; create new jobs and industrial development; and support efforts to create new housing options for low-income residents.

The Community

These goals reflect the conditions in the larger Near North River Industrial Corridor. The corridor, located along the Chicago River, stretches for about 3 miles just north of Chicago's downtown. It includes Goose Island and the Clybourn and Elston industrial areas. Covering parts of three wards, it contains a total of 30,000 mostly industrial jobs representing all major categories of manufacturing activity. Despite years of job loss and neglect by the city, it's still a strong manufacturing area.

The goals also reflect the dynamic between the industrial corridor and the bordering communities. Cabrini–Green is a large low-income public housing development. Lincoln Park is one of the wealthiest residential communities in Chicago. West Town is a neighborhood of predominantly working-class Hispanic and Polish residents who are rapidly losing ground to new, wealthier white residents. And River North, formerly a manufacturing area, is now a chic commercial, office, and residential area next to Chicago's downtown. Pressure from upscale retail, office, and residential development is converging on the industrial corridor, Cabrini–Green, and West Town from both Lincoln Park and River North.

Getting Started

The planning group felt that industrial retention should be the initial focus of the LEED Council's work since, no matter how successful we might become, we'd probably never create 30,000 new jobs. They also agreed that our industrial retention work had to benefit area residents through increased local hiring. The other goals would be phased in later as this basic strategy was implemented.

I began an "industrial advocate" service, meeting with companies to find out what their problems were and trying to help solve them. In 1983 the Byrne administration agreed to support our industrial retention work through a $14,250 contract, which increased our access to the city departments. Some companies viewed this city connection with suspicion, whereas others felt that it increased our credibility. The contract eventually allowed us to hire another staff person and increase our contacts with companies.

In addition to assisting individual companies, we also began to organize them to take collective action. Our first organizing efforts focused on obtaining infrastructure improvements. We were lucky: the planning had already been done on a number of industrial street improvement projects, but the funding had never been allocated. When Harold Washington was elected mayor he began funding these repairs. Our organizing successes came quickly—and they were literally in concrete.

During this early period I joined the Community Workshop for Economic Development (CWED), a coalition of organizations involved in community economic development. I hadn't worked in community development in Chicago before, and CWED offered me a chance to meet people in the field. When the Washington campaign started, some of the people involved in CWED asked me to help write *The Washington Papers* on jobs and economic development. The process was an exciting one and helped me understand the relationship between various city policies and what the LEED Council was trying to accomplish.

The Washington Papers and CWED's early work looked at issues of empowerment and economic development together. Those involved were looking for ways to democratize the development process and widely distribute the benefits. This was expressed in the concept of "balanced growth," which meant balance between economic sectors and between neighborhood and downtown development. Our work also began to redefine economic development. Until this point economic development and real estate development were considered synonymous. When *The Washington Papers* moved the issue of jobs—numbers of jobs, the quality of jobs, and jobs for whom—to the front burner, the differences between real estate development and economic development became apparent.

The Industrial Displacement Issue

The LEED Council developed the industrial displacement issue within the institutional and community context described above and finally in the larger citywide policy arena. This process involved several steps: (1) organizing companies to oppose zoning changes, and conducting research to understand and define the problem; (2) creating the PMD concept; and (3) developing enabling legislation. Throughout, we needed to manage the community process that developed the PMD proposal, and build the community and citywide support bases needed to enact the proposal into law.

The Organizing and Research Stage

In 1983, about a year after the LEED Council was started, the first zoning change was requested for a residential conversion on Clybourn Avenue. Up until that point Clybourn had been an industrial street. We organized the companies near the proposed Clybourn Lofts and went to the hearings. The developers were very convincing. They argued that their housing was for artists and others who liked the idea of living in a manufacturing environment. As a concession to the manufacturers, the loft purchase agreements would indicate that the buyer understood this was a manufacturing area. Since the residents would be there at night, security would improve. And, because residents vote, the streets would get fixed. Finally, they argued that there was no other use for this vacant, multistory industrial building. So we agreed to the conversion.

However, a couple of months after the first occupants moved into the development, companies began receiving complaints and three or four additional zoning changes were requested. Development hit the area at a startling rate, and before long every building on the market was "priced for conversion" to residential, office, or retail use—not for manufacturing.

The LEED Council continued talking to the manufacturers, going with them to hearings on proposed developments, and trying to get a handle on the phenomenon, which we ultimately called *industrial displacement*. We learned that, contrary to popular opinion, many companies did not want to leave the area. We began to understand how industrial displacement happens. Then, we started explaining what we were learning to others. The idea of industrial displacement was not easily accepted. The prevailing view was that all industry *wants* to leave the city and that Chicago would inevitably have a service-sector economy because all manufacturing is either dying or dead. Nobody had thought about industrial displacement as a *cause* of job loss or relocation.

From our vantage point, the city government was pursuing contradictory policies. On the one hand, the administration wanted to retain the manufacturing base here and was funding industrial street improvements, company expansions, and the LEED Council. On the other hand, it was granting zoning changes from manufacturing to other uses without question and destroying the future of manufacturing in the area. These zoning changes were creating a new dynamic. Manufacturers could no longer afford expansion space, and new manufacturers couldn't move into the area. Investors were buying property and holding it until redevelopment arrived at their doorstep. Then they would sell it for other uses at higher prices.

In the Near North River Industrial Corridor, industrial land sold for $6–9 per square foot. For retail use, it commanded $12–20. For residential use, the price was as high as $40. Manufacturers could not compete in the office, retail, or residential markets. As change continued, they faced growing operational problems and conflicts with their new neighbors.

For example, manufacturers operate under performance standards. A manufacturer next to other manufacturers operates under one set of standards for noise, vibration, odor, etc. If a manufacturer is located next to a business-use site, it operates under another, more stringent set. And a manufacturer next to a residential-use site operates under yet another *more* stringent set. So, for example, a steel mill in Lincoln Park that has been operating for a hundred years under the "manufacturing next to manufacturing" standards can suddenly, if a zoning change is granted, find itself in violation of the law. In the case of the steel mill, it's technologically unfeasible for it to meet *either* of the other two standards. In other cases the standards can be met but the company incurs increased operating costs that its competitors in other manufacturing areas do not have to assume.

Uncertainty became another major problem. More and more companies in the industrial corridor were afraid to continue investing here. Investments in maintenance or expansion could be foolish if, in six months or five years, incompatible uses were developed next door. Major capital investments take years to pay for themselves. A stable industrial environment is a requirement for capital investments to take place.

As we worked with the companies, the causes of industrial displacement became more clear and zoning fights were consuming more and more of the LEED Council's resources. We needed a strategy to *solve* the problem, because we couldn't continue fighting zoning changes on a case-by-case basis. We might win battles, but eventually we would lose the war because we couldn't create a stable industrial environment. One by one companies would leave. We had to get to a point where we could propose a solution.

The idea of industrial displacement got its first positive reception from the R&D Division of DED. Bob Giloth, the deputy commissioner, had worked in Pilsen, another community near the downtown area, and had encountered the same issues there. Other colleagues in community development, with less direct experience of the same phenomenon, were harder to convince and tended to question our observations rather than support our efforts to understand the process. I was very frustrated by this, because although I had expected it to be difficult to convince others, I had counted on support from our friends. So, I began working just with the R&D Division to conduct research on industrial displacement. The purpose of the study was both to understand the issue better and to give the issue credibility.

We worked on the study for a long time exploring what had happened to companies displaced by redevelopment from River North and projected what could be expected in the Goose Island/Clybourn areas. The work was split between LEED and the R&D Division. Later the Center for Urban Economic Development at the University of Illinois at Chicago (UICUED) joined the research team. UICUED's role was to find out if other cities were experiencing the same phenomenon and what they were doing about it.

I was scraping together the staff time to do the research whenever I could. Our city contract did not include funding to do research. The Field Division of DED, which monitored our city contract, tolerated the industrial displacement work but didn't recognize it as part of our industrial retention responsibilities. It didn't fit into their categories, and initially they were angry that I was working directly with another division of DED. They required delegate agencies to access other divisions through them. To me community empowerment meant that community groups were equal players and should be allowed to access DED's resources the same way that everyone else did—directly.

Building a Solution: The PMD

When the first draft of the research paper was complete, we sent it out for review. One copy went to Marty Oberman, the alderman in the 43rd ward, where most of our zoning battles had occurred. He was beginning to understand the issue and was concerned about having to face continuing battles with no policy guidance from the city administration. Fortunately, right before we finished the first draft of the research, two things happened to underscore the magnitude of the problem in his ward:

First, a new residential conversion was proposed, but it faced opposition by a number of companies. The developer argued that residential was the only viable use for the building. But an industrial broker had informed us that an industrial bid had been made for the property. Armed with this information, we went to the hearing, and the alderman agreed to give us three weeks to produce an industrial bid. If we could produce such a bid, he wouldn't support the zoning change. When we found a suburban company that wanted to relocate to the area, the developer withdrew his request for a zoning change and developed the property with commercial and office uses allowed under the existing zoning. Nevertheless, we had proven to the alderman that an industrial market did exist in the corridor—even for multistory loft buildings.

Second, one of the companies closest to the redevelopment (who subsequently did leave the area) contacted Oberman. The owner explained in detail how the redevelopment was affecting his company and why he couldn't operate in the corridor much longer. This company employed 150 people and had been located in the area for years. The phone call made an impact. When Alderman Oberman received the research draft, he decided it was time to do something about the problem. He called a moratorium on zoning changes in the industrial area until a solution could be developed. Then he asked LEED, the city government, and his staff to come up with a solution.

At this point DED's role changed significantly. Until Alderman Oberman came on board, the industrial displacement work was an interesting idea being nurtured in the bureaucracy. But the administration wasn't really committed to the issue, and it did not take any real risks until that first alderman supported our work. This was the major turning point. Oberman gave the issue the legitimacy that provided the security needed for the city to proceed with the next steps. This was in early 1986, two and a half years after the first conversion on Clybourn.

In January 1986, at Alderman Oberman's request, we began to develop a solution to the industrial displacement problem in our area. We held meetings with the companies and developed a manufacturing district that would protect the industries. These meetings were significant for three reasons: First, the companies involved in the process began to feel as though they shared ownership of the solution. Second, a split developed between those who wanted to stay in the area and those who wanted to sell their properties at the highest (nonindustrial) price and leave. Third, the aldermanic office, R&D staff, and Planning Department staff involved in the process had their first significant contact with the companies and heard, first hand, about the problems they faced. This helped to cement our credibility and strengthen support in the government.

During the first nine months of our work on the PMD concept, industrial displacement was still viewed as a local issue. One zoning case emerged in the 42nd ward, and the first case occurred in the 32nd ward, further north on Clybourn. But both were in the larger industrial corridor that forms our service area. Nonetheless, the city government's involvement with industrial displacement changed dramatically during this time.

Up to this point, zoning changes were left to the discretion of the local alderman. In September 1987, the LEED Council was contacted by the Planning Department about a rezoning requested for Goose Island (located in the neighboring 42nd ward). The developer wanted to convert a multistory industrial building zoned for heavy manufacturing use to a mixed-use, work/live development called "River Lofts." Plan Commission approval was needed because of the river frontage. The alderman and the commissioner of economic development had apparently given the green light to proceed with the plan months before. When we discussed the proposal with the manufacturers on Goose Island and found strong opposition, a protracted nine-month battle ensued. After a series of hearings, the administration decided to support the industries. The alderman, who generally supported the administration, wanted the development approved. The Planning Department was charged with conducting negotiations between the developer, the local industries, and the LEED Council to reach a compromise. As a result of these negotiations, the development proposal was modified somewhat to address the company's concerns and the alderman agreed to support passage of a PMD on Goose Island to ensure its industrial future.

The River Lofts situation was significant for a number of reasons. The city government began to realize the implications of pursuing the new industrial displacement policies it had helped to create. For the first time it took significant risks to move the policy forward. The LEED Council learned what it took to provide enough community support to reduce the city's risks. And, through the negotiation process, the Planning Department, which had remained skeptical, became convinced that industrial displacement was really a problem and warranted its serious consideration.

Both the River Lofts case and the Clybourn Corridor PMD proposal, which had been approved at a community hearing in January 1987, received media attention. This broadened awareness of industrial displacement. As people began to hear about it, they also began to *see* it. Industrial displacement cases began to surface in other neighborhoods—

one in Back-of-the-Yards, and some further north. Industrial displacement had occurred before in Chicago, in places like Printer's Row and River North, and it was currently happening in other parts of the city. But until it was defined, it wasn't seen. Confirmation of the problem in other communities helped our legitimacy. It also added a year to our work.

The Enabling Legislation

As industrial displacement became obvious in other Chicago neighborhoods, we realized that we should be creating a tool that could be applied in other communities as well. We decided to draft the enabling legislation for the PMD to allow the creation of many districts; *then* we would go back to pass legislation for the Clybourn District. As a result, we went through the process of developing the Clybourn Corridor PMD and obtaining community approval *twice.* Too much time elapsed between the alderman's community hearing in January 1987 and passage of the PMD enabling legislation in April 1988. Furthermore, passage of the Clybourn Corridor PMD had to follow the rules now set forth in the enabling legislation. In October 1988, the Clybourn Corridor PMD finally became law.

This was a period of a lot of change and frustration. In April 1987, Alderman Oberman was replaced by Alderman Eisendrath. Almost immediately after Eisendrath took office, the Law Department staff, which had been consulted early in the process, decided that the structure of the enabling legislation was unworkable, but they let our revision sit in their offices for four months without comment. In August 1987, Bob Giloth, who had been the key city staffer pushing the PMD through the bureaucracy, moved from Chicago. Subsequently, the R&D Division that nurtured the PMD from its infancy shrank considerably. One of its staff, Greg Longhini, moved over to the Planning Department, a recent PMD supporter, to assume the main PMD staffing responsibilities. Finally, Rob Mier left DED for the Mayor's Office and it took considerable time for a new commissioner to be named. In the meantime, DED was severely understaffed.

The Law Department finally completed its review of the enabling legislation in September 1987. After a series of meetings it was finally ready for city council submission. Then, three weeks after Mayor Washington toured our service area and announced his support for the PMD, he died. Acting Mayor Eugene Sawyer was elected by a raucous and divided city council. At this point, the enabling legislation was finally ready to go—almost two years after Alderman Oberman had requested a solution. The newspaper, commenting on the fate of Washington's policies, reported the PMD to be "hanging in the balance." I had no idea what would happen. I couldn't believe how easily years of painstaking work—putting all the right pieces in place—might fall apart. Even if we would ultimately succeed, it would take months more of effort and energy to put all the pieces back in place.

The Ingredients of Success

However, the PMD didn't die with Harold Washington. It survived all the changes and actually improved along the way. The main reason for this was that, quite simply, it wasn't Harold Washington's PMD. He didn't publicly support it until three weeks before his death. By that time, stakeholders included not just the administration but also the companies, the alderman, community organizations, workers, and many others.

The Administration

The Washington administration made it possible to develop the PMD, but it originated in the community. Parts of the administration wanted to support it and took stronger and stronger steps to do so as we were able to produce the expanded bases of support that minimized the risks of each step. Other parts of the administration were dragged along kicking and screaming by those who were supporters. The policies established in *The Washington Papers* and then "Chicago Works Together," I and II, the city's development plan, were held over the heads of the bureaucracy more than once to induce cooperation.

The role of the supporters in the administration was to coach us, help us, and give us legitimacy when they could, and to pave the way in the bureaucracy to take each successive step. Our role was to know our community, know what was needed, and to build the base of support that could keep the process moving. We made the policies real. Our agendas and priorities didn't always match, and there were many tense moments along the way.

The Companies

Once the decision was made to develop enabling legislation and build a citywide tool, we had to build a broader base of support for the PMD. The company managements remained the critical spokespeople in the process and were more and more important in the process as it went along. They were the people who gave the issue validity. I could explain the problem, but until real, profit-making manufacturers who wanted to remain in the industrial corridor spoke up, much of the public was skeptical.

The companies played a key role. Getting them involved in public processes and helping them articulate the issue was no small task. We did succeed in building leadership among a core group of manufacturers, and over time they became the key spokespeople about the issue. For example, until 1986, nobody had heard of A. Finkl and Sons. At Alderman Eisendrath's urging, they hired a public relations firm and ultimately assumed a high profile and a leadership role in the community. Finkl's public relations firm was also instrumental in lining up experts in the field to do research and to testify in support of the PMD. By the time the PMD passed, Finkl was a household word in Chicago's economic development circles.

The Alderman

Alderman Eisendrath was critical to the success of the process. He understood the public relations aspects of the issue and used this knowledge to help overcome the negative perceptions about the PMD and its policy implications. He helped make it a mainstream issue. Eisendrath wanted the PMD to be more than right, he actually wanted it to be elegant—and succeeded in improving it markedly. Finally, it was his leadership that kept the PMD alive in the confusion after Mayor Washington died.

Community Organizations and Coalitions

As other community organizations and business organizations began to see this problem in their communities, they began to help broaden the issue, each in their own way. Both of the citywide coalitions of community economic development organizations found ways to support and further the issues underlying the PMD. The Chicago Association of Neighborhood Development Organizations (CANDO) initiated the Securing Older Buildings Project to identify other techniques to control land use and to explore ways to reuse older industrial buildings for industrial purposes. CWED began a Local Development Issues Working Group, designed to help other groups address development issues in their communities.

The community groups supporting the PMD were a diverse lot. They were from white ethnic neighborhoods, poor minority communities, and manufacturering areas. Ultimately every community group in the wealthy Lincoln Park neighborhood bordering the Clybourn Corridor PMD supported its passage.

Workers and Unions

We also developed strategies to involve workers in the issue. A small study that we conducted with five companies on Goose Island indicated that their 385 employees came from all 50 wards of the city. We asked the companies to have their employees write their aldermen (city council representatives). We also began to develop some connections into the unions, through the companies that supported the PMD, through the city government, and later through community groups that had union and worker contacts.

The Press

Another critical role was played by the press. There were a few friendly reporters and editors who helped enormously. In particular *Crain's Chicago Business* played a crucial role in educating the public about the issue and why it was important. Its staff wrote a series of editorials and a number of articles that supported the issue. They kept the PMD in the public eye at critical times. The *Reader*, the *Booster*, and a number of other smaller publications also played important public education functions. The two major Chicago newspapers, on the other hand, tended to look for and cover any controversy related to the issue rather than playing educational roles.

The Results

Building this base that spanned different interests provided new ways to influence the support of others. It offered a wider range of options. When we were trying to change the *Chicago Tribune's* editorial position, we could now send people that they might listen to more readily than others. So, one by one and piece by piece, different groups came on board and the base expanded.

Once the enabling legislation was ready and the support base was lined up, Mayor Washington finally came out and said, "Okay, I'm behind this." I was angry about his public silence for a long time. He could have saved us a lot of frustration and energy by legitimizing the issue earlier. Valuable time was lost. But, when he died, I was glad he *hadn't*. He forced us to do our homework and to build the base needed to make the initiative credible on its own.

As I now see it, we might well have gotten the enabling legislation and the

Clybourn Corridor PMD passed earlier with Mayor Washington's backing, but it wouldn't have been a process that changed economic development thought in Chicago. And it might not have found the common ground that brought so many different interests together. In the long run this loose coalition that joined together in support of the PMD may prove to be the PMD's most important by-product. Relationships were formed that could be critical to addressing other important issues related to Chicago's economic future.

Conclusion

The Planned Manufacturing District evolved out of a community process. We felt our way along; I had certainly never done anything like this before. We simply began to see and then to address a local issue. We had no master plan and no idea that our PMD work would lead to major city policy changes or spawn related work in and out of government.

Just what has and what has not been accomplished as a result of our work will be more clear in the years to come. Our success will be measured by whether the two additional PMDs needed in the Near North River Industrial Corridor are designated, by what happens to the industries and jobs in the PMDs, and by whether we can provide the manufacturers with the supports needed to complement the PMDs. It will also be measured in terms of whether the coalition that came together around the PMD stays together even if the political climate changes. Will it continue to grow? Will it take the issue further and in new directions? Can it evolve to address other critical issues? Will the economic development and land use policies that have emerged from this process as acceptable mainstream thought remain there?

The success that we know we've had was not easy to achieve. The process of developing the PMD and changing city policy was essentially one of forging new ground and then giving that ground to other people. When we started, industrial displacement was a LEED Council's issue. This is obvious from the press accounts. Every article mentioned LEED Council or Donna Ducharme. Today's press accounts rarely mention the LEED Council. Instead, it's the mayor, the commissioner, the alderman, this company president, or that expert. The issue has been kicked up a few levels.

This change had to occur for us to be successful. City policy wouldn't have changed without it happening. Now there are probably ten people who rightly believe that the PMD is the result of their efforts. In order to become an important issue, more people had to own it. In order for it to have spin-off policy and program impacts, other people had to develop their own cut on the issue. For example, the Economic Development Commission funded an industrial land use plan for Chicago's North Side in 1989. The need for the plan and its contents clearly evolved from the work we've done on industrial displacement. It succeeds in taking what we've done a few steps further and has been a valuable vehicle for involving the real estate industry in the process. In 1990, similar plans were formulated for the South and West Sides.

A number of community and economic development organizations have also developed *their* own cuts on the issue that reflect their own agendas and constituents. Some of them have been more closely reflective of our work than others. All of them have expanded the base and taken the issue in new directions. The LEED Council does not control the agendas or strategies of these groups but does try to establish a cooperative atmosphere.

The PMD has helped, along with the continuing work of other groups, to change the prevailing assumptions about what economic development really is and about what constitutes a healthy balanced economic future for the City of Chicago. It has also helped change the locus of decision making about development choices in communities. Opponents of these changes portray initiatives that have recalculated the benefits of different development choices or "democratized" development decision making as essentially political and unprofessional. They deny that their positions perpetuating the status quo are also essentially political.

Perhaps the greatest accomplishment of the Washington administration's development policy is that it encouraged learning. It became acceptable to ask questions like "Who benefits from this development choice?" and "Are there other ways to do this?" It also recognized that *all* development decisions are essentially political because they are decisions about who will benefit and about how these benefits will be distributed. The PMD process verified that well-formulated questions and well-supported answers would be seriously considered and could actually alter city policies, actions, and plans.

The City and the Neighborhoods: Was It Really a Two-Way Street?

ROBERT BREHM

On a cold, gray, weekday afternoon in March 1983, Harold Washington made what was to be his most successful visit to date to the West Town/Humboldt Park community of Chicago. The purpose of the visit was a planned outdoor rally at the corner of North and Washtenaw Avenues, followed by a walking tour of the area. By midafternoon, a crowd was beginning to form on North Avenue, jamming the sidewalks and median strip. The organizers had done their job well: hundreds of calls had been made to anyone who might be interested in seeing the Democratic candidate for mayor of Chicago. Community groups, churches, social service institutions, and others were all represented. Whatever timidness these groups exhibited prior to the February primary was gone; Washington was the Democratic nominee, and in victory he had expressed his love and devotion to all Chicagoans and all neighborhoods. For the Latino, black, and working-class whites of West Town, this was something so new and exciting it had to be witnessed in person and maybe even supported.

The handful of political activists who organized the rally knew that Washington had touched a nerve in the West Town community. But they also realized that as yet, the candidate had not reached the people of West Town directly. He had been to a few political rallies and small meetings, but if the people of this area were to share in the victory and ultimately in the ongoing struggle a Washington victory would represent, the activists knew there had to be more direct contact. The media were totally unable or unwilling to communicate Harold's message effectively. If he had a chance to meet and talk with these people on their own streets, talk about the problems this community had in common with others, how they were left out when the political machines controlled city government and resources, and talk about the need for black, brown, and white to struggle together, then maybe he could spark a fire that would help the infant independent political movement in West Town get going. At the same time, it wouldn't hurt the organizers' political careers if Washington could get a rousing welcome from a primarily Puerto Rican crowd.

By the time Washington arrived, a few hundred people had gathered. People crowded the median and sidewalks, some carrying signs and others chanting "Harold!" The candidate finally arrived, and his aides helped him on to the open back of a small truck to make his speech. Local Puerto Rican leaders introduced the candidate, and the crowd mostly waited, shifting their feet in the cold, to see what this guy was all about. By the time he finished his short speech they all knew—and were his supporters all the way. He had spoken in his uniquely impassioned, articulate style of the injustices suffered by communities like West Town under current and previous city administrations. And he had spoken of his commitment to right those wrongs and to return city hall to all the people of Chicago.

As the rally broke up, an organizer told the crowd that Washington would join them for a walking tour, to begin three blocks away at Washtenaw and Potomac Avenues. While Washington rode in his car, most of the people began walking and the crowd grew as they walked. People were excited, jubilant; many commented on how this was just like campaigning in Puerto Rico, with candidates and their supporters often in the streets.

Organizers carefully planned the walking tour for maximum impact, both for residents and the evening news. It would start at the site of forty-five low-income townhouses under construction and would continue to other blocks with vacant lots that community groups hoped would also be developed into affordable housing. On the way, Washington could witness the drug dealing, garbage problems, unemployment, and poverty that dominate the everyday lives of the area's residents. At the same time, he could witness their commitment to making things better, whether through new housing, block clubs, community gardens, or youth agencies, and he could witness their bitter frustration with the political system that afforded them little, if any, support in these efforts. It would be hard to convince people that he was any different than other politicians, but he would try. After all, none had ever tried so hard or so successfully to convince non-whites that he truly was a "man of the people."

The walking crowd arrived at the site before the candidate. Among the nervous group of organizers wondering if Washington would actually come were a few staff and board members of Bickerdike Redevelopment, the local community development corporation responsible for the housing development. The political activists were nervous because they had convinced their friends at Bickerdike to participate in what could be construed as a partisan event on the basis that the community groups could use the tour as a chance to win a candidate's support for their good work. In this way, it would seem more that Washington was supporting affordable housing, rather than Bickerdike endorsing Washington. And the people from Bickerdike were nervous because they considered digressions into politics to be very risky; the only way for them to be legitimate was for all such activities to be geared toward making politicians more accountable to the needs of the community. If Washington were to attend the rally and skip the tour and meeting with the people (including a hoped-for commitment to helping build more affordable housing), then he would be acting like most other politicians and the justifications for Bickerdike's involvement would seem transparent and purely political.

After several minutes of waiting, Washington arrived in his modest campaign car with the accompanying police car, both approaching the corner driving the wrong way on a one-way street. Washington got out of the car, shrugged, and explained that they had gotten lost, that he should have taken one of the local organizers in the car with him. The tour began with Bickerdike leaders explaining the housing development around them. They emphasized their concerns for affordability, local employment, and community and resident involvement, and related stories about the years of organizing and planning it took to make the housing a reality. Harold took it all in, asking knowledgeable questions and promising to support Bickerdike in its efforts to develop more affordable housing in the community. This all depended, he told the crowd, on winning the general election in April. Then he laughed and flashed that characteristic grin, and everyone cheered.

The day's organizers then led the mayor-to-be on a brief tour of the area. During the four-block walk, Harold talked informally with those who were introduced or who simply walked alongside, all the while waving and smiling to the people who came out on their front steps or leaned out of upstairs windows to see him. Harold agreed with those who said city services like garbage pickup, street repairs, and police and fire protection were abysmal. He commented on how remarkable it was that the people of this community had been able to do so much positive work with so many negative forces working against them. And he cautioned people, as he often did, that there was a long fight ahead of "us," that all of this wouldn't suddenly go away when "we" took over city hall. In his own way, filled with humanity and humility, he charmed everyone.

The walk over, Harold got back in his car and quietly drove off. As the crowd dispersed, the political and community organizers shook hands and congratulated each other on a good afternoon. Turnout was good, lots of press showed up, and the people seemed really impressed with the candidate and the commitments he made. That afternoon, someone leaked to the press information about the Republican candidate's past history of psychiatric care. That story dominated the day's news. Pictures of the rally were run by both *Newsweek* and "60 Minutes," but not a single word or picture appeared in the local media. The political activists had to measure the success of their rally in terms of the boost it would give their local political operations and in the sense of goodwill it generated among Washington and the community groups. The community groups would measure success in terms of Washington's support for their work and the extent to which his visit helped people see just how different this politician was.

Harold Washington was elected mayor of Chicago just a few weeks after this rally. He served until his tragic death about four and a half years later. My memories of Harold Washington are that he was one of the finest, most committed public officials I have ever known directly or indirectly, as well as the most dynamic and inspiring movement leader I have ever experienced. My recollections of the city administration of Mayor Harold Washington are not nearly so positive. City government was certainly much more open and honest than under the administrations it followed, which were controlled by the political machine of the local regular Democratic party. But other gains are not so clear.

Given the shortness of his term in office, the strength of his opposition, the inertia of the city hall bureaucracy, and the weaknesses of many of his appointees, it hardly seems possible that Harold Washington could have accomplished anything meaningful for those who originally supported him. Unfortunately, his progressive philosophy was not effectively translated into government practice. Not much of lasting value was accomplished in terms of community involvement in planning and development. In fact, Harold Washington's most meaningful contributions came in his role as a grass-roots political leader rather than in his role as the highest elected official of a major American city.

In his role as mayor, however, Washington has provided us with some valuable lessons. Students of progressive governance will probably analyze the Washington administration to try to extract lessons for the future. This account is an attempt to contribute a community activist's experiences to that effort, mostly by recalling examples of how the Washington administration failed to achieve its stated goal of community involvement in policymaking and resource allocation. These experiences raise several questions about the record of the Washington administration as a participatory, progressive government. Was Washington really different from other politicians—both regulars and reformers—who came before him? In what ways did his supporters expect him to differ, and were those expectations reasonable? When were the interests of the Washington administration and those of community groups like Bickerdike the same, and when did they diverge? How about the divergence of community groups' interests from those of their constituencies, and what effect did this have on Washington's interaction with his political base? To what extent did the people, policies, and actions of the administration contradict the rhetoric of Harold Washington as activist, candidate, and even mayor? Did that rhetoric serve as an adequate guide for the administration? And did the Washington administration suffer from a necessary or inevitable divergence between "movement" and "government"?

The answers to these questions are addressed in this chapter, but not conclusively. It all happened so fast, everyone involved was too busy to reflect, and it all ended so abruptly that to try to answer these questions definitively would be not only vain but also dishonest. What follows, then, are simply the thoughts, observations, and remembrances of a community activist who interacted with Mayor Washington and his administration and experienced the joys and frustrations that came with that interaction.

Community Groups and City Hall

Harold Washington set out to do more than simply represent the interests of all Chicagoans while serving as mayor. He pledged to involve all communities in government, from identifying the problems they experienced to helping design and carry out city efforts to address those problems. This was an important way in which Harold went beyond other reform candidates: he wasn't just going to do right for his people, he was going to get people to do right for themselves. Seldom in Washington's term as mayor, however, did the administration communicate this to his base in West Town as well as he did himself at the rally.

A vehicle was needed to involve the mayor's base in the neighborhoods in the coalition he was trying to form to put his campaign promises into government action. There was much discussion early in Washington's first term of creating local planning boards for that purpose. It is not clear why this idea was dropped. Some people who were involved in the discussions, attribute it to considerable disagreement among activists—both those working in city hall and those still on the "outside"—as to how much power to give the planning boards and how the members would be selected. Some wanted the planning boards to be given broad powers in an attempt to institutionalize community involvement and put into practice the ideals expressed in Washington's campaign. Others feared the same institutionalization, thinking that the boards could effectively cut off most of the community from the involvement in government enjoyed by the boards themselves. It is too bad the local planning boards were never tried; the experience of attempting to structure community involvement in city government under a receptive administration would have been very valuable in analyzing the practical problems inherent in such a unique political environment.

In the absence of local planning boards or some other new structure, existing groups assumed the responsibility of involving their constituencies in city government. Many had done so for years and were anxious to try it in a friendly, rather than actively hostile, atmosphere. Others had been involved on friendly terms with previous administrations and hoped to continue in their quiet, nonpublic way to influence city policy in their favor.

And still others had never interacted with city hall in the past but heard Harold's challenge to get involved and decided to do so. There were five basic types of groups that were poised to become involved with city hall in a way that served their communities' interests: churches and related groups; advocacy groups representing a particular race or ethnic background; labor groups (particularly those concerned with job loss through disinvestment and plant closings); independent political organizations; and community groups. These varied actors often overlapped; community groups in particular often tried to involve many of the others. This chapter focuses primarily on the relationship between community groups and the Harold Washington administration.[1]

For purposes of this discussion, "community group" refers to those organizations that have at least the following characteristics in common: (1) a nonprofit structure; (2) a defined geographic area of concern, smaller than the city as a whole; and (3) a concern for the welfare of their community's residents and an organizational mission to somehow address the needs of those people. There are hundreds—maybe thousands—of groups that fit this basic definition in Chicago. The list includes all sorts of groups, from activist organizers, to housing and economic developers, to social workers, to mutual aid societies, to health services providers, and so on.

Bickerdike is generally known as a relatively honest, community-based Community Development Corporation (CDC) with an emphasis on community empowerment through development—one of about a dozen such groups in Chicago.[2] The labels are offered to help characterize the perspective of these comments on the Washington administration. For example, dishonest community groups existed before, during and after Harold Washington's tenure in city hall. There is no apparent pattern to the level of success enjoyed by such groups under various administrations. On the other hand, it is significant to look at the Washington administration's dealings with legitimate CDCs, and particularly in terms of any preference on the part of policymakers for dealing with those who were or were not community based and empowerment oriented.

In general, progressive CDCs like Bickerdike got along great with Harold Washington. Many leaders of these groups got involved in the campaigns, organizing rallies and other public events for the mayor. He, in turn, treated them with genuine respect and affection. The same cannot be said for these groups and Washington's city hall administration. City hall appointees and activists eyed each other warily at first, each seeming to acknowledge the limits of the common bond. After a brief initial period, community activists often complained that most Washington appointees never treated them with respect. Activists resented what they perceived as the policymakers' role in preventing the "progressive coalition" of city hall and community activists from becoming a reality. The relationship gradually deteriorated from there and never really recovered. There are several reasons for this. Groups like Bickerdike were used to distrusting all-powerful institutions, and particularly city hall. City government had mistreated their communities and residents for decades, never supported the groups themselves (outside of grudgingly acting as a conduit for federal grants), and was commonly thought to be corrupt and self-serving. City government under Harold Washington was far less corrupt than its predecessors, and it served poor and working-class Chicagoans and their neighborhoods fairly; moreover, the mayor himself supported progressive CDCs. But these distinctions alone did not change the fact that as mayor, Harold Washington took on a new role as chief executive of a city with some 3 million residents—a role that severely limited his latitude in recognizing CDCs as active participants in a governing coalition.

The wary community groups were quick to sense retreats from Washington's professed fairness and support in the words and actions of the people appointed by him to important positions. And those same appointees, well aware of the groups' fondness for activist organizing attacks on injustices suffered by their communities, were wary of the progressive community groups. On another level, several city hall appointees were former community activists themselves or had been peripherally involved in community development issues. These new bureaucrats and the staff of community groups knew each other, and each expected friendly relations. They were both quick to anger whenever the other took some action that was perceived as unfriendly. For example, the former activists working in city hall seemed to prefer dealing with individuals they knew personally. This led to resentment when a community organizer or CDC staff person insisted on a public meeting with the city official in the interest of community involvement and empowerment organizing. And similarly, community activists resented the officials when they took some action affecting the community without discussing it with the community group first. As for those new city hall appointees with no history of commonality with progressive community groups—such as those at the Department of Housing and holdover staff from previous, unfriendly administrations—they and the activists distrusted each other almost from the start. There was one similarity in the way community groups were dealt with by all city officials: to city hall the group was personified in its key staff—usually the director—for better or worse. Groups that are not community based usually don't mind this characterization, as it is often accurate and always more expedient for everyone. For those groups concerned with community control and empowerment, downtown's insistence on dealing with a lone staff person can be a real problem, one that is ignored if everyone at city hall is an avowed enemy, and a real stickler when they are supposed to be friends.[3]

But we're jumping ahead a little. How did self-proclaimed "independent" and "progressive" activists get so caught up with city hall insiders—wasn't this a big change from the past? In fact, it was such a change for most of us that our inexperience led to many of the mistakes that were made. Next time, if there ever is a "next time," perhaps those mistakes will have made us more experienced in dealing with a "friendly" city hall and we can do better. But in 1983 no one knew what to expect, and those of us who had fought for years against oppressive policies of neglect and disdain for the basic needs of people and demanded responsibility on the part of public officials were excited about the prospects.

For many years prior to 1983, most progressive community groups stayed far away from any involvement in politics or city government. Activist organizing groups like the Northwest Community Organization, which founded Bickerdike in 1967, steadfastly refused to accept any sort of government funding. Most CDCs used government funds, since those were the only source of development subsidies available. Still, in the case of progressive CDCs, they did so cautiously, wary of the lessons of the early Model Cities programs where cities often used the federal funds to buy off community activists. And many times, the city only funded a local CDC after an organizing campaign in which an activist community group charged the city with misusing federal funds intended to benefit the group's community.

Forays into independent or reform politics were rare but not unheard of. Sometimes, a community leader would catch the electoral politics bug and convince people that a reform candidacy against the political machine was a natural complement to their community organizing work and that a legitimate challenge could be mounted. In those cases, in part because of their familiarity and respect for their fellow activist-turned-candidate, community groups crossed the line into electoral politics, but they did so cautiously. The first reason for this caution is that it is illegal for most nonprofit organizations that receive government and/or private grants to become directly involved in partisan political activities. This problem could be legitimately avoided if the group itself was not directly involved and if its resources were not used in a political campaign. If the members of a group wanted to volunteer for a candidate, that was perfectly legal.

The other and more important reason for their caution was a belief in a simplistic but all-too-often accurate credo: Politics and government in Chicago do not serve the interests of the people. So, the belief continues, if you get involved in politics, you have to be willing to give up your concerns about the interests of the people in order to survive with other politicians. Sure the groups would have liked to delve deeper into the complexities of the public sector, to examine carefully the distinctions between truly oppressive governments and those that served their constituents, but too often the groups were underfunded and overworked, and the problems faced by their communities never seemed to abate. To get directly involved in occasional independent campaigns could mean sending out mixed messages about the basic corruption of political institutions. Community groups often had great difficulty rallying their constituents around even basic issues. Many thought the price to pay for saying "Not all politics is bad; let's try this out and see what good comes of it" was not worth the potential benefits of an isolated independent campaign.

Prior to 1983, most community groups in Chicago were never or hardly ever involved in electoral politics, and almost all of the honest community-based groups were never directly involved in government. Those groups whose leaders even accepted appointment to a city commission under mayors like Richard J. Daley or Jane Byrne were labeled "political" or "sellouts" by other groups. (These groups often earned the labels by acting as puppets of politicians, who in some cases used them to disrupt the work of more independent groups.)

The candidacy and subsequent election of Harold Washington changed all that, perhaps forever. In the black neighborhoods, Washington's candidacy was a political happening of almost revolutionary proportions. How could any honest community-based group in the black community not respond to that movement? Here was an incredible, exciting example of mass activism, and few self-respecting organizers were going to sit back because of some tired notion that "politics is not for us." This time the stakes were too high to ignore: this was a chance to really kick the white machine in its butt, and maybe even take over the mayor's office in the bargain. Didn't that represent community involvement and empowerment?

Outside the black community, however, the choice was not so clear. Bickerdike works in the West Town neighborhood, a community of about 130,000 people on the Near Northwest Side. The population is about 65 percent Latino (mostly Puerto Rican), about 25 percent black, and the rest white. Activists in this area were quick to see the real differences between the Harold Washington campaign for mayor and other independent efforts of the past: they liked what the candidate was saying and were really inspired by him. The people of West Town, however, were slower to react. Among voters, there were those with a history of voting with the machine (the majority in almost every previous election), those who were not yet or never would be ready to vote for a black man (not the majority but a distressingly large group), and those either too disenchanted to vote or disenfranchised by racist voter registration policies. After Harold's victory in the February primary, his campaign started to catch on. Still, there was little in the way of political organization in the area to turn that growing excitement into electoral results. In the black wards, in addition to the fervor Harold himself generated, most of the political ward organizations aligned with the machine switched to support Harold after the primary, and this greatly enhanced the vote totals for him. In West Town and elsewhere, supporters of Harold Washington were still the lonely opposition, often fighting against formidable organizations. It took four years, a court-ordered redistricting, and the election of an alderman aligned with Washington before the voters of West Town started honoring Harold with election day victories. Still, the vote count for Harold or any of his allies never exceeded 70 percent of the votes cast in any election in West Town; in most of the black wards his totals approached 100 percent.

Following the election, Harold was magnanimous in reaching out to the people of West Town. The political pundits said he needed the Latinos as a "swing vote"; he said, we're all brothers and sisters in the same struggle. Activists and groups from West Town may not have enjoyed the same status as those from communities that overwhelmingly voted for Harold, but just the same they were initially welcomed as friends and supporters. And the political strategists dominating the formation of the new administration clearly believed that the more they talked as if we were friends, the better our relationship would be. That was flattering. Combined with the general euphoria among community groups (even those who supported Harold but sat out the elections), it was a heady time for community activists.

The first letdowns were not long in coming, however. One early disappointment was the administration's series of "Neighborhood Forums." These were billed as putting into action the rhetoric of open government and community self-determination. In reality they were highly organized charades, which would have been accepted by Washington supporters had they been campaign ploys but, occurring as they did soon after the election, the forums in fact caused many a rude awakening to what life with Harold might really be like. If a group wanted to participate in a forum, they had to first submit their questions to the city staff, who would then negotiate which questions would be used at the forums. These negotiations took place at a meeting of the participating groups organized and controlled by the city staff. Bickerdike and several other groups in West Town declined to participate in what they saw as a poor excuse for community planning. And groups that had supported machine administrations in the past and only recently decided to express support for Washington flocked to the forums and were welcomed with open arms. Just the stumbling of some overzealous activists turned into bureaucrats and political operatives, we thought.

Always hopeful, in spite of early disappointments like this one, I remember being excited the first time I dialed a city phone number and a familiar voice answered. I also recall just as vividly my surprise when my call elicited an attack on me and fellow community activists who—according to the political organizer on the other end of the line—expect too much and are too impatient. True perhaps, but this was within weeks of Harold's inauguration and the call was meant to be congratulatory. What had we done to deserve this? Were community groups jumping all over the infant administration, showing a lack of appreciation for the complexities of governing a big city? Not much, and hardly.

What did community activists expect of the new administration? First, we expected to be treated differently from the past in our dealings with city hall. For example, if we applied for a housing loan, we expected not overnight improvement in the bureaucracy but a gradual improvement, and at least some responsiveness from new appointees when we sought their help in overcoming a bureaucratic obstacle. We expected an increase in respect for our efforts and an end to the attitude of many in prior administrations that CDCs were irresponsible spenders of the bureaucrats' money. And we expected to become involved in helping shape city policy as it related to community development. We and our counterparts in the new administration were equally unaware of how to go about involving the communities, but it seemed clear almost from the start that we expected more of a genuine partnership in this endeavor than they did.

Exorcising the Demons Within

From the very beginning, the city hall administration of Harold Washington was on the defensive. This posture made it difficult to be an outside "friend" of the administration: public criticism was out of the question, and private critical suggestions or analysis were poorly received. Paranoia seemed to permeate most dealings with the struggling new administration: on the one hand, they were afraid of making embarassing or damaging blunders; on the other, we were afraid of losing favor, of being labeled a political enemy because of some criticism or refusal to follow the administration's line on an issue. The demons responsible for these fears were real; the overreaction to them by administration officials and their overuse by political people greatly contributed to the lack of joint, cohesive effort by the administration and its outsider friends and supporters.

The two most frequently cited obstacles to the young administration achieving its stated goals of progressive development policies and community involvement in government were the political opposition's control of the city council and the Shakman consent decree of 1983 regulating political hiring and firing. These were real and quite limiting: nothing could get past the city council without majority support, and suddenly the city council wanted an active role in government for the first time, such as approving all city loans for development. On the Shakman side, the Washington administration was stuck with a work force of about 40,000, most of whom were political hacks of the opposition but who now enjoyed the court's protection against political firing. In short, Washington could not get his policies approved by the city council, nor could he get "their" people out and "his" people in. These were serious constraints. Just the same, many outside supporters quietly grumbled that the administration was paralyzed by them, when in fact there were other steps that could be taken. Supportive community groups felt they could have been treated as real partners in a struggle to wrest control of city government from the opposition, thereby establishing the progressive coalition as a major force within the Washington administration.

Many in the administration were too obsessed by their own "demons within" to take such positive, productive steps as building a stronger coalition of supporters. Harold's victory seemed so slim, his hold on government so precarious, that most of his appointees seemed to live in fear of doing anything that would give the opposition (which for many included the media and white liberal supporters of the mayor) a chance to criticize the administration. For example, the Department of Economic Development (whose Commissioner Robert Mier was red-baited by the media at the time of his appointment for his background in left-of-center academia) and the Department of Planning (whose Commissioner Elizabeth Hollander came out of a background of promoting the civic-mindedness of downtown real estate and corporate interests) both worked overtime to avoid any possibility of being perceived as being "antidowntown" or "antibusiness." Both labels were worn by Washington in the eyes of the media and most business interests, and these officials were not about to exacerbate that problem for their new boss. Another obsession of many in the new administration was a simplistic categorizing of everyone they dealt with—insiders and outsiders—into supporters and enemies. No matter what a loyal supporter did and said most of the time, the first hint of variance from constant, unquestioning, and unequivocal support was cause for suspicion, challenges to one's loyalty, and most likely reduced access. (In time, factions within the administration began to treat each other the same way, but early on it was clearly "them vs. us.") In retrospect, it is somewhat easy to see how these fears and concerns—both those that were justified and the others—contributed to strained and unproductive relationships between administration officials and outside supporters. During the early years of Washington's term as mayor, however, it seemed more of a nagging problem, a frustration to be overcome jointly by good people inside and outside city hall. After all, the outsiders have a few demons of their own to deal with (all government and politics are bad, for example), and most were so proud and excited about Harold Washington's presence in city hall that they too were guilty of varying degrees of reactionary response to criticism of the administration.

Community Groups and City Hall: Working Together?

So chances were taken, especially early on. With the adrenalin still pumping from the electoral victory and the continuing political struggle, some bold initiatives were attempted. One of the earliest was centered on the announcement by its multinational parent that Playskool would be closing its Northwest Side factory and moving operations out of state. Hundreds of jobs were to be lost permanently. Community, advocacy, business, and labor groups—already trying with some difficulty to start an "Early Warning Network" to address job loss through sudden plant closings—seized on the Playskool announcement to attempt to bring the problem to the attention of the public and at the same time galvanize a true coalition to fight plant closings. Tax-exempt Industrial Revenue Bonds (IRBs) had been issued by the city under Jane Byrne to finance capital improvements at Playskool's Chicago plant at a below-market interest rate. In order to get the city to issue the bonds, Playskool said in its application that it would create additional jobs. Such economic development subsidies to major corporations had been called giveaways before, but this was a uniquely clear example of a company taking public funds, supposedly justified for their impact on job creation, and not only not creating additional jobs but actually closing the plant a short time after receiving the loan.

The advocacy and community groups involved saw this as an opportunity to force the issue of reform of the city's use of economic development subsidies. They found willing allies in the city's Department of Law and Department of Economic Development (DED). These allies were easily convinced that confronting such an obvious example of corporate callousness would go unchallenged by corporate leaders, business groups, and the press, who liked to portray themselves as genuinely concerned for the well-being of Chicago and all Chicagoans. Without Playskool, any attempt to tighten the job-creation requirements for receiving public funds—a reform consistent with Washington's economic development platform—would have been a plodding, frustrating affair. City hall reformers would have been afraid of alienating the business sector and press by giving the impression of attaching too many strings to the release of public funds to the true benefactors of Chicago's economy. With such a blatant abuse on record, who could oppose a few modest changes in the program, including such things as stronger certification and reporting requirements?

The advocacy, community, and labor groups were itching for a chance like this to put some of Washington's policy commitments into action. The local business group was angered by an outright lie by one of its members: Playskool had told them repeatedly that it was not moving. And the community groups and union local covering most of the Playskool workers were concerned about the loss of hundreds of jobs that would affect them directly. But time was short, and few among this ad hoc coalition really believed that Playskool could be prevented from leaving. Just the same, organizers and activists love a good fight, especially one where the other side does something so obviously evil.

The brief time available between the company's announcement and the start of layoffs was probably a blessing. At first there was a lot of excitement and camaraderie. City officials and activists alike felt and acted as though they were on the verge of a major breakthrough in the fight against plant closings, and everyone cut each other a little slack. But conflicts soon arose on several fronts. The union local was unable to prevent its international from negotiating for the contract at the Massachusetts site to which Playskool was moving. Nor could it generate much interest in the battle among its members. None of the local's leadership spoke Spanish, while an estimated one-half of the work force spoke little or no English. In fact, the only times union participation at rallies or picket lines exceeded a handful of officers and stewards was when bilingual community group volunteers did the recruiting. A few activists felt the Washington administration was dragging its feet, thinking the city could and should just step in and save the day, not to mention the jobs. The administration, in turn, admonished the groups to "Get out the troops!"—demonstrating a somewhat patronizing attitude toward organizing. (Mier in particular seemed to think that by giving the activists a "kick in the pants" he could get them to "produce" thousands of people at rallies, thereby giving Washington a public justification for suing the company.) The business group, on the other hand, frequently balked at participating in organizing strategies, fearful of alienating member businesses and thinking some of the coalition's members a little too radical for their tastes.

Everyone was stretching the limits of previous dealings with the others involved, some enthusiastically and some cautiously; but everyone also seemed to be holding on to a little of the historical mistrust, as if to have a reason for blaming others if the effort failed. Maybe this hedging was unwarranted, but it was an indication of the defensiveness and uncertainty that dominated so much of the interaction between the administration and community groups.

To everyone's credit, these conflicts were kept private, while a carefully orchestrated multipronged strategy achieved some success. The city—for the first time ever—sued a company over its failure to perform under an IRB financing agreement. The coalition organized rallies and pickets at toy stores that carried Playskool products. Coming just before Christmas, the specter of Playskool workers not being able to afford toys for their children at Christmas provided some powerful imagery—just enough to guarantee great media coverage in spite of the divisions within the coalition and the weaknesses of the organizing effort. Organizers' talk of a Christmastime boycott of Playskool toys helped fire the media hype, but a proposed symbolic torching of Lincoln Logs (a Playskool product with an Illinois flavor) never materialized. The coalition encouraged sympathetic friends around the city, and in some cases from other cities, to express their support, and one group of clergy even intervened in the city's court case. In the midst of all this activity and attention, the union local was quietly upping the ante for the workers' severance package.

As expected, Playskool left Chicago. The struggle to keep it, however, earned at least one lasting victory. A major multinational corporation was publicly exposed as a thief: caught stealing public subsidies intended for inner-city redevelopment and job creation, and damaging the Chicago economy in the process. Not a new charge if you hung out with radical activists or read leftist journals, but certainly the first such exposure in the mainstream press and in public opinion. Activists and reform-minded public officials have since been able to invoke images of corporate abuse, bad city policy, and layoffs by the hundreds whenever Playskool is mentioned in policy debates or organizing. All community organizing is part grass-roots mobilizing and part smoke and mirrors—in this case the latter has had the more lasting effect. The city's active role added legitimacy to the organizing effort and sent out a message that this new administration was ready to challenge past policies, and to do so in partnership with community activists.

The real Playskool story does not end there, however. While not in any way detracting from the symbolic victory, the follow-up has been seriously lacking. Soon after the company and the city settled the court case, and the company repaid the IRB loan in full, the coalition began to pull apart. In addition to personal and philosphical differences, the groups started to go in different directions. The union local focused on the settlement benefits (among them some limited retraining and job referral assistance) and then disappeared. The business and labor advocacy groups focused on their roles in any redevelopment of the site. The community groups who stayed involved pushed for controls over eventual users of the site requiring them to hire ex-Playskool employees for a portion of their work force. And the Commissioner of Economic Development Mier seemed to simply want something to happen at the site which he, and therefore Washington, could take credit for. Ultimately the fragile coalition was unable to maintain a common bond among the divergent interests.

Everyone involved should have done more to overcome these differences but did not, for reasons ranging from too much other work to indifference or opposition to others' concerns. The business group, for example, was legitimately concerned about security and maintenance at the vacant site, fearing that visible deterioration would inhibit marketing and perhaps encourage other neighborhood businesses to leave. Their director, however, was opposed to community group participation in the marketing of the factory—opposed even to their participation in setting guidelines for the marketing effort. The city, despite a professed commitment to the ex-Playskool workers (or at least to unemployed workers in general with similar skill levels and backgrounds), permitted this conflict to fester, and eventually allowed the marketing to go ahead with modest attempts to address the work force issue but without the participation of the groups most concerned with that issue. Again, the young Washington administration found itself avoiding conflicts with the business community, no matter how much their criticisms might be unreasonable or contrary to the Washington platform. The plant is now partially occupied again, which is good for everyone. Maybe someday the city will fund a study to find out if any ex-Playskool workers have landed jobs at the reopened facility.

But perhaps the most telling point as to the transitory value of symbolic victories like these came to light at a recent seminar on economic development under Washington. A former city official who helped write the IRB reforms in the wake of the Playskool fight surprised most of his well-informed audience when he reported that those reforms had been tabled by city hall, even before Harold died, and in fact had never been made into law. Thus, a brief struggle that started out as a fresh, exciting example of a progressive city hall working with community groups and others on an important issue ends up as an example of the weaknesses of that coalition under Harold Washington. Had there been a real partnership committed to the same goals, someone, somewhere, sometime in the years between the Playskool closing and Harold's death would have tried to get the two forces working together on passage of the IRB reforms, and they would probably have succeeded.

Linked Development: From Bold to Buried

Governments are often adept at burying politically sensitive issues by appointing special commissions to study the matters. The government is credited with taking the issue seriously, and the most vocal protagonists on the issue usually reciprocate by quieting down long before the commission's report is issued. Judged in those terms, formation of the Mayor's

Advisory Committee on Linked Development was a good tactical move, but not one that says much for progressive economic development or planning under Harold Washington. In sharp contrast to the dramatics of the brief Playskool struggle, the city government used the prolonged deliberations of the advisory committee to bury the linked development issue.

A coalition of grass-roots community groups from the white middle-class areas on the city's Northwest and Southwest Sides first raised the issue of linked development in Chicago. These groups had a long history of organizing, direct action, and racism. The latter was perhaps an unfair perception, but they did not help their image any by forming the Save Our Neighborhood/Save Our City (SON/SOC) coalition soon after Washington's victory in 1983. They aggressively pushed the linked development issue into the public spotlight. They were able to get lots of press for their early efforts; the Chicago media really ate up the idea of an all-white group challenging Harold Washington to help their neighborhoods. Was Harold really for all Chicagoans? Was he really for neighborhood growth even at the expense of downtown? They had Harold on the spot: if he did not respond in a positive way he could be accused of ignoring white neighborhoods and proneighborhood policies at the same time.

Many close to Washington, however, actively opposed the concept SON/SOC was proposing: impose a "linkage fee" of $5 per square foot of new office space, with the funds used for neighborhood redevelopment. Some Washington appointees, like Mier and Hollander, had their backgrounds and demons to deal with. Other high-level appointees in places like Housing, Planning, and the Mayor's Office were simply not sympathetic to concerns of poor people or neighborhoods in general, and did not want to spoil the opportunity to use their appointments to set themselves up for life in the good graces of Chicago's corporate world. These officials spoke out against linkage; they seemed afraid that city hall support of a linkage fee would damage the mayor's chances for reelection and their own positions within the administration.

Some of us thought the issue had real organizing potential, in spite of its suspect origins: the striking contrast between the glistening new glass towers going up in the Loop and the decaying physical structures in the neighborhoods would be a good catalyst for grass-roots action. And the concept was simple: Why shoudn't the wealthy developers and their tenants pay for housing and job development in the neighborhoods? After all, hadn't the neighborhoods been "paying" for decades for downtown improvements through disproportionate allocations of tax resources?

There were a few negatives, however. The most important was an almost complete unwillingness on the part of community groups supportive of Harold to become embroiled in a public fight with him that might undermine his attempts to wrest power from the opposition. SON/SOC had already chosen to play the issue out as if it was simply the neighborhoods vs. city hall. They acted as if all Harold had to do was say he was in favor of it and linked development would become a reality. To add to our misgivings about jumping on their bandwagon, there was the perception of SON/SOC as harboring many racists, as well as the fact that some groups they had previously coalesced with felt that SON/SOC could not be trusted. Also, there were some nagging doubts about the concept itself. What if downtown and city hall said, sure, we'll give you a piece of the spoils from downtown growth, but we want you community types to stop complaining about unrestricted growth, the proposed 1992 World's Fair, etc.? And in fact, if linked development was a reality, many community activists would feel torn between opposing growth that was bad for the city, or perhaps misused public resources, and supporting that same growth because some of the monetary benefits might flow to the neighborhoods. What on the surface looked like a classic "Robin Hood" strategy could be seen as a not-so-progressive sellout to corporate greed and downtown growth at the expense of the neighborhoods. Fortunately, none of the pro-downtown representatives on the committee—either from the private sector or city hall—had the foresight to see the long-term value to them of supporting linked development. Instead, their reactionary posturing about "killing the goose that lays the golden egg" still serves to galvanize neighborhood activists in opposition to schemes like stadiums and World's Fairs and the like. And finally, linked development had the potential for raising only a small fraction of the funds needed for community development.

When I was first approached in the summer of 1984 to accept an appointment to the Mayor's Advisory Committee on Linked Development, I did not see any of these issues so clearly, but I was still confused and torn. On the one hand, I still thought linked development had great organizing potential, not by going after city hall but after the developers themselves. This would avoid the problem of publicly criticizing Harold or his administration and could even provide him with the public support sufficient to enact a linked development program. By joining the committee, I knew I was signing on to a long, quiet process that would preclude any organizing work by the committee members. You could not very well agree to sit on a task force, it seemed, and at the same time trash it by going public with attacks on its members or premise. On the other hand, it was flattering to be asked. In spite of a nagging sense that they wanted you there just to keep you quiet, it was only a little more than a year since Harold took office and we were all still a little high from the victory and the access it gave us. Also, I didn't really want to see nonwhite communities like West Town join in a public organizing campaign with SON/SOC that was directed at Harold. By sitting on the committee, at least I wouldn't be left out of the deliberations, and maybe I could even help Washington by redirecting the community activism for linked development away from him and toward the developers, where it belonged. It took a while to decide, but eventually I decided that if this was what Washington was going to do about linked development, I wanted to be there.

The notebooks handed out at the first committee meeting in October 1984 included the following "Goals for Mayor's Advisory Committee on Linked Development," written by the Department of Planning and attributed to the committee chairman, a black banker named Walter Clark:

> 1. To establish a linked development program for Chicago which will generate a pool of seed capital of $5,000,000 to $10,00,000 annually for neighborhood development and revitalization.
> 2. To establish this program in a genuine spirit of cooperation, recognizing that our goal is to strengthen Chicago's neighborhoods, but not to the detriment of our Central Business District.
> 3. To help break down the "us versus them" perception between the neighborhoods and downtown.
> 4. To develop a program that responds to neighborhood needs on a fair, priority basis, with clear and workable criteria for eligibility.
> 5. To arrive at our final recommendations to the Mayor by consensus, to the extent possible, while still respecting minority points of view.

Here we have something for everyone going in, and just enough contradictions and difficult goals to ensure that little would come out at the end. For example, if the community activists wanted to cite the monetary goal, the downtown developers could counter that we all had agreed not to weaken downtown to help the neighborhoods. Even then it seemed improbable that a group with such a mixed bag of participants and goals could work out a solution by consensus.

To make matters worse, it seemed that the committee members were picked to provide "balance," which translated into an inordinate amount of disharmonious debate, further rendering it impossible to produce a "clear and workable" program that would provide "$5,000,000 to $10,000,000 annually" to be raised in a way that did not turn out to be "to the detriment of our Central Business District." In the eyes of some who clearly opposed any form of linked development, the committee was stacked with community types. In truth, six representatives of actual community groups sat on the original eighteen-member committee. Another three were clearly sympathetic, coming from groups like the League of Women Voters and other citywide groups. Another six represented developers, lawyers, banks, a union, and a business group, who had all expressed their opposition to any linked development program that downtown had to pay for in any way. The remaining three members either did not participate or did not express an opinion early on. The first action taken by the committee was to make the committee more "fair" and balanced by including more downtown developers and their supporters. The suggestion was actually made by a person from a community group (who later championed the idea of community group support for the then fading World's Fair in exchange for a piece of the fair action going to community groups), and the chairman and city commissioners were so excited they nearly tripped over each other in their efforts to get the suggestion into the record without a formal vote. A couple of community activists questioned the idea, eliciting a chorus of complaints and threats to quit from the developers and their supporters, that not only succeeded in quashing opposition to the idea but also set the tone for the Committee's future deliberations. So, a few developers were added, among them people who grew to be favorites of the progrowth and pro–World's Fair crowd in city hall, all the while crying about the supposed conspiracy between Harold Washington and the community groups to make paupers out of all downtown developers and turn the Loop into a slum.[4]

The incessant whining by the developers and their support groups—both in committee meetings and in the press—proved to be highly effective. While community activists were enjoying their access and avoiding both public and private criticism of city hall, the Washington administration was busy meeting with these aggressive developers and generally doing everything it could to disprove the conspiracy theory. Aside from a few private meetings with city officials to express concern, the community representatives and their supporters never really challenged the city on its role, concentrating more on the deliberations on the various program proposals and on making sure the votes were in place to pass the best ones.

The linked development task force was also an example of another characteristic of the relationship between community groups and the Washington administration. There was no room in the committee process for grass-roots participation. Individuals participated, ostensibly as representatives of the groups they belonged to. The committee, however, did not operate as a body of representatives who had to go back to their groups for authorization to vote a certain way, but rather as a group of individuals who were expected to act as informed proponents of the interests they served and who were authorized to act on their behalf. Meetings were held at 8:00 A.M. on weekday mornings, and the few times community activists tried to delay a vote until they could get back to their groups, they were left out of the voting altogether. And there was another, more subtle way that participating in the committee cut activists off from their community base: city officials and the community representatives knew each other personally in several cases from before Harold's victory, and there still existed the presumption of friendship and allegiance to the same cause. So when a commissioner called, we usually agreed to a private conversation rather than insisting on an appearance at a community public meeting where the official would be put on the spot to publicly commit her/himself to a position. The downtown interests constantly invited city officials to their functions to discuss controversial issues, and they never hesitated to quote city officials in the press expressing their support for downtown development and their commitment to avoid doing anything that might slow it down. Of course they supported linked development, city officials would tell their skeptical audiences, so long as it did not take anything away from downtown.

We could have played the Washington appointees for fools and hypocrites for trying to dance around issues of at least symbolic concern to their political constituency, or exerted pressures strong enough to counter the developers. But we didn't. Instead, we allowed the myth of city hall—community group collaboration ("conspiracy" to the opposition, "progressive coalition" to us, but still a myth either way) to grow, further weakening the potential for any real, productive collaboration.

As the Linked Development Committee's work wound down toward a majority vote in favor of the original $5 per square foot linkage fee, a sudden mad scramble for an alternative program ensued. This effort, led by the developers and staffed by the Department of Planning, clearly worked against most of the stated goals of the committee (breaking down the "us vs. them" perception, for example); and rather than fostering collaboration among community groups and city hall, it led only to increased suspicion and mistrust. Eventually, a minority report was published calling for a voluntary linked development program wherein developers, while not required to do so, would contribute to neighborhood development. The sponsors of this proposal refused or were unable to back up the idea with dollar commitments, and it was a real revelation to see city officials promoting the program. Community activists on the committee managed to convince Commissioner Mier of DED that we would publicly criticize the administration if it bought the voluntary concept, and that he could be a hero if he convinced Washington that the mayor would look bad if that happened. Up to that point, city commissioners had been calling community members of the committee and pressuring them to vote in favor of the voluntary program, stressing that it was less than a year to the next mayoral election and that a committee vote in favor of a linkage fee would damage Harold's chances for reelection. With help from a few city council members (aldermen) the community groups had ties to, Mier was able to get Washington to call off his people, telling them he supported the linkage fee proposal. It was a brief, bitter struggle within the "progressive coalition," but it never went public. Then, as if by unspoken agreement,

Washington, Mier, the city council, and most of the activists on the committee allowed the issue to fade out of the spotlight until after Harold's reelection. Given the other controversial issues (such as proposals for a home equity program and for new sports stadiums) that were intentionally strung out by Mier and others until after the 1987 elections, it would not be surprising if the pitch to Harold in favor of the linkage fee included a promise to stall the whole thing for several months.

Chicago never adopted a linkage fee of any kind. However, some say lessons were learned from this process that led to more modest gains. These include a so-called voluntary linked development program whereby the city brokers free consulting hours from downtown developers for the benefit of CDCs. Ironically, one of the few things developers and community activists agreed on in committee deliberations was the futility of such a program, based on the developers' lack of experience in community development, and the insignificance of such technical assistance in making development projects financially feasible.

Enterprise Zones: The Coalition Stumbles

Another, less public attempt to forge a progressive coalition among city hall and community groups was focused on the question of enterprise zones.[5] This concept, which involved lowering taxes and wages in the zones to promote economic development, was first advanced on a large scale by the "supply-siders" in the new Reagan administration, and when Harold Washington took office it was still just an idea at the federal level. While some states—including Illinois—had passed enterprise zone legislation, the idea was still new and untested. Community groups across Illinois argued against the idea and formed the Community Workshop on Economic Development (CWED) in the hope of creating a statewide force to influence public policy in this area.

When Harold Washington ran for mayor in 1983, several people active in CWED became involved in the campaign. In fact, the Washington position papers on economic development were taken to a large extent from CWED working papers and position statements. Rob Mier, who as a technical assistance provider was an associate member of CWED and involved in writing for both CWED and the Washington campaign, was able to convert that involvement into an appointment as Washington's new commissioner of DED. He brought with him others who had a background in CWED or with groups that belonged to that coalition, among them two deputy commissioners: Arturo Vázquez and Robert Giloth. Giloth, a community activist in Chicago for many years, worked in and then headed the Research and Development (R&D) Division of DED. Vázquez was put in charge of the Field Division, which dealt directly with those community and business groups that DED contracted with under its delegate agency program. The R&D Division was responsible for some creative approaches to making the progressive coalition work. While many of these efforts, like Playskool, were flawed, at least there seemed to be a genuine commitment to testing the practical and political limitations of such a coalition. Vázquez, on the other hand, seemed to aspire to a personal empire of groups that collectively represented little that was creative or progressive. A sympathetic visitor from outside of Chicago during Harold's first term commented on how exciting it was that DED was taking bold steps to involve grass-roots community groups in governance and planning. Not quite. The majority of the DED delegate agencies were industrial or retail chambers of commerce with boards composed almost entirely of businesses and little, if any, involvement of the residents in their areas. Their programs were limited in scope, focusing on such things as sidewalk sales, facade improvements, and city services in industrial areas. A handful of the business groups were different, trying hard to form a bridge with community groups and resident interests. DED also funded a few other agencies, including Bickerdike, that did not fit the mold. The business groups were often successful at attracting or retaining businesses in their areas, something which benefits the residents also. But their continued dominance of the delegate agency roles under Washington said more about the programmatic inertia at DED than it did for any attempt to forge a real working coalition among community groups and city hall. And since DED's interaction with community-based groups was dominated by its dealings with local business groups, which had little if any base among residents, DED was not even indirectly dealing with Harold's political base when it worked with these groups.

This was particularly evident in DED's bungled attempt to turn the free market nightmare of enterprise zones into a progressive economic development tool. "Politically, we're stuck with enterprise zones," DED said, "so why not try to work together to control the potential negatives and maybe even turn them into something positive?" It sounded like a real turnabout from the pre-Washington days of ripping the entire concept as a threat to the creation and retention of livable-wage jobs, but what the hell, these were our former allies, so we thought it was at least worth considering. From the very first meeting, however, it was clear that no such reversal of enterprise zone effects was possible or even important to DED. Vázquez controlled DED's dealings with community-based groups for the most part, and he organized the enterprise zone meetings for DED. The first meeting I attended included a representative from a local agency active in job training and placement, and representatives from industrial groups in the two enterprise zones to the west and south of West Town. Ironically, these two business groups were known for their particularly strong opposition to community group involvement in local economic development and to any community oversight on their members' use of public subsidies. These groups were not inclined to go along with any of the ideas for making enterprise zones more progressive, which included: goals for affirmative action in the companies receiving benefits, set-asides of subsidies for training local residents, and community accountability. When the meetings stalled, Vázquez shrugged and said that if the "community" disagreed, there was nothing he could do.

The state enterprise zone legislation provided for the creation of nonprofit "Designated Zone Organizations" a majority of whose boards were to be residents of the zones. The zones to the south, west, and east of West Town were drawn by the city administration in advance of these meetings and excluded almost every residence in the area. Requests to redraw the boundaries to include the residential portions of the area (so that even without DED's help we could still pursue some community accountability over the use of subsidies) were ignored, as were we troublemakers ourselves after a while.

Having plenty else to do, not wanting to fight with our "friends" in city hall, and having only participated to begin with after being coaxed by DED, we dropped quietly out of the enterprise zone picture. Within a couple of years many of the business groups were openly criticizing DED for the manipulative, patronizing way in which they were treated—not just on special projects like enterprise zones, but across the board. Ironically, Vázquez tried to enlist groups like ours to head off this criticism, arguing that these critics were trying to say they represented the interests of Chicago's neighborhoods. We agreed that the critics did not distinguish between themselves and those groups which had actual community bases and control. But their message was still largely true: regardless of whether you were probusiness or proworker, or some of both, and regardless of your concept of community control, if you were from a neighborhood group, DED did not treat you like a true partner in pursuing local economic development strategies.

Harold's Legacy:
How Deep Did the Commitment Run?

The West Town Housing Phase II development of 178 new and rehabilitated housing units, which Harold Washington promised to support in his preelection tour of the neighborhood, had still not begun when he died four and a half years later. This project lost the only supporter it had in the administration. Primary funding of $11.75 million had already been committed by the U.S. Department of Housing and Urban Development (HUD), and the city had committed an additional $1.65 million as a second mortgage which was critical to the overall financing. Since making that committment, however, the city's Department of Housing (DOH) had thrown up multiple roadblocks making it impossible for Bickerdike to use the funds and begin construction. Only Harold's unwavering support and our ability to go to him directly with our concerns kept the project from falling apart altogether. When he died, we had just made some progress in negotiations with DOH. We immediately decided that we should close, if at all possible, with the DOH loan in its then current form, even if it would be costly in the long run to do so. And after borrowing another $1 million from a bank, we closed in February 1988, and the first units were occupied in August of the same year.

Why did it take so long? First, construction prices kept going up and the level of federal subsidy did not. The federal funding for this project was appropriated before Ronald Reagan took office, and only remained owing to the protection of a court-ordered settlement of the *Gautreaux* desegregation case. The Reagan administration, while forced to comply with the settlement, was not about to help release the funds by sufficiently adjusting the subsidies for inflation. After all, it had cut the program entirely in 1981. Worse even than the federal government's refusal to increase the funding were its continual threats to cancel the funding commitment and thus the project if certain deadlines were not met. While certainly within its power to do so, these threats magnified the significance of delays caused at the city government level.

Another, more serious delay was caused by the city council's refusal to sell five vacant lots to Bickerdike in the gentrifying "Wicker Park" area of West Town. City practice—unchanged under Washington—had always been to allow the local aldermen the power to veto any sale of public land or any zoning variance in their own wards. The alderman for this area at the time was Terry Gabinski, a white machine stalwart whose mentor and boss is none other than Congressman Dan Rostenkowski, chairman of the House Ways and Means Committee. They opposed Bickerdike and low-income housing in general, preferring instead to support the speculators and developers who had dreams of the area becoming the next yuppie haven. First they blocked the sale of the lots outright, then told us we had to go to public bid, and then simply opposed the sale when we were the high bidder. At their request, the city council opened the bids and decided to accept none of them. This final rejection came at a time when the city was preparing for special aldermanic elections in February 1986 in several wards where a federal court had ruled that the existing ward maps had been drawn to deny black and Latino representation.

Luis Gutierrez, a community activist who had been on the Bickerdike board, ran and defeated the machine candidate and became alderman in May 1986. This was a victory for the people of West Town and for activists and Washington supporters all over the city: the special elections resulted in Washington finally breaking the 29–21 stranglehold his opposition had on him in the city council by giving him at least 25 supportive votes. (In one of the most dramatic retreats from Harold and the things he stood for, Gutierrez supported Richie M. Daley, son of the late Richard J. Daley, in the mayoral campaign of 1989 that returned the white machine to power in city hall). But in 1986 Gutierrez was still the "people's candidate," espousing support for a true progressive coalition of blacks, whites, and Latinos, and of city hall and community groups. He also campaigned on a platform that included support of affordable housing, and within two months of his election the lots were sold to Bickerdike.

During the three years between Harold Washington's election and the special elections giving him control over city council, the administration did little to help us get the lots. Sure, the council always respected the wishes of the local alderman (in this case a member of the opposition), but the 29–21 stalemate was not as absolute as it seemed. Deals were cut all the time, among them several with Rostenkowski himself, who was in a position to either help or hinder the city's efforts to get federal funding for everything from bridges to stadiums. The closest DOH came to including the Bickerdike lots in one of these deals was to have the neighborhood's alderman, Gabinski, in for a catered lunch. They served him pierogi, a tasty Polish dish, but made no progress.

By the time the community finally elected Gutierrez and Bickerdike bought the lots, construction costs on Phase II had risen even further. The city increased its funding commitment to its final level, but then made it nearly impossible to use the funds and topped that off with talk of there not being enough money in any of the DOH accounts to actually fund the project. The roadblocks at DOH ranged from simple matters of bureaucracy and incompetence to real differences in the approach to housing subsidies and development. The latter is more important and unique to this situation, but at times it seemed the incompetence was so prevalent that DOH could not help a project even if it wanted to.

The Harold Washington appointees at DOH did not trust or like dealing with legitimate community groups. The first commissioner, Brenda Gaines, and her successor, Bess Donaldson, both came out of years in high-level administrative positions at HUD. They had no experience with community groups, and few if any ties to Harold's base aside from the fact that they are both black. Like Vázquez at DED, they saw themselves as rulers of a private army of scores of community groups funded by the city, most of whom were first funded under former Mayor Jane Byrne, but many of whom were added under Mayor Washington. Most of these groups provided "soft" services such as housing referrals and related counseling. When it came time to deal with experienced housing development organizations with some ideas of their own on how best to use subsidy funds to create affordable housing, they became defensive, paranoid, and downright hostile. Just as with other city hall problems, we did not take these public, although the identical treatment of community groups and misdirection of subsidy dollars under earlier mayors would certainly have prompted pickets and an extended public compaign to try to force some change. But the more we kept the struggle private, the more DOH took advantage of that, dividing groups by threatening their funding and implying that any criticism of DOH—no matter how private and constructive—was in fact criticism of Harold and would hurt his chances of reelection.

The programmatic differences we had with DOH centered on their embracing of policy themes like "leveraging." Any liberal supporter of good government knows that there is a scarce amount of public funds available for subsidized housing and that the more a city can leverage private dollars with public dollars, the further those public dollars will go. But what these people and their friends in the private residential development business fail to acknowledge is that there is a direct and inverse relationship between the amount of private, unsubsidized dollars used in a project and the affordability of the housing units in that project. Sure, more units can be built when bank loans are combined with public subsidies, but those units will probably be affordable only to middle-income people if the leveraging goes too far. There are many who would argue that this is fine, that in the end the supply of housing is expanded and everyone benefits. Unfortunately, these sort of trickle-down approaches represent more of an excuse to subsidize middle-income housing development than they do a progressive approach to city government.

In conjunction with their attempt to maximize private involvement in DOH-funded projects, Gaines and Donaldson were keen on, in their own words, turning DOH into "more of a bank than a government funding agency." This meant increasing the interest on the DOH share of a funding package, thereby further increasing the debt service on the development and again driving up the cost of the housing to its occupants. But to DOH this meant providing income to the city. (When housing groups suggested to DOH that the city should segregate these repayments in a fund to be used only to finance low-income housing and not administrative costs at DOH, they flatly refused.) This banker mentality was the problem with the Phase II loan: with the repayment requirements, the DOH loan was unacceptable to HUD and was so burdensome on the project's operating budget it scared off investors.

Prior to Harold's death, we realized that dealing with DOH had become almost impossible and vowed that if we ever got Phase II funded we would never try to use their funds again. When the mayor died, we scrambled to close our project with whatever they were offering, fearful that without Harold Washington to go to we might lose it all. At DOH, practice clearly contradicted the Washington image and platform, and under a new mayor, black or white, the things Harold stood for would no doubt get lost in the rush to please private developers and downtown banks. This was a scary notion for any progressive CDC with a project awaiting city hall approval at that time. Fortunately, the final compromise worked, and the project is now a reality. But instead of Bickerdike having funds to reinvest in its community, DOH will be slowly repaid its funds to use as it sees fit.

Conclusion

Alderman Eugene Sawyer, a black few would call progressive, was elected acting mayor after a raucous, divisive city council meeting shortly after Harold's death. He immediately set out to consolidate his power, rightly assuming that he would be forced to run for office in a special election within a year or two. He had won the acting mayor position over another alderman, Tim Evans, who was supported by most of the Washington block in the city council, and many Washington appointees had expressed support for Evans. María Cerda, a Puerto Rican woman who headed the Mayor's Office of Employment and Training (MET), was one such appointee and was one of the first to be fired when she refused to pledge support for Sawyer in the anticipated mayoral election. Ironically, Mier, who claimed that as a close advisor of the new acting mayor he was responsible for the firing, suggested as her replacement his former deputy Vázquez, who in turn pledged his political support to Sawyer as a condition of the promotion.

Were those who stayed on just keeping the seats warm until another of Harold's ilk could regain the mayoralty for progressives? In several cases, that was probably true. Esther Nieves was appointed executive director of the Mayor's Commission on Latino Affairs by Washington after María Torres stepped down. Rather than resign when Harold died, she stayed on and challenged the Sawyer administration to continue the progress Harold had initiated in the city's treatment of Latinos. And when Sawyer proved unresponsive, the commission went public with its criticism—a bold move for a city-funded commission. But in other cases it seemed like officials, including former activists, were mostly concerned with protecting their own positions and maintaining their recently acquired lifestyles, complete with power, media exposure, and bloated salaries.

Activists throughout the late mayor's base saw personal concerns over-riding loyalty to the Washington movement when officials like Mier accepted positions in the Sawyer administration, which had been voted into office by Washington's most ardent opponents in the city council. For those activists who questioned the allegiance of some high-level city offi-cials to the Washington platform, these defections seemed proof enough of the shallow connection between Harold Washington and some of those he hired to carry out his ideals. By the time of Harold's death, it was clear that the commitment to his approach to government and to his political base varied from one department to another, but nowhere was it deep enough to outlast his tenure. Putting aside the intentions and personal motivation of those who espoused a committment to Harold and his platform, in many instances their performance after his death undermines their claim to have been truly committed to the concept of a progressive city government.

But Harold Washington succeeded in other ways, having a great impact on the lives of those he represented. His victory was clearly the result of a grass-roots movement. The primarily black and Latino poor and working-class Chicagoans who voted for Harold have experienced a great victory against a formidable opponent. More people were caught up in the Harold Washington elections than in any other social movement in Chicago in re-cent years. Such a mass experience of a positive campaign is what empowerment is all about. However intangible and unmeasurable the ben-efits of empowerment, they are nonetheless very real and invaluable to those who experienced the movement of Harold Washington.

To some this may seem like an unbelievable contradiction. How could we have thought of him as so good and valuable in one way while so ineffec-tive in another? For many of us who worked both with Harold Washington the leader and with his city hall administration, this was a contradiction that troubled us constantly. In this chapter I have tried to address several questions with respect to one disappointment community activists experi-enced with the Washington administration: the administration's record on involving Chicago's communities in a progressive coalition with city hall. So how did Harold's vision of progressive change via a coalition of city hall and community people get distorted and frequently lost altogether? There are several possible explanations, of which the following are just a few that seem applicable to the area of community development.

First, the vision was not clearly enough articulated for those who were appointed to put it into practice. Campaign speeches were sketchy on the issue of how Chicagoans at large would be involved in setting the city's agenda. The transition team, which outlined the early positions of the ad-ministration, was a huge, disorganized body to which most members brought their own agendas, rather than a mandate to translate the new mayor's ideas into policy positions. Two development plans were written, known as "Chicago Works Together" and "Chicago Works Together II." These clearly stated a progressive development policy emphasizing job creation, balanced growth, and citizen participation. The plans were not so clear as to how to achieve these goals. Unfortunately, it seemed that many policymakers paid little attention to what the plans said, choosing instead to wear their "Chicago Works Together" lapel pins as proof of their loyalty to the slogan.

Second, several key appointees did not share the vision. Some, like Hollander at Planning, were liberals, at best, who saw little value in broadening community involvement so long as the "right thing" was done by city hall. Others, like Mier and Vázquez at DED, seemed too preoccupied with their own self-image as development commissioners in a historic progressive city government to allow for genuine participation by outsiders. And still others, like Gaines and Donaldson at DOH, came across as upper-middle-class professionals who had for too long been thwarted in their attempts to rise in stature and power to let organizations of poor people hold them back.

Why did Washington appoint people like this? That is very hard to say. Perhaps they pledged their commitment to community involvement and simply never carried it out. Or maybe in the rush to assemble a new government that was both progressive and competent, the rookie mayor and his aides did not ask for such a commitment, or asked and did not carefully challenge the appointees on the point. At the time, few would have suspected that anyone interested in an appointment to a development department would have anything but a sincere commitment to neighborhood development and community involvement. After all, the public at large knew that Harold Washington stood for those things, so how could a potential appointee not share his views?

Third, community activists were not treated as true partners in policy formulation. There were a few examples of communication and cooperation, but there were many more examples characterized by suspicion, mistrust, and defensive posturing. Without most of the activists in communities supportive of the mayor working effectively with city hall, it was impossible to generate broad community involvement.

Fourth, the communities and their activists shortchanged themselves by not challenging these impediments to community involvement. Sure we complained, but rarely did we pursue the issue in a sustained way that could have contributed to some progress. And when occasionally some activists tried to help city hall pull off a charade of community involvement on a particular issue, rarely were they challenged for becoming like puppets of city hall and therefore blocking real community participation.

And, lastly, there was no discipline at city hall or among community groups to enforce adherence to the all-too-vague vision of a progressive coalition. When Harold Washington was approached directly about a case of one of his appointees acting counter to his stated development or process goals, he usually intervened to bring that person into line with the administration's public position, while pledging loyalty to his appointees. Various members of the administration came to be bell ringers on issues like job creation, displacement, etc., and spoke out in internal debates when the mayor's position on those issues was about to be violated. But it seemed that Harold alone—among those in a position to do something about it—understood the difficulties community people experienced in dealings with his administration. He understood just how valuable to his political movement and to his government were those frustrated supporters, and he often sought to correct the problems that caused the frustrations. But he could not and did not stand vigil over his entire cabinet, checking their performance against his vision of a progressive coalition. If we consider this lack of discipline in light of the appointees' varying degrees of commitment to the process of community involvement, it is not hard to see how we failed to realize the mayor's vision.

Such musings can easily be dismissed as the rantings of a cynical, resentful, hardheaded organizer with more than a few personal scores to settle. Or they can be seen as that and more, perhaps shedding a little light on the nature of the relationship between Harold Washington's city hall and the communities that put him and his team there. None of this takes away at all from the value to Chicago and particular to its black and Latino communities of having experienced Harold Washington and his brief tenure as mayor. Comparisons have been made between the adulation and grief displayed when the mayor died with that shown the Reverend King or President Kennedy when they were assasinated. But when it came to fulfilling your dreams and putting your policies into practice, Harold, we hardly knew you.

NOTES

1.   This was not the only way community involvement occurred under Harold Washington, but it was a significant one. And many critics as well as supporters of community groups would argue that the kind of elitist exclusion of most of the community from the process, which some feared would happen with local planning boards, did occur in some communities where community groups worked very closely with city hall.

2.   This discussion focuses exclusively on those community groups that address the issues of housing and/or economic development in their communities. There

are probably some 150–200 such groups in Chicago, many of them cookie-cutter versions of a standard model, but most represent a hybrid of styles, activities, and philosophies. Three further distinctions among such CDCs are significant: First, while most are honest and genuinely try to fulfill their mission, some are basically corrupt, existing primarily for the personal enrichment of their staff or members. Second, among the honest groups are those who are relatively well-connected to their stated constituency ("community-based"), and those who are not. And third, among the community-based groups are those that believe that such things as community involvement and empowerment are as important as quantitative measures of their work, and others who define results solely in quantative terms while downplaying the importance of community process and control issues. While surely an overused and distorted label, CDCs committed to community control and empowerment are often considered more progressive than those which do not share those commitments, or which only give lip service to them.

3. A personal phone call or invitation to discuss an issue from a city commissioner is hard to resist, and few of us did. When we would try to shift to a more public approach, it was hard to accomplish.

4. Would a committee that had a membership more balanced between community and downtown interests have been more effective in developing a workable, meaningful linked development program? In order for balance to be a significant factor, each side must have something the other wants, as in an arbitrated contract dispute. In this case, we wanted resources from downtown development to go to the neighborhoods, and the downtown interests did not want that to happen. Had we organized a campaign of public pressure through picketing, media exposure, and the like for months before the committee was formed, we might have had some bargaining power. As it was, all we had was the good intentions of the Washington administration. Their move for more "balance," then, was a signal that they intended to let the two sides slug it out among themselves, with the city acting as impartial referee. Until that point, we had expected to be joining a committee with the firm support of city hall to produce a proposal to redistribute resources from downtown to the neighborhoods.

5. The enterprise zone concept itself was of lesser importance than other economic development issues the Washington administration faced. The experience of trying to forge a coalition on this issue, however, is illustrative of the weaknesses of the so-called progressive coalition.

Conclusion

WIM WIEWEL and PIERRE CLAVEL

The preceding chapters illuminate themes and questions that we raised in the Introduction and that are applicable to local governments, and especially progressive governments, generally. The two main points relate, respectively, to *politics* and to *governance*. The political issue of which these chapters give most evidence is the politics of social movements and its consequences: the remarkable electoral mobilization without which Washington would not have been mayor; the new substantive concerns introduced by these social movements, particularly the goals for race and class equity; and the subsequent clashes between those who sought to implement the neighborhood movement program and those who were less ambitious.

The second main point these chapters offer is an elaboration of what a progressive city administration, attempting to implement a neighborhood movement program, looks like in the process and substance of its governance. On the one hand, a pervasive theme is the difficulty of governance that resulted from the conflict as representatives of movement concerns took up roles alongside holdovers from the machine period and alongside reformers with more modest reform interests. But this social movement base was also an opportunity, and the Washington administration produced a significant response, which we can summarize in some of the categories delineated in our introduction: the task of setting the agenda for the administration; relations between the administration and its movement base; the administration's efforts to transcend this base; the development and utilization of progressive expertise; the handling of diversity; institutionalization of reforms; and the formation of extralocal coalitions.

The Politics of Social Movements

The combination of movement fervor, along with race and class issues, as well as the diversity of interests with often competing goals, led to much confusion as to how to interpret the Washington election. Is there an objective base, even now, from which to view the social movement character of Washington's political base? Doug Gills argues that Washington's election was made possible by the mobilization of a new social base, primarily consisting of the black population, but importantly augmented by the community and independent political movements. From this point of view, one could expect a class- or class/race/ethnicity-based politics, which would employ a clear "us vs. them" analysis, know where its true interests lie, and use compromise only as a tactical weapon in a struggle for ultimate control.

The alternative view is that the Washington coalition was merely a coalition of convenience in which several sets of disparate interest groups coalesced temporarily, in the never-ending game of shifting alliances under political pluralism. The rapid split after Washington's death of his coalition in supporters of Alderman Timothy Evans and those of Alderman Eugene Sawyer and the subsequent move of the Hispanic community and the Lakefront liberals to Richard M. Daley certainly suggested, to many observers, the plausibility of this interpretation.[1]

The foregoing chapters bear the marks of the particular electoral conditions that brought Washington to office in 1983 and that continued to exist outside and inside the administration. In our view, they bear out the notion that Washington's election was a movement election. Without the unprecedented mobilization that occurred in 1982/83 in the black and Latino communities, among poor whites and in the community-based organizations, and among white liberals, Washington would not have been elected mayor. As Gills writes, people who were politically dead came to life and worked for Washington's election. It would be hard to overestimate the fervor that pervaded the black population—rich and poor—in this election and throughout Washington's mayoralty. It needs saying that this politics was *different*: it was drastically different from the kind of demobilized, organization-dominated politics that had characterized Chicago for more than half a century, and it was also different from the reform politics that occurred in many other cities. Gills makes this clear; its effects pervade the other chapters as well.

The way the 1983 election was different was most obviously that it was a black mayor who won with black support; but there was also the well-developed program supplied by the community organizations, particularly as articulated in the Community Workshop for Economic Development (CWED) Platform in 1982 that had the potential to transcend race issues by articulating a class or economic justice program. These ideas, which came out of a particular segment of the several social movements that came together in the election, had the potential, seen by at least some in these constituent groups, to weld the coalition together, to transcend divisions that crippled the city politically, before and after Washington's term.

The divisions, nevertheless, were substantial. The movement base was not at all monolithic, but represented a variety of groups and categories, many of which had never worked together before and differed quite radically in their objectives.

As Gills writes, the core of Washington's coalition was the black nationalists who, with financial support from a small number of wealthy black businessmen, were able to start the voter registration campaigns that translated black demographic strength into electoral strength. White progressives and community organizations had quickly joined the emerging coalition, though many of the latter never quite lost their doubts about participating in an electoral campaign and putting their trust in politicians and "city hall." Antimachine white liberals were a third group in the coalition. Disgusted with the old machine, they were quick to interpret Washington's efforts to reward supporters as evidence of a new form of machine building. They also did not share the antibusiness and anti-downtown-growth views of most of the progressives and community people in the coalition. Finally, Latinos provided an important part of the margin of victory in the election, but they only had joined the coalition in substantial numbers after the primaries.

This diversity caused tensions even during the electoral period; but the anticipated rewards of election—with different meanings to different actors—kept them together.

Governance

Intensity, diversity, and a coherent community development program were assets in the electoral mobilization that Harold Washington rode into office. But these same features were a challenge to Washington's ability to govern, once in office. An important theme in these chapters has been the evidence they give of just how great a challenge it was.

How Hard It Was

Once in office, the Washington forces found that it was necessary to bring in an even broader set of interests for governance than the diverse coalition that had been involved in the electoral movement. This strained the new administration even further. There was a tension between the need to relate to the movement base and the need to transcend this base by expanding the coalition to gain sufficient electoral support, and then expand it even further to maintain sufficient legitimacy outside of the coalition to govern. Doing this inevitably engendered suspicion on the side of some supporters.

The conflict was worse because of the class diversity of the coalition. Timothy Wright's chapter lays out the fights within the Mayor's Office between the representatives of the black business elite and the more progressive elements which represented the poor black population. Robert Brehm similarly describes the leadership of the Department of Housing as "upper-middle-class professionals [unwilling] to let organizations of poor people hold them back."

Overlaid on this was the history of distrust that many community organizations had built up toward city hall. As several of the chapters indicate, it was an article of faith with these organizations, backed up by many years of experience, that politics and government do not serve the interests of low- and moderate-income and minority residents. Any community leader accepting appointment on an official city commission or task force was likely to be labeled a "sellout." Thus, to participate in Washington's campaign was a big step, and the groups were always ready to see signs of betrayal. Brehm's chapter documents its occurrence.

The tenuous role of Latino interests in the coalition was continually troubling. There had only been a limited amount of cooperation, and the issue of Latino representation in the campaign, the transition team, and the administration itself was contentious from the start. The ward remapping and election of 1986, which gave Harold Washington control of the city council, made support of the Latino aldermen even more clearly essential. María Torres's chapter indicates the conflictual nature of the relationship between the Latino community and the administration. Indeed, the Latino Commission's establishment proceeded in direct defiance of Mayor Washington's wishes, and the commission's activities and mode of operating remained a thorn in the administration's side. Subsequent events, during the elections of 1989, made clear that Hispanics were probably the weakest link in the coalition, as they cast the majority of their votes for Richard M. Daley.

As the chapters make clear, these conflicts are not the mere squabbling among like-minded people about the best course of action. Nor do they just represent the fragmentation often found in large cities.[2] Rather, they reflected deep divisions between those who felt the administration should make unequivocal choices based on its class or race/ethnic group basis, and those who preferred a more "balanced" approach: the older, liberal alternative that combined support for the growth coalition with a slight redirection of benefits to poorer neighborhoods, increased opportunities for minorities, etc. Many of those in the administration, such as the commissioner of housing, and probably Elizabeth Hollander, as well as the mayor's chief of staff and others in the Mayor's Office, were ideologically much more comfortable with the liberal approach, albeit with a minority-oriented twist. Indeed, some of them had come from places like Atlanta, where the model had been used at its most succesful by Andrew Young and Maynard Jackson.

In this latter view, government's role is not the pursuit of a movement's interests, but rather it is to be the expression of, or arbiter among, competing legitimate interests. Hollander's description of the way in which the business and real estate community organized itself to defend its interests bespeaks her basic belief in such a role. Conversely, in his account of the Linked Development Commission, Brehm speaks of his disillusionment upon discovering that the administration was adopting this role, intending to let the community organizations and developers "slug it out among themselves, with the city acting as impartial referee." Indeed, much of the disappointment that pervades Brehm's chapter and, to a lesser extent, Gills's chapter, can be seen as a result of their initial assumption that with Washington's victory, they had won the battle. Instead, all they had gained was the opportunity to participate in the fight.

Harold Washington himself appears to have been a strong believer in the process of give and take and competition among different interests. Apparently he relished having different members or factions of his staff argue extensively for their point of view, making up his own mind as late as possible. As Robert Mier and Kari Moe write, this method went back to Washington's days as a congressman, and he continued it in his transition team, where the debate included not just his supporters but also representatives from the business community who had opposed him. It also showed in the latitude which each of the Commissioners apparently enjoyed, with Hollander describing the extreme example of the public works commissioner directly undermining the administration's position on the new Central Public Library.

However, it may not have been just a preference for extensive participation and debate that led Washington to adopt this course; he probably also lacked the power to enforce a single point of view. Timothy Wright's chapter documents some of the wheeling and dealing necessary to govern, and also shows the serious conflicts within the Mayor's Office. Time and again, on issues involving the World's Fair, the Latino Commission, the Linked Development Commission, or the Planned Manufacturing District for instance, the mayor did not interfere with the deep disagreements within his coalition, nor take a strong early stance against, for instance, the real estate developers who definitely were *not* part of his coalition.

New Practices

But all was not conflict. The social movement base also presented Washington and the community development people in his administration with an opportunity, and the greatest importance of the Washington administration lies in what it showed about the potential for new processes of governance and the development of new programs. Because of Chicago's size and complexity, new practices had to go well beyond the experiences of the smaller progressive cities whose notable features we discussed in the Introduction. In turn, any future progressive administration, in Chicago or elsewhere, will confront new circumstances that will shape its opportunities. Nevertheless, a summary of the most important points and lessons learned will hold useful models for the future. Following are the most salient points.

Agenda Setting   The earlier discussion about agenda setting suggested the importance of staking out the terrain early in the administration and of having a clear program to solidify the base. The experiences of the Washington administration confirm this, and further show the importance of symbolism in communicating and developing the agenda.

Developing the agenda was an opportunity for solidifying the administration's base of support, as well as to reach beyond it. But there was a tension between the need, on the one hand, to reward supporters and deliver on the campaign agenda and, on the other, to increase legitimacy by reaching out to those outside the coalition and present a viable agenda for the city as a whole. This tension was even greater for an administration with a shaky coalition, which just barely eked out an electoral victory, as was the case for Washington's. Thus, the early period of agenda setting needed to give clear signals about the significant changes that the administration sought to bring about, without scaring the business and banking world so much that the City's credit rating would be endangered.

Any hopes of a honeymoon were dashed when at the first city council meeting Washington's oppponents reorganized the council to take control of all committees, creating the near-stalemate that lasted until the special elections of 1986. Thus, the first act of agenda setting came from the opposition, and it clearly signaled there was to be war. It also immediately called into question the new mayor's political savvy. The "council wars," as they came to be known, significantly reduced Washington's ability to "deliver the goods" to his constituency. At the same time, they served to demarcate friends and enemies unambiguously, in the "Washington 21" and the "Vrdolyak 29." This helped pull the coalition together and provided a ready explanation, and perhaps excuse, for the lack of early visible progress on much of the election platform.

This demarcation, while rooted in political and racial/ethnic divisions, also rested on clear substantive ground. In the area of neighborhood and economic development the new administration did not have to invent an agenda; it largely came in with a ready-made one. It would be hard to overstate the importance of the decades of work and experience in the neighborhood movement that led to the creation of the Washington agenda. Neighborhood organizations had an enormous experience, both in terms of substance and process. Unlike other cities, where community organizations have largely been involved in housing, Chicago's groups had, during the 1970s, begun to expand their involvement to issues of economic development, job training, and job creation. In addition, they had experienced the lure of resources and dangers of co-optation in the Model Cities programs, as well as the headiness and frustration of organizing campaigns. Finally, because of the size of the city and the number of organizations, there existed a relatively sophisticated infrastructure of training institutes, technical assistance and research organizations, coalitions, and knowledgeable funders. Thus, all the elements were in place for a significant leap forward. As several of the chapters mention, the formation of CWED and its platform formalized the agenda of the neighborhood movement at that time.

Although this agenda was modified in the transition process, it was largely adopted in the 1984 Development Plan, "Chicago Works Together." Procedurally, the creation of this plan was most important for its effect within the administration. Because it involved top staff from all the development-related departments in a series of lengthy planning sessions, it served to build internal understanding and consensus around development principles that deviated significantly from prior practice. Substantively, the plan included many programmatic initiatives that had already been started by community organizations and others. Thus, they could be pursued immediately, and as Robert Giloth's chapter shows, most of the initial activities of the Department of Economic Development's R&D Division derived directly from these ongoing initiatives.

The progressive substance of the "Chicago Works Together" plan was made even clearer by the publication in the same year of the "Make No Little Plans" document of the Civic Committee of the Commercial Club.[3] As Mier and Moe and then Giloth discuss, the differences between the approaches represented by these plans were captured by a number of metaphors, several of which had been used among community organizations before and now entered broader debate: neighborhoods vs. downtown; manufacturing as opposed to a service economy; "Chicago

Works Together" instead of "The City that Works"; and "betting on the basics" as opposed to "bowing out."[4]

The use of slogans and symbols to communicate an agenda is nothing new. The challenge for the Washington administration was to communicate a drastically new agenda and to change the process by which issues were debated. The importance of symbols in staking out the terrain recurs in a number of the chapters. It includes such traditional tools as using buttons and slogans, but also shows up in such acts as calling the first all-department staff meeting; organizing volunteer Saturday morning task forces; insisting from the very beginning on racial, ethnic, and gender diversity in all hiring, committee appointments, contracting, and purchasing; and using broad-based task forces rather than "blue-ribbon" committees to assist in policy development.

These representations of substantive differences through symbolic and real changes were not mere marketing ploys. As Miliband, Castells, and others have argued, an essential component of the process of social change is the creation of new culture and language.[5] Only when political, economic, and cultural/social changes happen simultaneously do lasting structural changes occur. Albeit on a limited scale, the Washington administration managed to change not just who sat at the table but also the terms and nature of the debate. Thus, agenda setting went beyond staking out new positions in familiar controversies; rather, it included generating whole new areas of discussion and new ways of communicating them.

The use of symbols could also backfire. Hollander proudly describes the Community Forums as a low-cost alternative to the establishment of mini-city halls, while still conveying the administration's openness to citizens. But Brehm considered these forums to have been a charade, and they soured his attitude to the administration early on.

Perhaps more importantly, those who invent and use the symbols and metaphors can become caught in their own rhetoric. For instance, Mier and Moe argue that the administration's ability to undertake large projects was hampered by the "downtown vs. the neighborhoods" emphasis in community organizing. This made every large project immediately suspect. The nature of the symbolic policy discourse prevented an adequate response.[6] Nevertheless, more often than not this sort of discourse helped set the new agenda.

Relating to the Base   As we noted earlier, the Washington electoral coalition consisted of a varied movement base with additional constituencies, such as white liberals. Once in office, the coalition was broadened even further and included more representation from, for instance, the business community. This raised the question of the relationship between the administration and its original movement base. Some of this has already been discussed in the context of the political conflict that characterized the administration, but there are some important administrative and governance issues as well.

The relationship started out with the movement base nourishing the new administration in terms of providing ideas and an agenda for both process and substantive programs, as detailed above. This agenda was carried in significant part by individuals who made the transition from positions with neighborhood- or nationality-based organizations or related agencies to leadership positions in the administration. Mier, Moe, Giloth, Torres, and Walker represent this group, and they clearly played key roles in changing the priorities of their departments and how they went about implementing them, as well as in formulating the administration's larger agenda.

Part of this new agenda consisted of delegating government tasks to not-for-profit organizations. The city rapidly developed a network of 350 delegate agencies, involved in economic development, housing, job training and placement, social services, and neighborhood planning. This made possible a great increase in the level of activity and sophistication on a decentralized level. Since the vast majority of these agencies had multiple sources of funding, they were not wholly dependent on the city and retained significant autonomy. Although this had some elements of "the new patronage," such a characterization is exaggerated.[7] While some of the funding represented rewards for political support, there were significant differences from the usual notion of patronage. The organizations were not nearly as dependent on the city as a regular employee is. Furthermore, the work to be performed was specified through contracts, rather than assigned on a hierarchical basis. Also, there was only very limited solicitation of financial contributions to political campaigns. Although these organizations could occasionally be counted on to "rally the troops," they represented an often recalcitrant army.

Nevertheless, parts of the administration made skilful use of their relations with constituencies to move their agenda forward. María Torres describes the struggle of the nascent Latino Commission to be given official status, and the role of Latino activists who had helped Washington get elected in applying pressure. Judith Walker describes how the system of contracting with outside agencies helped create a constituency for her department, and Donna Ducharme writes about the reciprocal interplay between organizing efforts and policy development.

This mode of operating was never worked out well, though. The administration officials who had been active in community organizations perhaps took it too much for granted that they would be trusted and continue to receive the support of their former colleagues. Under pressure to deal with an often hostile bureaucracy and placate the business and financial community, these new appointees did not always keep their constituents well informed about the constraints they faced. When they did, these constraints were often seen as mere excuses.

On the other hand, the community organizations were uncertain how to proceed. Especially in the beginning, they were inclined to withhold criticism for fear of embarrassing Mayor Washington. The notion of assisting the administration in its arguments with the business community or city council opponents by forming a strident and vocal "left wing" never took hold. Without clear communication about such a tactic any attempts to pursue it only soured the relationship with the administration.

Transcending the Base   Many of the tensions in attempts to relate to the movement base arose from the administration's need to transcend that base. Unlike the situation in several of the other progressive cities described earlier, Washington's base was already fairly broad and very diverse. The primary need for reaching beyond it arose from the realities of city finance. As Gills argues, without the support of LaSalle Street and Wall Street no mayor can run the city. Furthermore, some segments of the coalition wanted to reach out in any event, because of a basic belief in the pluralist system.

As Hollander suggests, Harold Washington and the business community never became very comfortable together, but toward the end of his first term the business community had learned how to live with him. The real estate, financial, and other business sectors all went through some form of regrouping and reorganization in order to accommodate themselves to the new administration. The appointment of Rob Mier as commissioner of economic development in 1983 had been met with a significant amount of red-baiting and panic, and segments of the business sector deeply resented the mayor's lack of support for the proposed 1992 World's Fair. Nevertheless, the first term showed that business had little to fear.

Part of the reason for the relatively harmonious relations was the luck of timing. Washington took office at the depth of the recession and rode an uninterrupted wave of recovery. Although economic restructuring continued to leave many of the city's poorest residents and neighborhoods on the economic sidelines, the corporate and real estate sectors experienced substantial growth. The percentage of purchases made from local firms increased from 41 percent in 1982 to 65 percent by 1987, benefiting the local economy as a whole, even though some city purchasing may have been shifted from larger to smaller and minority firms.[8] Real estate development in the Loop reached record levels during the first term and continued unabated into the second.[9] The business community wasted no time throwing its support to Richard M. Daley when the opportunity arose after Washington's death, but clearly they had reached an accommodation with him that could have lasted a long time.

In addition, the Washington administration appears to have had a salutary effect on the ability of the business community to organize itself effectively. One form that this organization took was increased cooperation with community organizations, sometimes assisted by the administration, sometimes entirely separate from it. One example is the Neighborhood Reinvestment Program, a joint effort of banks and community organizations, through which $135 million was pledged to neighborhood housing and economic development projects.[10] Another case is the Chicago Capital Fund, a venture capital company interested in relatively small Chicago-based companies, which was first initiated by representatives from community and social service agencies. Supported by the Department of Economic Development (DED), it obtained the cooperation of some of Chicago's leading business people and with an initial capitalization of $5 million has been operating since 1987. The corporate community has also contributed significantly to the Local Initiatives Support Corporation, which in turn invests in neighborhood projects. These and similar activities greatly expanded the range of contacts between neighborhood and business representatives. They also facilitated and legitimated the increasing involvement of neighborhood representatives on economic and business-oriented task forces, and participation by business on social service and neighborhood-oriented groups.

Perhaps the most interesting effort to transcend his base came when Washington took the issue of a General Obligation Bond for infrastructure improvements directly to the voters. As Mier and Moe describe it, opposition on the city council by the "Vrdolyak 29" quickly crumbled when a busload of administration officials showed residents of the white wards the benefits their aldermen were opposing. Nevertheless, the relation with these wards remained problematic, as reflected in a speech Washington gave to Save Our Neighborhoods/Save Our City (SON/SOC), the main coalition of community organizations in these neighborhoods:

> One of the greatest challenges of my administration has been reaching out to and appreciating the special needs and concerns of our city's predominantly white ethnic middle income neighborhoods. When it came to our city's Northwest and Southwest Sides, I found myself stuck in a dilemma. It was difficult to communicate the key principles of the reform program we are bringing to Chicago and more difficult to get a firm grip on the real problems confronting those communities. . . . You may remember that I was a target at the coalition's last convention in April. Tomorrow, I will be their toastmaster. This is truly progress.[11]

In spite of this cheery tone, relations remained difficult. This same coalition put the administration and its supporters in a box over the issue of linked development, as Brehm and Hollander describe. Unable to oppose such a neighborhood-initiated and neighborhood-oriented initiative, but distrustful of SON/SOC's motivations, the administration attempted to bury the issue in a committee and wound up angering everyone involved.

Nevertheless, the administration earned sufficient credit that the virulence which had characterized the 1983 campaign was absent in 1987. Washington's support in the white Southwest and Northwest Side wards hardly increased, but the number of votes for his opponent decreased. However, Washington did not really need their votes, nor those of the business community. All he needed was sufficient legitimacy so that he could govern and hang on to the base that elected him in the first place. His administration managed to achieve this in the first term.

Progressive Expertise   The question here is what types of special skills or values progressives bring to city government that differentiate them from other professionals, and what the relationship is between these skills and values and their background in neighborhood or other movement organizations.

Much of the expertise that the Washington team introduced to their departments was of a democratic "good government" type. This was motivated by a commitment to fairness and equitable processes, as well as by the need for institutional reform in order to be able to use the machinery of government for a new agenda. The administration inherited a city government that in many ways was reminiscent of feudalism more than modern bureaucracy. Secretive and personalistic approaches dominated in the city council, and the process in the city departments was very similar, as John Kretzmann's chapter shows. For many workers, job security depended on a personal political connection. Clear objectives, evaluation standards, or an open budget process were generally lacking.

The first task in this situation was not to introduce anything very progressive but to implement professionalism and standard bureaucratic procedures of accountability and evaluation. Although both Walker and Hollander describe the use of intradepartmental participatory approaches, generally this appears to have been limited. Indeed, when one of the editors of this book asked DED Deputy Commissioner Arturo Vázquez if he was going to introduce participatory management techniques, the response was that "from feudalism one first has to move to bureaucracy."

Among the main attempts to rationalize procedures was the introduction of "Management by Objectives," which largely failed, whether because of a lack of centralized follow-up or inherent weaknesses. More succesful was the establishment of subcabinets bringing together related departments. Also important was the formulation of "Chicago Works To-gether" in 1984 and its update in 1987. This improved the coordination among the departments involved and provided some clarity about goals and objectives; it was used to create a scorecard for the 1987 elections. Another major innovation was the development of an open budget process, including public hearings, and the submission of the budget in time for actual debate to take place.

Much of the contribution of the progressives went far beyond conventional professionalism. Their unique skills derived from their community work came most to the fore in two ways. The first is the level of sheer enthusiasm and commitment that they brought to the job. Each of the chapters displays the enormous extent to which participants invested themselves in their work for the administration. Clearly, these were not bureaucrats and technicians doing a job, but true believers pursuing a mission. Obviously, Harold Washington's own charisma was a key factor in bringing out such dedication. His unexpected death showed this very starkly, and the process of writing these chapters assisted several of the authors in reflecting on this period and coming to terms with its ending.

The second, more specific skill that participants brought from their neighborhood work showed up in the relations between the departments and their constituencies. The main manifestation of this is the plethora of task forces and special commissions described in these chapters. These participatory bodies clearly played an important role in the process of policy formulation, even though results were often painstakingly slow in coming, or absent altogether.

Like any administration, Washington's used the appointment of special committees for several different purposes. These include the desire for real input from affected parties; building support for a policy; and providing the appearance of action to defuse a difficult situation. For instance, in the case of the Linked Development Commission, the administration was responding to pressure from the white neighborhoods for a linked development program. As the chapter by Hollander shows, the administration itself did not have a consistent position and the participatory process was intended to postpone this inflammatory issue past the 1987 elections. On the other hand, Walker established a Service Providers Council to strenghten her position in the difficult process of changing the way her Department of Human Services operated. The Steel Task Force resulted from a campaign promise to focus on the metals industry and was clearly designed to help chart the city's course through the new terrain of sector-specific intervention.

The main risk of these participatory efforts was to raise expectations and then anger participants because these were not met, either because of the limits to what city government can do or because there never was any intention of doing anything. At their best, they greatly expanded the number of people with a stake in implementation of the outcomes and with an informed understanding of the issues and constraints. Both happened. On the whole, however, the participatory approach is widely seen in Chicago as one of the major contributions of the Washington administration, and a significant method of institutionalizing reform.

Dealing with Diversity   One of the key goals of the neighborhood movement was to incorporate diverse racial, nationality, and gender groups. Although we have focused here on Washington's neighborhood and economic development agenda, he first caught national attention because he was Chicago's first black mayor. In Chicago itself, too, the race issue was far more important than substantive policy issues in determining voting patterns and shaping people's perceptions of the period.

However, Harold Washington was not, and couldn't be, just a black mayor. Although the growth of the black population was a key factor in producing the necessary voting block, blacks still only constituted about 40 percent of the population, and less of registered voters. Thus, whether by choice or necessity, his coalition and government had to be multiracial and multiethnic.

This diversity was not accepted, or expected, by everyone. At election victory night Jesse Jackson stated, "It's our turn now," reflecting not just the hopes of some blacks but also the fears of many whites.[12] Certainly there was grumbling among blacks when whites were appointed to key departments such as planning and economic development, which were seen as particularly important to the black community.

On the whole, the appointments of top-level staff, as well as subsequent appointments to commissions and task forces, followed the pattern Washington had established during the campaign. For all committees and working groups the aim was to reflect the diversity of the city in terms of race, ethnicity, gender, class, and geography. Departments developed new procedures for doing this, and other organizations kept track of their progress.

However, the coalition between blacks and progressive whites appears to have been easier to operate than that between blacks and Hispanics, for several reasons. Blacks and Hispanics are in a more competitive situation with each other than either one is with whites. Blacks and whites did considerably better in obtaining top positions than Hispanics. As Torres describes, the Latino Commission and the broader Latino community repeatedly had to press their demands to obtain fair representation, and they never quite succeeded to their satisfaction. Black nationalists wanted to keep the maximum number of appointments for blacks and were reluctant to accord Hispanics minority status. In that sense whites were less of a threat, because they would not take up "minority" slots (although white women might). Also, whites are a more agreeable coalition partner for either blacks or Hispanics than they are for each other, because whites control more resources. Given the overriding importance of race, appointing progressive whites could be interpreted for and by the city's white population and business community as a sign of appeasement, stability, and continuity in a way that appointing even a conservative Hispanic could not.

Furthermore, even though there may be similarities in the socioeconomic conditions of many blacks and Hispanics, this has not led to a feeling of shared destiny. Racism toward blacks among Mexican-Americans, Chicago's largest Hispanic group, is not much less than among whites.[13] Without a Hispanic equivalent to white liberalism, there is little reason to expect much receptiveness on the side of blacks to cooperation with Mexican-Americans.

These limitations should not let us lose sight of the positive accomplishments in the area of interracial and interethnic relations. Gills describes the importance of the experience of multinational coalitions in making the Washington movement possible, as well as the continued importance of racism as an obstacle to its success. Mier and Moe are impressed by the conscious effort from the beginning to reflect the city's diversity in Washington's issues teams, but also speak of how they "constantly struggled with finding language and metaphors . . . [for] a multirace, multiclass development environment." Finally, with fewest illusions, Torres documents the continuous dual battle, on the one hand, to keep the Hispanic community supportive of Washington and, on the other, to get sufficient Hispanic representation in the administration to make supportiveness worth it.

But diversity definitely was a hallmark of the Washington administration, and it set a new standard for achievement in this regard. In its own hiring, the city's purchasing, and the example it set in voluntary appointments, it made a strong break with the past and became a touchstone for subsequent administrations.

Institutionalizing Reform   The Washington administration was able to institutionalize many aspects of reform in spite of formidable obstacles. Important barriers to success existed within the city bureaucracy itself and from the remains of the machine constituency. In addition, there were the pernicious effects of racism, which deepened the division in the city council and kept the electorate divided. Also, Washington had only limited and indirect control over large policy areas such as public housing, education, and the park system, all of which had their own governing boards. Finally, a Republican governor and president were not particularly kind to a Democratic mayor.

In view of these problems, what is remarkable is the extent to which various parts of the economic development program were able to take root at all. This happened through several mechanisms. The key ones were the development of new organizational structures; changes in service delivery processes through subcontracting and delegation; the legitimation of broad participatory processes; direct executive orders and legislative action; and support for outside initiatives.

Giloth describes the creation of the R&D Division within the Department of Economic Development—a protected enclave free of operational responsibilities, which was able to support selected parts of the Washington economic development and neighborhood program by funding research and demonstration projects. Many of the projects and programs it supported or initiated have thrived, although the unit itself was decimated when Richard M. Daley became mayor.[14]

Other methods of reorganizing to institutionalize reform have been discussed above, as in the funding of the extensive network of delegate agencies by the Economic Development, Housing, Human Services, and Planning Departments and the Mayor's Office of Employment and Training. These agencies have evolved to become a source of representation and power next to the elected city council member (alderman), and so far have been able to maintain most of their resources under the new administration.

Legislative changes and executive orders were used to change the city's purchasing and hiring procedures to include more women and minorities. This led to dramatic results in these areas, and the policies were reaffirmed when Richard M. Daley took office. Nevertheless, the achievements have begun to slip from the levels reached during the Washington administration.[15]

Another aspect of institutionalization is the extent to which new items for the reform agenda continued to be generated outside of the administration itself. Many of the projects that the R&D Division worked on had been initiated by community and research organizations. Torres's description of the Latino Commission and Ducharme's experience with the Planned Manufacturing District are other examples of the extent of continued issue development and policy creation outside of government. The latter, especially, emerged from neighborhood experiences and required considerable struggle to gain legitimacy even as an issue. Ultimately, Ducharme argues, the lack of initial support forced her to build a stronger case and may have helped the legislation survive continued opposition. Hollander suggests, plausibly, that the 1989 movement for far-reaching decentralization of the school system would not have been possible without the climate created by the Washington administration. Similarly, in 1990, under pressure from a new coalition, the Neighborhood Capital Budget Group, the city began holding hearings on the Capital Budget, which had managed to remain largely a black box even during the Washington administration. Finally, the present "good government" management of the Chicago Housing Authority, although more top—down, may reflect a belated infusion of some of the progressive expertise that earlier helped improve the functioning of city government's departments.

One main area in which the Washington administration was unable to institutionalize reform was in the handling of large projects. Mier and Moe and then Hollander acknowledge this, regretting their inability to develop fully an approach to making major development projects fit into Washington's neigbhorhood and small projects agenda. The main elements of such an approach were public participation and linked development— ways in which benefits could be skimmed off a large project and be redirected to poorer neighborhoods and residents. There were some successes, such as the community consultation around the issue of installing lights at Wrigley Field, and the design—build competition for the Central Public Library. For the construction of a new football stadium the Chicago Bears, the city, and some community organizations were able to reach an agreement, but it was turned down by the state legislature. There was also continued community opposition and the city never established site control. Nevertheless, some of the principles contained in the agreement continue to be used by the community in its negotiations for other uses of the site.

Other projects were even less successful. In the early days of the administration, the renovation of Navy Pier fell victim to the "council wars." The administration was internally divided and perceived as indecisive on the proposed World's Fair; its stance earned it both the enmity of those in the corporate community who had staked much personal prestige on the fair and disillusionment among the community organizations that actively opposed it.[16] Thus, while Chicago now has a few more examples of how large projects should or should not be handled, the process by which the costs and benefits of such projects might be determined and distributed fairly never became sufficiently developed and established.[17] As a result, the current fights over the expansion of the McCormick Place exposition center and the construction of a third major airport on the South Side follow the old pattern of community groups on the outside, without adequate information or chance of participation, trying to determine and expose the true costs.

In spite of the weakness of the administration in this regard, on the whole these chapters offer considerable support for the proposition that even in a relatively short period a reform administration can bring about significant and lasting changes. The key mechanisms for this were the legitimation of broad involvement, through both subcontracting and consultative structures, backed up by the necessary organizational and policy changes. These mechanisms then enhanced the ability of progressive elements to continue to pursue their agenda, even after the administration itself has disappeared.[18]

Coalitions Outside the City Ultimately, a key element in the contribution one administration can make to the institutionalization of comprehensive social change depends on the external connections that administration and the movement that elected it establish outside of the city. Given the limits to local autonomy, a municipality must have a national strategy as well as a local one.

The foregoing chapters do not cover this area well, but the Washington administration probably had a more conscious and active national strategy than any previous Chicago government. Pursuing a regional, state, and national legislative agenda was one of the five formal goals of the 1984 Chicago Development Plan, and Harold Washington personally played an active role in this. Washington had very high visibility outside of the city and even internationally, and several of his staff frequently spoke and wrote about Chicago's experiences for outside audiences. There is little evidence, though, of any significant new coalition work, or of any support by the administration for any of its constituencies to form broader coalitions. Indeed, one of the purposes of the present volume is precisely to overcome this isolation and increase the exchange of experiences between progressive cities.

General Implications

What do these chapters suggest for those in Chicago or elsewhere who propose to embark on—or find themselves thrust into—something similar to the experience described in these pages? On the one hand, they sum up to more than the categories we have listed in the Introduction and the summary above. What follows is a set of observations that comes from this summary, but also from reflections of the way Chicago transcends the experience of other places:

The Movement Base

Washington's election and his administration's programs were possible only because they built on a long history of demographic, economic, and political change, as well as movement growth and development. In this respect Chicago goes far beyond the sorts of movement base reported in the Introduction, and perhaps beyond that experienced in any other city in the nation. The type of change from the past represented by the Washington administration did not spring full blown from one event or one organization or individual; it reflected years of coalition building and networking that created the necessary climate and resources.[19] Thus, there was a continuity of both the networks of people and the substantive, programmatic emphases between the movement and the governance coalition. Without it, electoral victories are likely to be lost quickly; Jane Byrne's election in 1979 and her subsequent compromises with her opponents in the city council are one example of this. In contrast to that experience, the "council wars" in the early years of the Washington administration had a substantive focus in the reform and neighborhood agenda, and no compromise occurred; they did not get settled until special elections gave Washington control.

Movement vs. Government

One of the themes we have emphasized is that of the need to distinguish between the various parts of Harold Washington's movement and his broader electoral and governing coalitions. One of the questions to be asked is whether, given the administration's relations with its base and its accomplishments, it was worth it for community organizations to divert resources and deviate from their previous very limited involvement in electoral campaigns?

Interestingly, even the most disillusioned of our authors ends his chapter almost suggesting he would try even harder next time: "When it came to fulfilling your dreams and putting your policies into practice, Harold, we hardly knew you." The community movement as a whole appears to have answered the question positively. During 1990, all the major coalitions banded together to formulate a "Neighborhood Agenda" aimed at the 1991 mayoral and aldermanic races. It was a process reminiscent of the development of the CWED Platform in 1982, but significantly involved no less than seven coalitions. The work culminated in a Community Congress, which established the enduring stake of the neighborhood movement in the electoral process alongside the enduring emphasis on community organizing. It also showed the advances made during the previous eight years in the organizations' strength, the sophistication of their work and organizing, and understanding of the political process.

Based on these chapters, we think that the entrance into electoral politics by the neighborhood movement was not a mistake. There certainly were costs, and the benefits would have been greater if not for Harold Washington's relatively short tenure in office. But we think that what happened was that, with enormous effort, the neighborhood movement supported a city administration in a series of innovations that projected a new way of doing business, and that this would in the long run help the city and the movement.

These chapters give ample evidence of ways in which the administration benefited from and provided resources to its movement base, and of some of the ways in which individual commissioners and departments used the base to provide political pressure. Largely by omission, they also show the problems caused by the lack of strategic or tactical discussions between the administration and the movement base. It would seem important for a progressive administration to maintain communication networks that would make such discussions possible. This would also clarify the distinct roles of the administration and the outside organizations and make clearer that, while the neighborhood movement had representatives within the administration, it did not constitute the whole of the administration.

Movement vs. Pluralist Leadership

The authors of these chapters repeatedly note the extraordinary nature of Harold Washington's personal characteristics and the level of commitment he inspired. The chapters are suffused with an awareness of the strength of Washington's personality and clearly show the zeal which those within the administration brought to the task. For several of the authors the experience caused changes in their own beliefs.

But there was another dimension as well. One of Washington's leadership characteristics was his ability to get interests to the table that would otherwise not have been in the game at all. In this his administration differed from the pluralist model, in which leadership concerns itself with the mediation of existing pressures, not the creation of new ones.

On the other hand, Washington let various often conflicting constituencies fight out their positions—once given access—before deciding which to support. In retrospect, this was still the best approach. It gave enough space for the movement actors, who then developed raised expectations for earlier and more decisive action on their behalf. But perhaps this is the best a progressive mayor—as opposed to a movement leader—can do. He or she can bring new people to the table but cannot always favor one side.

But there is again the problem of developing a sophisticated sense of the boundary between movement and government. Any progressive mayor who wishes to cultivate the support of a movement base should pay special attention to communicating these rules of the game.

Building Diversity

For many, the hallmark of the Washington administration was its attempt to transcend a narrow base by reaching out to other racial, ethnic, and ideological groups. This was reflected most clearly in the electoral "Rainbow," and followed up in the administration's affirmative hiring policies and its appointments to boards and task forces. Its lasting effect is difficult to ascertain. The administration's experiences make clear that achieving and maintaining diversity entails a constant effort over largely unknown terrain.

These chapters reflect one clear success—the effects of instituting administrative and political procedures in the several agencies represented here, which resulted in substantive advances in affirmative hiring procedures and the treatment of black–white issues. Partly this would be obvious, given the symbolism of a black mayor and the electoral mandate for equal treatment. Another part is the commitment by these authors to a community agenda, as opposed to a bureaucratic one, which often entailed race-sensitive procedures. But the other part was in the adoption or invention of administrative procedures that constantly reminded people in these agencies to be conscious of race. These chapters present evidence of such procedures, and there is material in this experience that can be replicated elsewhere.

There were also failures, as in the area of black–Hispanic relations. Cooperation between these groups is essential to the development of progressive coalitions in the United States, but the sensitivity of the subject among progressives appears to have limited analysis of the issue. Unfortunately, the Chicago experience shows more about the difficulties and pitfalls than about how it might be succesfully accomplished.

A perhaps more positive result was achieved in the relations with the business community—another kind of diversity. The state of the economy was a very significant factor in the administration's ability to reach succesfully beyond its initial base to the business community. If there had been an economic downturn, Washington would no doubt have been blamed for its local manifestations and relations with the business community might have been considerably worse. Furthermore, the increased sophistication of community organizations and increased receptiveness of the business community helped these organizations in some cases transcend their previous antagonistic relationships.

View of History

The most fundamental question raised by these chapters for many persons will be whether Harold Washington represented much in substance, apart from his personal charisma, his representation of minority populations, and his procedural reforms. There is a significant segment of opinion that he did not. A weeklong series of *Chicago Tribune* articles in the summer of 1988 stated this view: Washington's community development agenda was a naive attempt to indulge the fantasies of neighborhood organizations about having a real role in development decisions; the attempt to maintain high-paying manufacturing jobs within the city was not only futile, it blocked the progress that might come from commercial real estate development and residential gentrification; and the community development strategy was, in any event, not a real grass-roots movement but the creation of a small number of university-trained ideologues.[20]

These chapters suggest another view. We present them as closer to the truth than what the *Chicago Tribune* suggested. We hope that, at a minimum, Chicago can keep and nurture the history these authors have begun. If it does keep it, the city will be the richer for it.

NOTES

1. Many black city council members had no choice but to participate in Washington's coalition, but they chafed under it. The afternoon of Washington's death one of them was quoted as saying that the mood among several of them was "Hallelujah, we're free." See Bruce R. Dold and Ann Marie Lapinski, "The Making of the Mayor: Sawyer Vote Arranged in Parking Lot," *Chicago Tribune* (December 6, 1987), 1, 22–23.
2. See Wallace Sayre and Herbert Kaufman, *Governing New York City* (New York: Russell Sage Foundation, 1960) on New York City, and Francine Rabinowitz, *City Politics and Planning* (New York: Lieber-Atherton, 1969), more generally.
3. Commercial Club, *Make no Little Plans: Jobs for Metropolitan Chicago* (Chicago: Commercial Club, 1984).
4. See also Robert Giloth and Robert Mier, "Spatial Change and Social Justice: Alternative Economic Development in Chicago," in Robert A. Beauregard, ed., *Economic Restructuring and Political Response* (Newbury Park, Calif.: Sage, 1989), pp. 181–208; and Ann R. Markusen and Virginia Carlson, "Deindustrialization in the American Midwest: Causes and Responses," in Lloyd Rodwin and Hidehiko Sazanami, eds., *Deinstrialization and Regional Economic Transformation: The Experience of the United States* (Winchester, Mass.: Unwin Hyman, 1990), pp. 29–59.
5. Manuel Castells, *The City and The Grassroots* (Berkeley: University of California Press, 1983); Ralph Miliband, *The State in Capitalist Society* (New York: Basic Books, 1969).
6. For an elaboration of this point see Robert Mier, Wim Wiewel, and Lauri

Alpern, "Decentralization of Policy Making under Mayor Harold Washington," in Kenneth Wong and Laurence Lynn, eds., *Policy Innovation in Metropolitan Chicago* (Greenwich, Conn: JAI Press, 1991, in press).

7.   See Gerald Suttles, *The Man-Made City: The Land-Use Confidence Game in Chicago* (Chicago, University of Chicago Press, 1990), p.267, where he describes Washington's relations with community organizations as patronage.

8.   Wim Wiewel and Nicholas Rieser "The Limits of Progressive Municipal Economic Development," *Community Development Journal* 24, no. 2 (1989), 111–119.

9.   Wim Wiewel, "Economic Development in Chicago: The Growth Machine Meets the Neighborhood Movement," *Local Economy* 4, no. 4 1990, 307–316.

10.   For a complete description see Marc Weiss and John Metzger, "Neighborhood Lending Agreements: Negotiating and Financing Community Development," Occasional Paper Series No. 88–06, Lincoln Institute of Land Policy, Cambridge, Mass., March 1988.

11.   Mayor Harold Washington, Remarks at a press conference, Save Our City Coalition, Chicago, September 29, 1984.

12.   For instance, Suttles suggests Jackson's statement was a regular chant and argues that the patronage which was once an obstacle to blacks' political representation became, under Washington, "the instrument to perpetuate it." See Gerald Suttles, *The Man-Made City*, p. 267. Robert Mier rebuts Suttles's claims in "Inept Elitism from a Would-be exposé: A Review of *The Man-Made City*," *Chicago Enterprise* (July/August 1990), 27–28, and in "A Review of *The Man-Made City*," *Journal of the American Planning Association* (Summer 1991).

13.   It may be even worse among Cuban-Americans, who have been politically the most conservative Hispanic group. However, in Chicago their numbers are far smaller than those of Mexican-Americans and Puerto Ricans. See on the general issue the article by Gary Rivlin, "The Blacks and the Browns: Is the Coalition Coming Apart?" *Reader* 17, no. 7 (November 6, 1987), 1–33.

14.   In addition to Giloth's chapter, see for more detail Kenneth Reardon, *Local Economic Development in Chicago, 1983–1987: The Reform Efforts of Mayor Harold Washington* (Ph.D. dissertation, Cornell University, 1990).

15.   *Chicago Sun-Times* (April 11, 1990), 1; *Chicago Enterprise* (February 1990).

16.   See Robert McClory, *The Fall of the Fair* (Chicago: Chicago 1992 Committee, 1986).

17.   This was not just the Washington administration's fault. In 1986 the Metropolitan Planning Council started a Capital Projects Committee charged with the task of developing a broadly acceptable methodology for assessing the impact of large public projects. In spite of a good background paper (Larry Joseph, "Impact Analysis of Urban Economic Development Projects," Center for Urban Research and Policy Studies, University of Chicago, 1985), the committee met only a few times and disbanded without coming to grip with the issue.

18.   See, for application in a different context, the development of the concept of "non-reformist reforms" by André Gorz, *Strategies for Labor* (Boston: Beacon Press, 1964).

19.   See, for instance, John McCarthy and Mayer Zald, "Resource Mobilization and Social Movements: A Partial Theory," *American Journal of Sociology* 82

(1977), 1212–1241, and Edward J. Walsh, "Resource Mobilization and Citizen Protest in Communities Around Three Mile Island," *Social Problems* 29 (1981), 1–21.

20.   See John McCarron, "Chicago on Hold: Politics of Poverty," a series, *Chicago Tribune* (August 28–September 4, 1988). Also see Philip W. Nyden and Wim Wiewel, "Introduction," in Nyden and Wiewel, eds., *An Urban Agenda for the 1990s: Research and Action* (New Brunswick, N.J.: Rutgers University Press, 1991).

Index

Washington's electoral base
    overwhelmingly black
w/ critical support
from poor whites &
    latinos